FRAMED

Iaia Filiberti & Debora Hirsch

FRAMED

100 round trips to Hollywood

CHARTA

design
**mario piazza
letizia abbate
(46xy studio)**

scientific coordination
federica cimatti

editorial coordination
**daniela meda
filomena moscatelli**

copyediting
emily ligniti

copywriting
and press office
silvia palombi

us editorial director
francesca sorace

promotion and web
monica d'emidio

distribution
antonia de besi

administration
grazia de giosa

warehouse and outlet
roberto curiale

**edizioni charta srl
milano**
via della moscova, 27 20121
tel. +39-026598098
+39-026598200
fax +39-026598577
charta@chartaartbooks.it

**charta books ltd.
new york city**
tel. +1-313-406-8468
**international@
chartaartbooks.it**

www.chartaartbooks.it

we wish to thank
federica cimatti
germana negri tedeschi
patrizia nuzzo
federica olivares
giovanni pippi
marco ronzi
eva scharzwald
paola ugolini

special thanks to
maggie cardelús
antonio somaini

**this book was made possible
thanks to the support of**

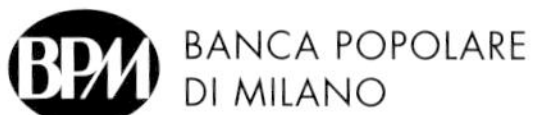

Ai miei cinque uomini:
Luciano, Alberto, Marco,
Giulio e Vero.
E a una sola donna, Giulia.
Iaia

A Pietro e… a Pietro,
a Titti e Cesare,
genitori e nonni di Pietro.
Debora

Iaia Filiberti and Debora Hirsch
Introduction

The books speaks of births, deaths, awards and illness, stardom and tragedy in the lives of 100 actresses that were once successful in Hollywood, even for a short period of time.
We try to lead the readers to unmask the forces at work behind the image and see these 100 actresses for who they really are, individuals at times strong, at times weak, at times fortunate, at times unlucky, who in a phase of their lives sought to be a part of American stardom, but for one reason or another abandoned that dream.
The carefully and shrewdly constructed Hollywood studio photographs have a quality of permanence, as though somehow protected from the cruelties that hang over the ordinary person. This could not be further from the truth.
Each star is presented by a text, a glimpse into their real lives. It takes but a second to unveil the lure of the image and find ourselves facing our own vulnerability and ephemerality.
The images of the book are presented in ovals that connect to Western memorializing traditions. The same happens to our related art installations. We want the readers to accept these women as people like us, somehow related to us, who were drawn into an elaborate forcefield of power and interest that rendered them even more fragile . . . or not.
Careers ended up in the void, disappeared black and white faces, forgotten stories.
We unexpectedly found a box of Hollywood collectible cards with actresses from the 1920s to 1950s, and we conceived a complex project trying to reconstruct, like a jigsaw puzzle, the life and career of each one. From a static condition of oblivion they come back to light for very brief moments in the book, and maybe after those faces will once again be forgotten.
We reinvented the word "framed" to define the sudden stop of the artistic career of those actresses.

Exchanging Cards

Changing the Hollywood collectible cards
We randomly picked fifty actress cards and then,
like kids, started to play and change them.

Iaia Filiberti: I want Irene Dunne . . .
Debora Hirsch: Irene will stay with me
forever. She is similar to Norma Shearer who
decides to quit at the top and have a new life.
Compared to Shearer, she goes much further
. . . to become a champion of philanthropy and
charity, and not just the wife of a very young
ski instructor.
IF: Irene was a very devoted Catholic and you
know me . . . I have already Dolores Hart and I
want Irene. I can give you everything for her!
DH: I know your faith in God and that you try
to evangelize. I appreciate it but you know
that it is not the same for me. I could give
you another Catholic, Jeanne Crain, who had
seven children and never divorced.
IF: No matter I want Irene!
DH: Sorry, no. You already have Dolores Hart
and also June Haver, be happy with what you
have.
IF: Right, I buy Jeanne Crain. What do you
want for her?
DH: I want Tilly Losch or Susan Fleming, both
painters like me.
IF: You got it, Tilly Losch for you.
DH: Iaia, I know you love Clara Bow much
more than Susan Fleming because she sleeps
with Gary Cooper, so it's a deal?
IF: I cannot refuse. Keep those painters!
DH: Do you remember that Lupe Vélez also
sleeps with your Gary Cooper?
IF: How could I have forgotten? But Lupe
committed suicide and, what's more, a
gorgeous suicide. I do not want her at all.
DH: Better for you, so that you do not get
frustrated. I would never let her go. She is
my heroine. To plan a gorgeous suicide . . . so
dramatic, so kitsch, so desperate. I love her.
IF: Great, at least for once we do not have to
fight.
I want Constance Bennett, the best poker

player in Hollywood, and you know my passion for playing cards.

DH: Constance must stay together with her sister Joan Bennett and with the two other card players, Anna Quirentia Nilsson and Kay Francis. That I already have. By the way I went to a French casino last weekend.

IF: I hate you even because you are not a very good card player like me! I'm bored with you. Now I try with another category. I already have Lizabeth Scott and Tallulah Bankhead, give me Alexis Smith right now.

DH: I want to keep "I wish I were a man." She is as tall as me and she has an incredible personality. Give me Lizabeth Scott, because with Barbara Stanwyck she took part in one of my favourite movies, *The Mystery of Martha Ivers*. For Lizabeth, I can give you Belita, Joyce Olden, and the beautiful Sheila Terry . . .

IF: Are you joking with me or what . . .? For them let's speak later. Now let's finish this category. Give me Alexis Smith and stop it.

DH: What do you give me for her? Gene Tierney?

IF: You want to play tough . . . but why not? Done. Let's move on. I want Louise Brooks.

DH: Of course you want her. Look at you! You look like her, but that's exactly why I want to keep her. Listen to me: I love symbols, Louise is an icon, a myth of freedom and courage. How can I leave her? And for whom?

IF: She is the gorgeous symbol of the jazz period. You know that I have had this haircut because of Louise since I was 11 years old? Come on, look at you with your blond and long hair. Do you want Veronica Lake?

DH: Silly girl, I already have her.

IF: I want Louise and I give you two.

DH: No, five and you know perfectly well that Louise is worth more than five others.

IF: It's fair . . . I give you three sexy ladies like Corinne Calvet, Martine Carol, Yvonne De Carlo, and I add . . . Virginia Mayo. Four for one, what more do you want?

DH: Well . . . no comment . . . I'm tired, I'll do this gift for you.

Since you have June Allyson and Jane Powell, I can offer you another girl-next-door to complete the group. I have Nancy Olson, an Oscar nominated actress, Julia Adams, and Sandra Dee.

IF: Oh, what a hard seller you are! Be ashamed of yourself! None of us is able to do housework and you know it! Why should I keep this group? Maybe I'll take just Sandra Dee, but for other reasons.

DH: What reasons?

IF: Sorry Deb, but you know we all have secrets.

I adore the grace of Cyd Charisse. She is so classy and so professional. May I have her?

DH: Yes.

IF: So quickly . . .?

DH: In Marilyn Monroe's last unfinished film, Marilyn plays a mother far from home for some years who comes back to find Cyd Charisse in her place. Being a mother of a seven-month boy I think Marilyn is at her best in this role. All the lights shine on her, Cyd just disappears.

IF: Everyone disappears for you compared to Marilyn.

DH: Exactly like Bette Davis for you.

IF: For Cyd . . . you can choose Deb.

DH: I have no doubt, the rebel Frances Farmer. I want to put her next to another rebel, Louise Rainer.

IF: You got it. I have Marisa Pavan, Pierangeli's twin sister. I give her to you so you keep the family together.

DH: Oh how sweet you are . . . but no. Pierangeli makes me nervous. I hate all these love stories that do not realise their full potential leaving someone always thinking about what could have been.

IF: Each one has to be the mentor of oneself.

DH: I agree. What a sad story! All her life with a broken heart for James Dean until her suicide . . .

IF: You have to respect the memory, but above all you have to respect the gift of life.

DH: Let's change subject, it makes me sad. When I think about some of our ladies, those who changed their lives, such as Norma Shearer, Rosalind Russell, or Susan Kohner, who quit at the top to have a second life . . . you realize we did the same thing Iaia?
IF: Yes . . . so funny! You studied engineering and I studied criminal law, we both managed companies . . . and then we switched to art . . .
DH: . . . And we are mothers. My first child after nineteen years of marriage, and it is wonderful!
IF: And I, two kids with different dads, and it is wonderful!
DH: Please give me your two Dorothies, Comingore and Dandridge.
IF: You forgot Dorothy Lamour.
DH: Come on Iaia! How can you compare a blacklist victim, a victim of racism with a victim of exotic typecasting?
IF: Take it or leave it.
DH: Done. Make your last selection for the three Dorothies.
IF: Haya Harareet, Constance Smith, Heather Angel.
DH: You are completely crazy! Of course I accept, at least I was expecting you to ask me for Simone Simon.
IF: Ok give me her immediately.
DH: Do you also want the key?

Iaia Filiberti, born in Milan, Italy. Graduated in Criminal Law in Milan and received her Master's in Brussels, Belgium. Currently lives and works in Milan and Stresa, Italy.
www.iaiafiliberti.it

Debora Hirsch, born in São Paulo, Brazil. Graduated in Industrial Engineering at USP, São Paulo, and received her MBA at SDA Bocconi, Milan. Currently lives and works in Milan and São Paulo.
www.deborahirsch.com

They have both participated in numerous solo and group exhibitions worldwide.
Framed is an art project they have developed together since 2007.

Maggie Cardelús and Antonio Somaini

One Hundred Comebacks

What is a star? Or better, what *was* a star within that classical Hollywood cinema which between the 1920s and 1950s had generated a real star system? Writing in 1957 from a country, France, which at that time was witnessing the blossoming of the stardom of Brigitte Bardot, Edgar Morin presents his answer from the vantage point of what he calls "an ethnography of non-primitive societies"[1]: an ethnography which aimed at unveiling and analyzing the archaic which is still woven within the texture of Western modernity. "The star—writes Morin—is on the border between the aesthetic and the magic. She overcomes the skepticism of the spectator-consciousness, which always knows that it is participating in an illusion."[2] Starting from the theses he had presented a year before in his *The Cinema, or the Imaginary Man*,[3] Morin considers the phenomenon of the stars as emblematic of that coexistence of the modern and the archaic in which lies the power of cinema. A modern divinity, the star is at the same time a product, a construct, meticulously crafted and planned in all its manifestations, and a cult object. It is both the focal center of a cinema conceived as entertainment industry and the symptom of a persistent need for magic that haunts modern society.

At the time that Morin was writing *The Stars*, the star cult proliferated in a variety of forms that accompanied and reinforced what viewers saw at the movies. The film star—whose life was obsessively followed and literally consumed by a public who needed to project itself and identify with the star's exemplary life of romance and excess— radiated his or her glow through print and

1. E. Morin, *The Stars* [1957], translated by R. Howard, foreword by L. Mortimer (Minneapolis – London: University of Minnesota Press, 2005), 88.
2. Ibid., 85.
3. E. Morin, *The Cinema, or the Imaginary Man* [1956], translated by L. Mortimer (Minneapolis – London: University of Minnesota Press, 2005).

television, gossip columns and advertising. The images of these carefully constructed intermedial divinities meandered through and infiltrated a wide range of channels that pulled them off the screen and brought them closer to their public. One of these material channels, thousands of miles away from Hollywood, were small, collectible photo portrait cards that circulated during the 1950s and 1960s in Italy, a country then thriving in its post-war economic boom. This is where Iaia Filiberti and Debora Hirsch's *Framed* finds its starting point, in the unexpected rediscovery of an old tin box full of well-worn star cards.

The driving force behind the circulation of star images, what made them so desirable, was the face: the star's face, that sees beyond the frame and gives herself over to be looked at in the small surface of the trading card or on the page of a book, often looking straight into our eyes. The faces in the portrait gallery of *Framed* are at times radiant, at times dreamy, provocative, but always *intense*. The star, as she appears in these images, is a creature that sees, feels, wants, loves, hates with unrivalled intensity. Her facial expression, often filled with light, has to clearly reveal the exceptionality of her life, an exceptionality that is only rarely aided by props or extravagant decor: Dorothy Dandridge's grand piano, Alexis Smith's gun, Dorothy Lamour's chains, the light rays that radiate from behind Sheila Terry's provocative pose . . . In most cases it was the face, the make-up, and the pose alone that transmitted the star's aura and prestige. Taken together, the poses that we see in the *Framed* photos constitute a small atlas of star *Pathosformel*. Although it is a random repertoire, it is still indicative of the formulas that codified and conveyed the pathos of the Hollywood star. The star's moving and fluctuating screen presence crystallizes in a single image that must be emblematic and able to synthesize stardom in a single expression, an inclination of the head, a hairdo, a dress.

"The star is made from a substance compounded of life and dream,"[4] writes Morin. This dream in *Framed* is redreamed a second time. In this piece, as in others in contemporary art, the classic Hollywood movie world is handled as a massive cultural image bank whose latent energy can be freely accessed and reactivated. It is an archive of the imaginary that has to be explored and re-edited in order to rediscover the stories that have yet to be told. "A great actress is a woman capable of incarnating a large number of different roles, a star is a woman capable of giving rise to a large number of convergent stories,"[5] writes Malraux in 1939, a few years before publishing his *Musée Imaginaire* for the first time. *Framed* is, in a way, a small, private, portable museum of the imaginary. It emerges from an attempt to make use of the large archive of reproductions of the stars, represented here by the small collection of trading cards, with an almost archeological or taxonomical spirit. The goddesses of this small pantheon are mostly minor divinities that in many cases were only briefly under the Hollywood spotlight, disappearing rather quickly from the screen and then vanishing into oblivion. Their fleeting success is underlined by frames that are both celebratory and funereal. The texts that accompany the images meticulously reconstruct the reasons why these actresses abandoned the stage. Behind the glowing faces, the radiant smiles, the provocative eyes, the meditative and intense poses were often lives in shambles: multiple marriages, drugs, alcohol, depression, illness, suicide . . . None of this is visible in the images alone. All that is left of them as Hollywood stars are these faces, these masks, these icons born of a specific time and place,

4. *The Stars*, Op. cit., 85.
5. A. Malraux, *Esquisse d'une psychologie du cinéma*, introduction by J.C. Larrat (Paris: Nouveau Monde, 2003), 65.

compelling enough to induce Filiberti and
Hirsch to attentively and repeatedly reframe
these photos in an ongoing project that pays
homage to these irrecoverable lives. One
should look at this book as the most recent
manifestation of this work in progress. For this
reason, we would like to return to the small tin
can of star portrait trading cards.

"Collect the photos to make a complete artist
series." "With these original photos you will make
the best collection of stars in cinema history."
"Send us 100 loose photos for verification. We
will send them back to you with a magnificent
290mm soccer ball." "17. Haya Harareet in the
film *Ben-Hur* (MGM)." "67. Inger Stevens in the
film *The World, the Flesh, and the Devil* (MGM)"
… These texts, written on the backs of the
cards, show the ways in which the Hollywood
myth insinuated itself into the very fabric of the
everyday. The myth here finds a foothold in the
rituals of collecting and card trading, and were
even given away at the supermarket as discount
points: 100 star cards would win you a soccer
ball, a mother's dream for a son's dream. Printed
in the thousands, the star cards assumed a
trade value that could be exchanged between
collectors, used to play games, or traded in for
other merchandise. The star cards—miniaturized,
made manageable (handled, swapped, ordered),
and given specific trade value—gave the
collector the illusion of ownership and power.
More importantly, perhaps, they maintained,
even enriched the aura of divine stardom.
Their accumulation and circulation offered
their owners the opportunity to cultivate an
"infinite time of *rêverie*,"[6] which like a continuous
daydream created a sense that this world of
small and governable images would acquiesce
and divulge the secrets of their universe.

The cards rediscovered by Filiberti and
Hirsch had moved through different spaces

6. S. Stewart, *On Longing: Narratives of the Miniature,
the Gigantic, the Souvenir, the Collection*, 6th ed.
(Durham, NC: Duke University Press, 1993), 65.

of exchange in the post-war years in Italy to
be collected by one person into the unified
space of a vintage Japanese camphor tin, a
serendipitous choice when one takes note
that in the first half of this century 80% of all
camphor produced went into the production
of film and celluloid, and like the Hollywood
monopoly on film stars, Japan had the
monopoly on camphor. The artists chose to
carry these images into various other spaces
over the next two years, choosing to abandon
the disarray and intimacy of the tin box.

For their first project, they chose to ignore
the varied sources of the cards and selected
100 images from the camphor box, enlarged
and cropped them into 25 x 16 cm ovals, set
them behind thick oval plexiglas, and hung on
the wall, each framed by a large adhesive frame
shaped like the ones we see in the book. The
images were organized on the walls in a grid
and we were informed, with accompanying text
handouts (similar to the ones we find later in
the book), of the various facts of their lives and
were forced to recognize that these women
were only ordinary human beings with dreams
and plenty of failures. Some of the installation's
defining words were order, silence, memory,
vulnerability, homage, and untouchability.
Walking through the space of this paper and
plexiglas cemetery we saw a progression of
tombs that made one think of the unfulfilled
ambitions of these actresses, or perhaps of
their rejection of a system that they found
intolerable. On the one hand we were asked,
through the texts, to get close to the real lives
of the women behind the star image, while
on the other hand their new scale and fixed
placement behind 2.5 cm of plexiglas denied
us the quality of the original print, as well as
the accessibility and intimate manageability of
the trading cards. We were shut out from the
rêverie and promise of knowledge provided
by the materiality of the miniature and given
instead real knowledge of the women's lives. It
is as though the act of giving up the secrets of

the stars made the photos give up their scale, tactility, intimacy, and magic.

Filiberti and Hirsch then continued to work on their project and for a time set aside the tin box and returned to the films in which their 100 stars were cast as leading ladies. The artists chose one film segment per star and edited the 100 segments together into an approximately 30 minute video sequence, each segment accompanied by an edited version of the original text. It seemed like the artists had carefully selected the segments like scholars examining the prophesy books, to identify for each star the precise moment that foretold her impending fall from stardom. Here the stars were reclaimed for the present in a compelling operation of returning them to the screen where, as viewers, we were teased by their 20 seconds of magic but not allowed to fully indulge because we were again constrained to participate in the drama of their biographies as real people and made hyper-aware of their performances as career swan songs.

Filiberti and Hirsch continued to develop *Framed* by returning again to the original material and recontextualizing it into another form, this book. Our divas are now returned to print on paper and we are given a new set of conditions in which to examine the images. Like the trading cards, we can feel a sense of ownership, and like the trading cards, we are allowed to return to them over and over again. We may choose to read or ignore their biographies. The book format allows us to easily examine the pictures because they are neither miniatures nor walled-in by 2.5 centimeters of Plexiglas nor disturbed by overlaid text. The images reassume all the compelling quality of the archaic, magical presence described by Morin, a presence deposited over time on the surface of the glamour shot. In the light of what we know of the film and installation versions of the work, these photographs aren't obliged to foretell the future, nor are they inaccessible visual epitaphs organized in rows, but they

stubbornly inhabit a liminal zone between life and death. We are poised in an uneasy balance between the magic of the image and the facts of the text and can lean one way or another depending on our inclination. The book form of this project is perhaps the format that most successfully re-evokes the tensions these women actually lived as they attempted to find a balance between their real lives and their careers as actresses.

Iaia Filiberti's and Debora Hirsch's ongoing project *Framed* and the images of stars that emerged from the Hollywood golden age are inextricably, vitally, linked by the continuous shift between movement and stillness, life and death, and the power that this connection has to generate fascination. From the motion of the actual films to the stillness of the glamour shots, back to movement and stillness through their circulation in their intermedial forms during the subsequent decades, these images start and stop up to the moment when Filiberti and Hirsch step in to reclaim the portrait cards and return them to circulation in a new context, the art world, that repositions the images in a new space of signification as the real lives and deaths of these stars come into play. Here we are asked to look at them as both stars and women in installation form, as a found-footage video, and now as a bound book, and each step of the way the passage from movement to stillness, from one form to another, demands a rereading, a reconsideration of how all the elements discussed thus far are held in a balance and how they express the complexity and contradictions inherent in the visual manifestations of the movie world. All this depended on 100 stars taking 100 round trips to Hollywood. Unlike real lives, the images continue to come back, pitting stillness against movement, and will continue to do so as we leaf through the pages of this book.

one

No More Calls

Anna Quirentia Nilsson

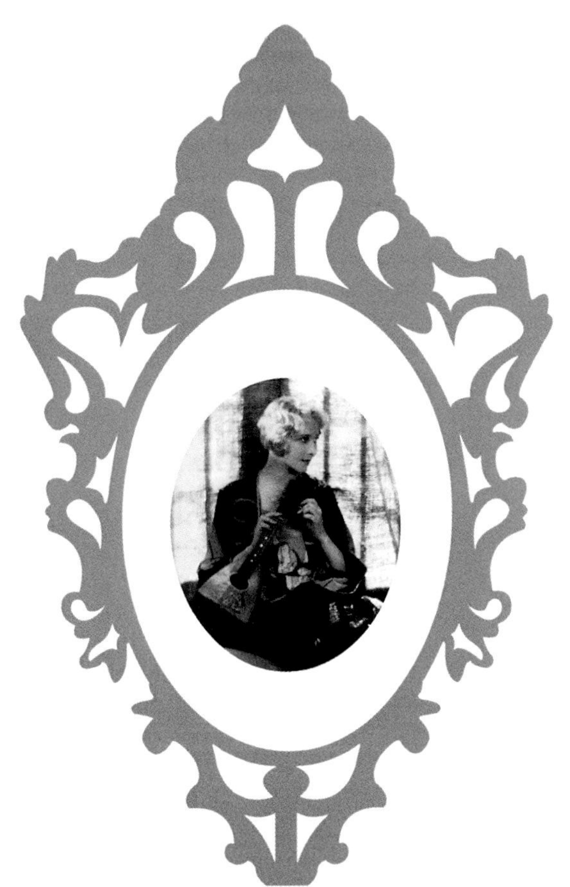

From . . . to . . .

"It seems like most of her films are lost.
I've only seen her playing cards with Gloria
Swanson and Buster Keaton in *Sunset
Blvd.* (1950). She was beautiful, though!
How Sweden can provide Hollywood with
stardom—Anna Q. Nilsson, Greta Garbo,
Victor Sjöström, Ingrid Bergman . . ."
(martinklasch.blogspot.com/…/swedish-
actresses-anna-quirentia.html)

From Sweden to Hollywood.

From nursemaid to silent film superstar.

From Metro to Paramount from
First National to Warner.

From a serious horse-riding accident
to a short comeback to the screen.

From the silent era to the advent of the talkie.

From sound to small and even
often uncredited parts and cameos.

From the first Swedish actor and actress
to get a star on the Walk of Fame to oblivion.

Belita

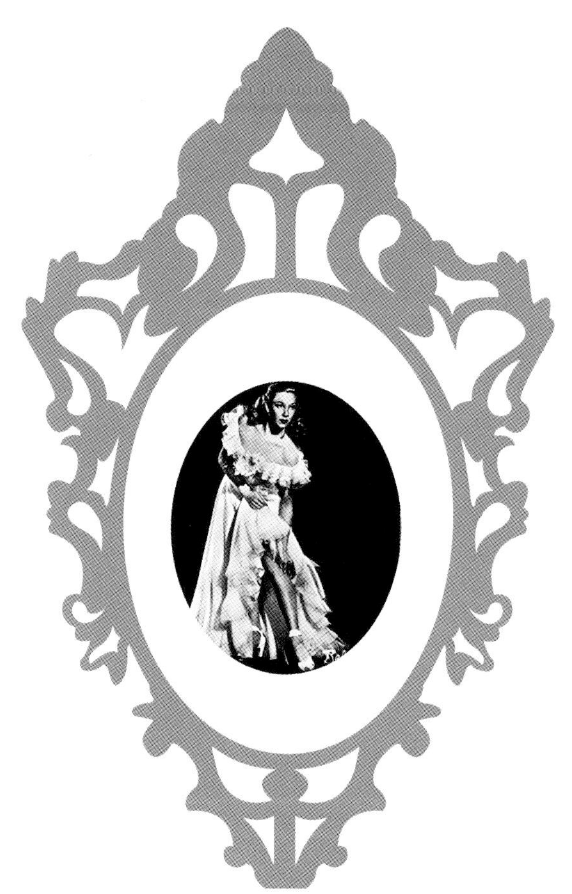

Belita the Ice Maiden

She hated the ice

At age 12, she is selected for the Olympic Games skating contest at Garmisch-Partenkirchen, Bavaria. She wins 16th place and takes 4th place in the British figure skating championships.

At age 18, she spends five years under contract to Allied Artists. Her salary is reportedly $2,000 a week, all of it taken by her showbusiness-oriented mother, because it is against the law to pay minors.

"I hated the ice. I hated the cold, the smell, everything about it. I only did it for the money."

She appears in films including *Silver Skates* (1943), *Lady, Let's Dance* (1944), and *Suspense* (1946), a good mixture of ice-skating and film noir proving a hit at the box office.

Belita's career starts to drop in the 1950s at age 30.

Constance Smith

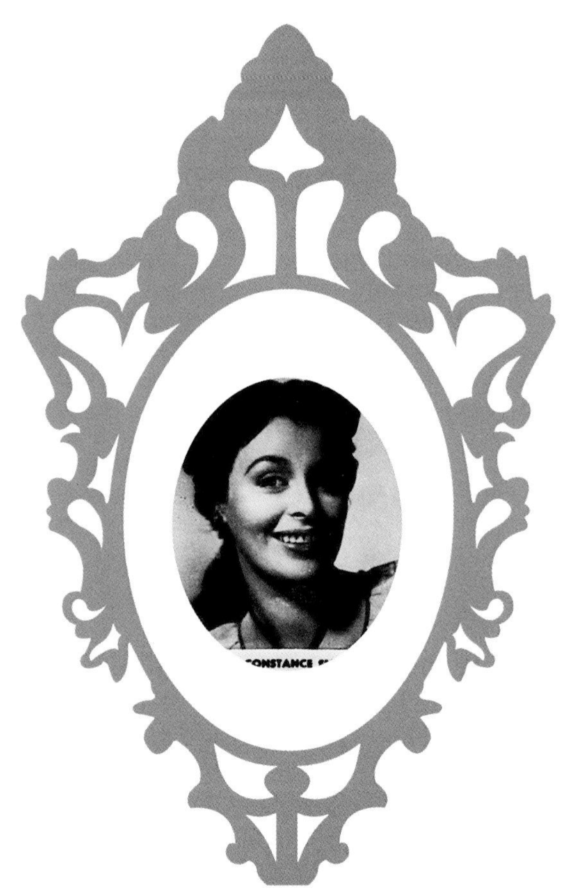

Anybody any information?

Any information on 1940s Irish actress Constance Smith?
Any online biographies: she was a neighbor of my mom.
I know she's dead now . . .

Best Answer - chosen by Voters
Wow! That's something.
(uk.answers.yahoo.com/question/index?qid).

Short film career
Constance is most active in the 1950s, appearing in Hollywood features such as *Man in the Attic* (1953) but, quite soon, she is unhappy about her career: she quits 20th Century Fox and finds a new agent, without any success. At age 31 she makes her last film appearance in *Conspiracy of the Borgia* (1959).

Long love affair
She falls in love with director Paul Rotha. They immediately plan to get married. He wants to postpone the date because both are already married. She stabs him twice and is charged with attempted murder and put into custody for three months. Finally, the wedding . . . after fifteen years. She is 46 and he is 73.

Haya Harareet

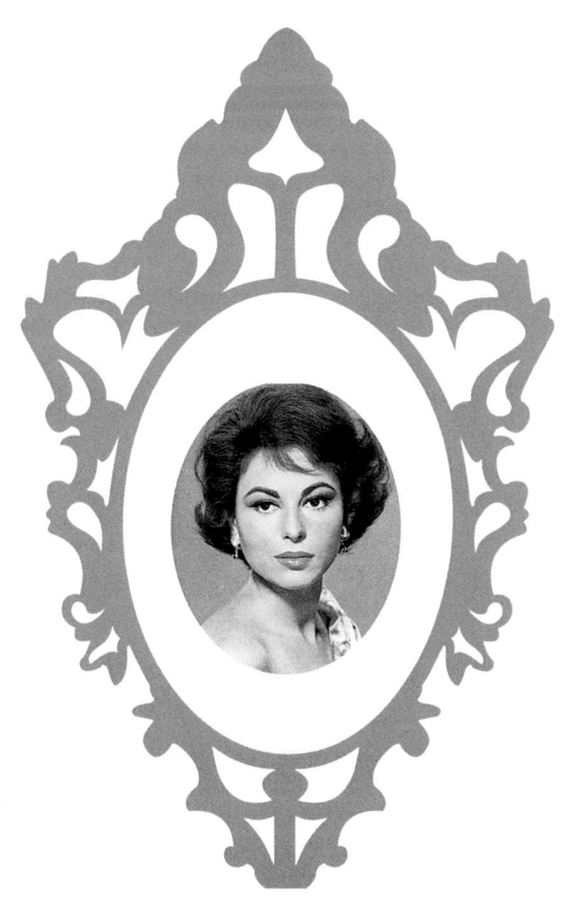

From *Ben-Hur* to vanishing

At age 23 she is Esther in the *Ben-Hur* (1954) colossal opposite Charlton Heston. This young woman is mysterious. She is the ultimate Christian, whose faith is ultimately the message of the movie.

"Wonderful actress. I fell in love with her since I saw her in the film *Ben-Hur* with Charlton Heston. I was in love with her immediately. Has unique and beautiful eyes and a charming look. She could be my mother, but that matters if it is really a big star. I would like to know of it, across any updated biography."

"Does anyone know if there is such a biography? Where do you currently live in England or Israel . . . It's great to know that Charlton Heston and Haya Harareet are the only ones in the movie *Ben-Hur* now living."

"Sorry . . . just Haya Harareet is alive . . . but it has been many years since we have not heard from her."

"I just hope that my heart is with the right to say that she still live."
(HH fans, www.flickr.com)

Heather Angel

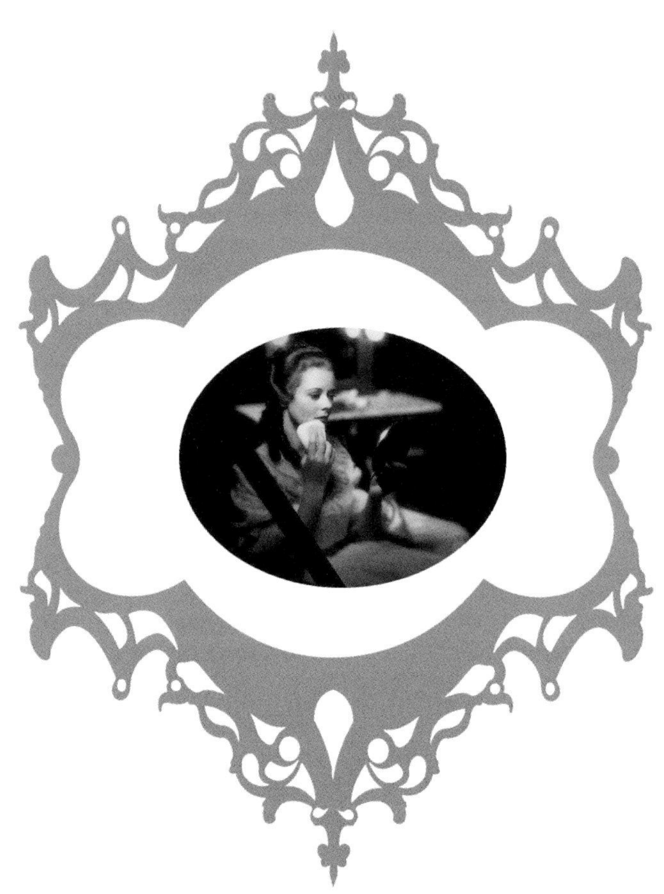

Like an angel you are somewhere

Never gonna ya do it
A world below
Heather angel you are somewhere
On the show
Don't you think you would find
Where to go
I want to go dancing on the other side
I want to buy a phonograph
But the money's gone
He bought books and records
I don't care about that
I just want to be alive
And go to the other...
I don't want money or books
Have to decide
Passive
And you were shot in the name of it
And then you'd see yeh, yeh
Then you'd see
The relationship
And walking I see you in the clouds
And I fall for
I would fall for you
I would . . .
Forever
Goodbye, bye
Goodbye
Stop stop

(Sonic Youth, "Heather Angel," 1997–1998)

Inger Stevens

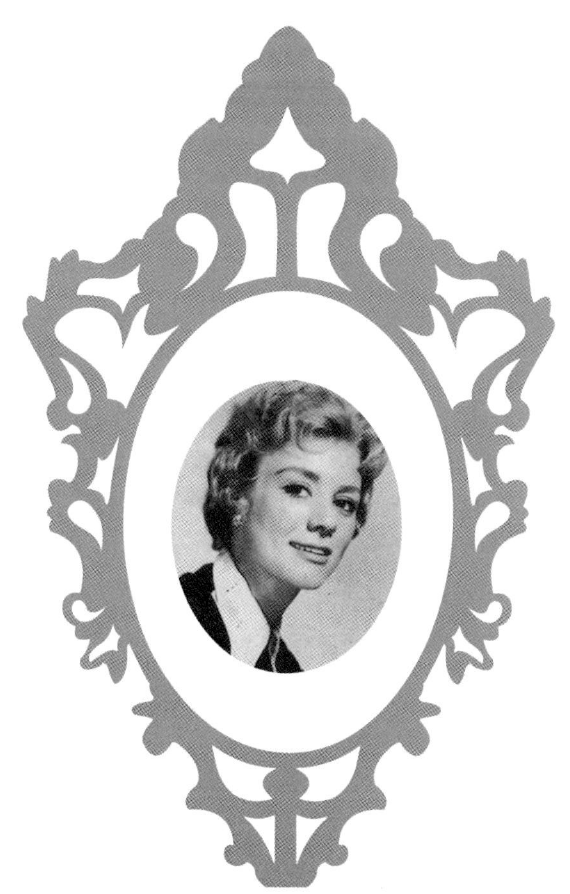

Grand Central Station

"A career, no matter how successful, can't put its arms around you."
She studies at the Actor's Studio but she debuts in the business through television programs and commercials and summer stock until she finally gets her big chance in the movie *Man on Fire* (1957), with Bing Crosby, at age 22. Several roles in major films follow but there are less than ten. However, she has success with her leading role in the ABC television series *The Farmer's Daughter*, with William Windom, and she has roles in episodes of *Bonanza, The Alfred Hitchcock Hour, The Eleventh Hour, Sam Benedict,* and *The Twilight Zone.*

"You end up being like Grand Central Station with people just coming and going."
Everything starts from her sad childhood thanks to her mother who abandons her when she is 6 years old for another man. The father moves alone from Stockholm to the US. He remarries and rejoins the family after four years. Inger's innate sadness and abandon fright never leave her.
She has serious set problems each time she begins falling in love with her co-stars such as Bing Crosby, Anthony Quinn, Dean Martin, Harry Belafonte, Mario Lanza, and Burt Reynolds.

"And there you are left all alone."
She attempts suicide several times: when her relationship with Crosby is over after filming *Man on Fire* (1957), another time with sleeping pills and ammonia and even while filming a scene from *Cry Terror!* (1958). Rod Steiger and her are nearly asphyxiated by carbon monoxide fumes in a tunnel and Inger initially refuses medical treatment saying she want to put an end to it.

She commits fatal suicide with barbiturate poisoning at age 36 in 1970.

At the moment of Inger's death it is discovered that she had been secretly married to African-American actor Ike Jones for nine years. The marriage is kept clandestine for fear that Ms. Stevens's career would be penalized due to the public's disapproval of interracial marriages. The couple is estranged but not divorced. Mr. Jones asks to be named administrator of her entire estate but the court decides for half. All the money is devolved by Jones to mental health organizations and children's charities.

Jeanne Crain

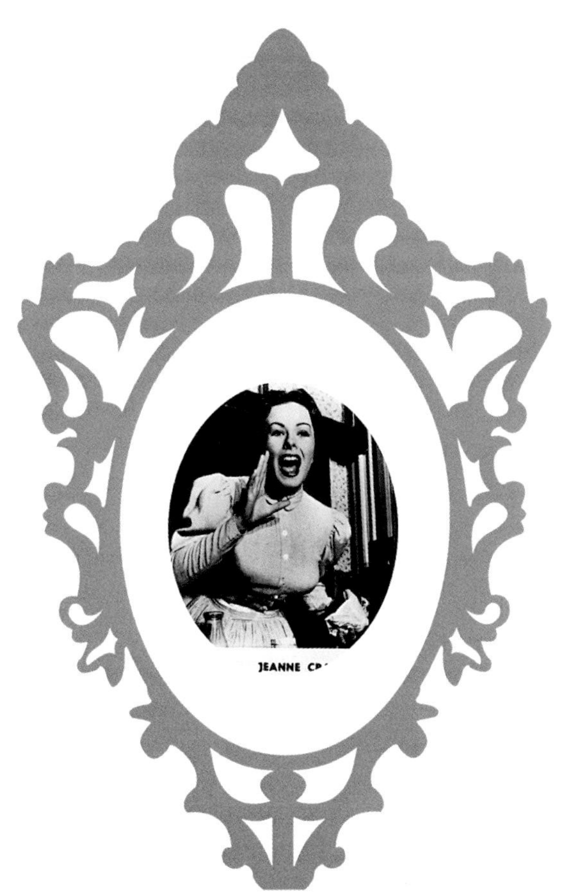

So devoted

Born in California to Irish-Catholic parents she is very devoted, too. As a lifelong devout Roman Catholic, Jeanne Crain Brinkman and her husband Paul Brinkman remain married, though they live separately in Santa Barbara, until their death. She has seven children.

She is ambitions and takes a screen test for Orson Welles for the role of Lucy Morgan in *The Magnificent Ambersons* (1942) but Anne Baxter gets the part.
She has an Oscar nomination as best actress for her role in Elia Kazan's *Pinky* (1949), and the other four candidates are:
Olivia de Havilland, the winner, Susan Hayward, Deborah Kerr, and Loretta Young.

Pinky is the story of a light-skinned African-American woman who, for love, passes for white. The film is acclaimed by critics but finds opposition in the South, especially because a white man in the film wants to marry Pinky despite knowing her heritage. The US Supreme Court declares the movie unconstitutional and Jeanne starts to be a star at age 24: she receives more than 6,000 roses a week!

"I loved being at 20th Century Fox.
After all, I started at 15, and I grew up there.
But there comes a time when an actress stays too long in the same place. People get used to having you around, and they can't think of you in a different light."

She is a typical 20th Century Fox girl, charming, youthful, and pretty and after the glory she is "no more calls" at age 35.

Joyce Holden

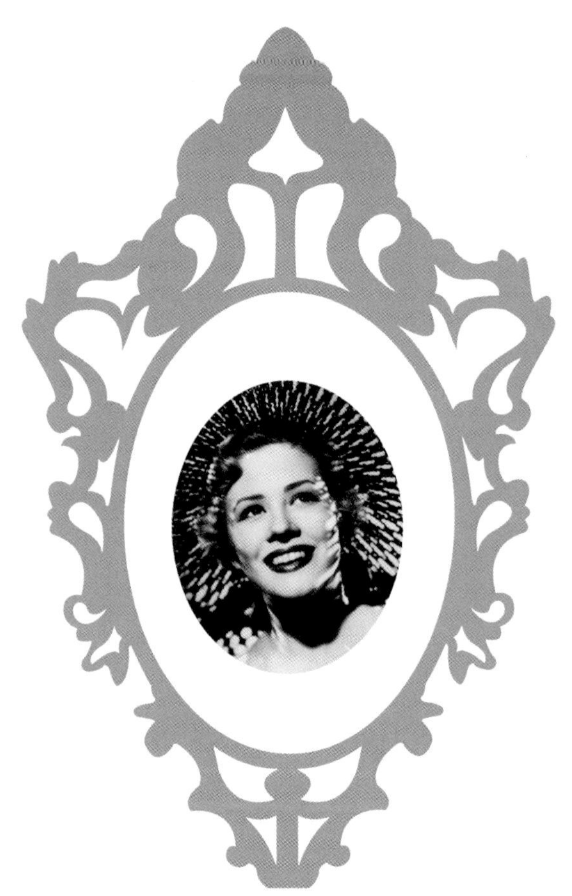

Terror at last?

"I found stage work very unrewarding.
I do not like the idea of repetition
too much. Doing the same thing every night
for months and years . . . it loses
its challenge."

At age 3 she starts learning how to stay
on stage and, with her stage mother, they move
to Hollywood after her parents' divorce.
At age 19 she signs with Universal and she
debuts in the comedy *The Milkman* (1950).
She has a seven-year contract but the studio
drops her option after five years.
She makes only a handful of films during
her ten-year career, including *Girls in the
Night* (1953) and *The Werewolf* (1956).

At age 28 the last film: the American
international horror flick *Terror From the
Year 5000*.

"I feel sorry for young actors today.
Where do they learn everything? Where are
they allowed to take ballet and horseback
riding, and do live shows and USO tours?"

Julia Adams

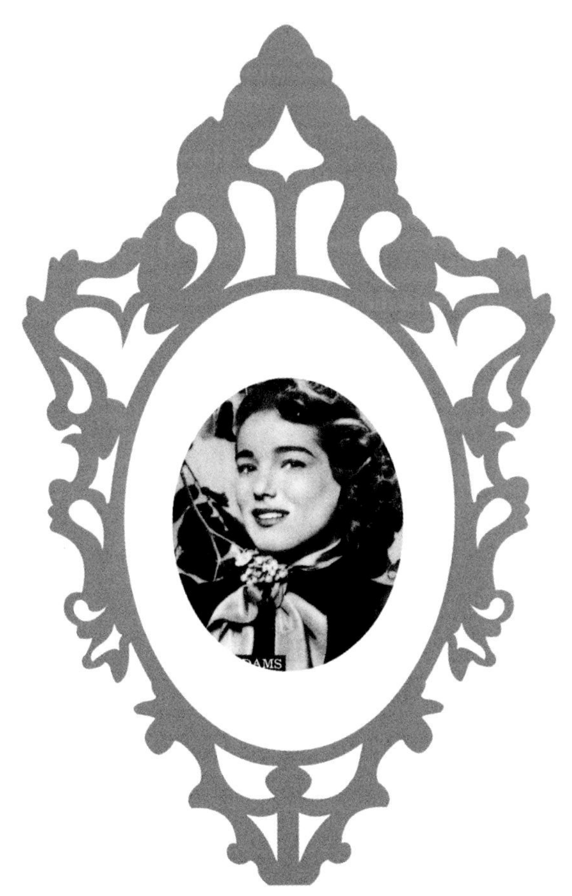

Betty, Julia, Julie? No . . . Kay

No matter what you do, you can act your heart out, but people will always say: "Oh, Julie Adams . . . Creature from the Black Lagoon."

Betty begins her film career in B-movie Westerns as Betty Adams. Universal changes her first name to Julia at age 23. Later she is Julie. Anyway she becomes Kay Lawrence, a leading lady of horror films.

Julia, at age 28, is featured as the bathing beauty Kay Lawrence in *Creature from the Black Lagoon* (1954), Jack Arnald's monster film, one of the first Universal Pictures in 3D. It is a huge hit that produces two more sequels, *Revenge of the Creature* (1955) and *The Creature Walks Among Us* (1956). A scientific expedition looking for fossils in the Amazon River discovers a prehistoric Gill-Man in the Black Lagoon. The explorers are able to capture the monster but it breaks free. The Gill-Man is in love with the beautiful Kay and returns to kidnap her and he has right because Julie's legs are considered "the most perfectly symmetrical in the world," insured for $125,000.

Kathryn Grayson

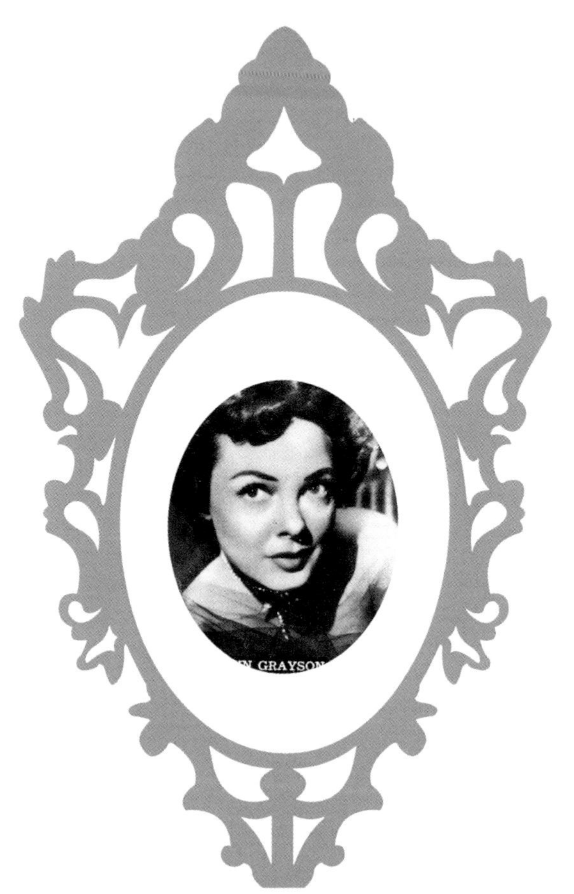

Just my voice

She dies at age 88, survived by her
daughter and her several grandchildren
and great-grandchildren.

She leaves MGM at age 31 and makes just
one more film.

She goes on working in night clubs,
summer-stock circuits, some variety-show
appearances, and in some operas.

She is at the top with her roles in *Show Boat*
(1951) playing opposite Ava Gardner and
Howard Keel and in *Kiss Me Kate* (1953).
She sings the hit "Anchors Aweigh," in which
she co-stars with Frank Sinatra.

She has a coloritura soprano voice and,
at age 19, she debuts in a B-picture but soon
she is cast opposite some of MGM's top
musical stars of the 1940s, such as, Gene Kelly
and Mario Lanza, with whom she never has
a good relationship, mainly due to Lanza's
hot temper and alcohol abuse.

As she sings on the radio with her coloritura
soprano voice, an MGM talent scout calls
her and quickly signs a contract, including
acting lessons and countless publicity photos.
She is a singer. She wants to sing.
She is a reluctant movie star.

Kay Aldridge

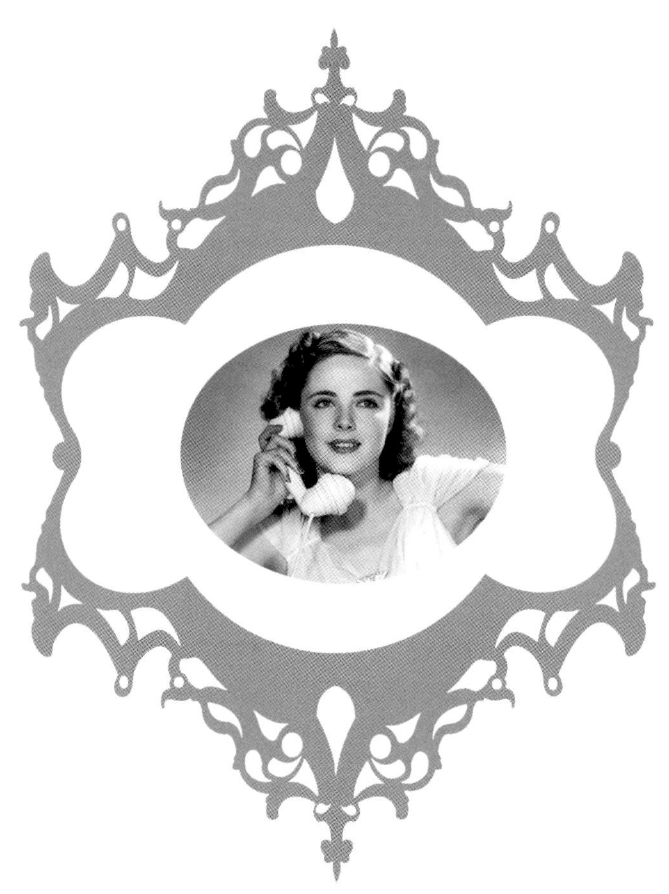

The black and white cliffhanger serial queen

20th Century Fox: just an up-and-coming starlet with minor and decorative roles.

Her A-movie career does not pan out. She is among the actresses screen tested for the part of Scarlett O'Hara in *Gone with the Wind* (1939).

Republic Picture: at age 25 she becomes the black-and-white B-serials queen thanks to this company specialised in serials of the type that have dramatic cliffhanger scenes at the end of each episode.
Now Kay is Nyoka Gordon, one of Republic's biggest hits. Kay is very popular among serial fans.

And serial again
Kay's next serial is *Daredevil of the West* in 1943.

Kay's final serial is *Haunted Harbor* in 1944.

Kay, later, goes on charming the guests at many serial conventions and discusses her serials with her fans.

Cliffhanger fans are still in love with Kay Aldridge.

Martine Carol

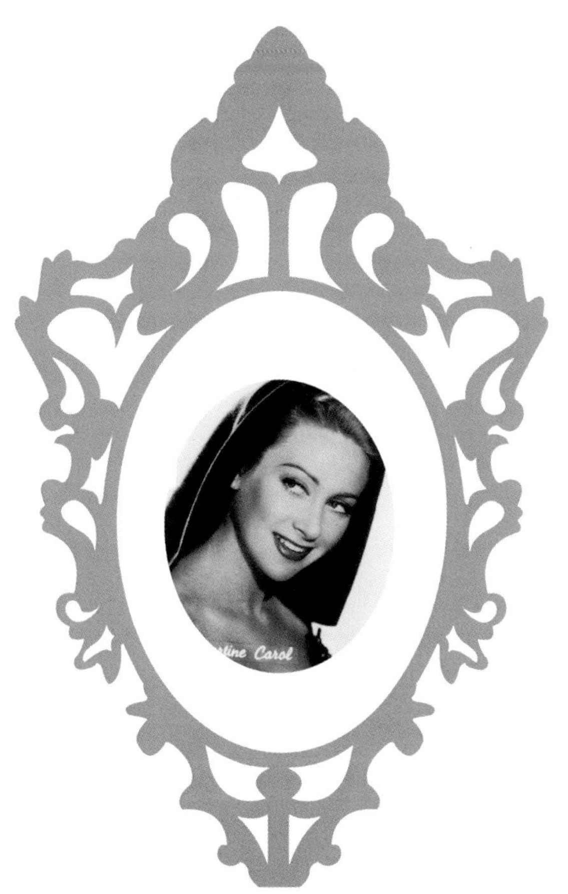

Brigitte's shadow

She is born Maryse Mourer, the name she uses early in her stage career.

She is Martine Carol, the name that this voluptuous blonde uses for her screen debut at age 21.

She is Caroline chérie, the seductive aristocrat of one of her best films, *Caroline chérie* (1953), which makes her France's biggest box office attraction in the early 1950s.

She is overshadowed as a sex symbol with the rise of Brigitte Bardot and her career falls suddenly.

She plays just a title character in *Lola Montès* (1955) by Max Ophüls, but Bardot is starring in Roger Vadim's . . . *And God Created Woman* in 1956 . . . and a real super star icon is born, BB! This film, about an immoral teenager in a respectable small-town setting, is a huge international success that puts BB on the map. The explosive sexuality of the French movie can be compared to the US "flapper" sensation in the 1920s.

She is 35, BB is 22 and her kingdom is untouchable.
She is depressed and a drug addict.
She tries a very strong diet, which does not help her breakdown.
She marries four times, first with Stephen Crane, an American actor and restaurant manager, previously Lana Turner's husband. When Georges Marchal, her first lover, chooses Dany Robin she attempts suicide in the Seine River in 1947. It is a taxi driver who saves her.

She tries a movie comeback without any success.
She dies of a heart attack at 45.

Sheila Terry

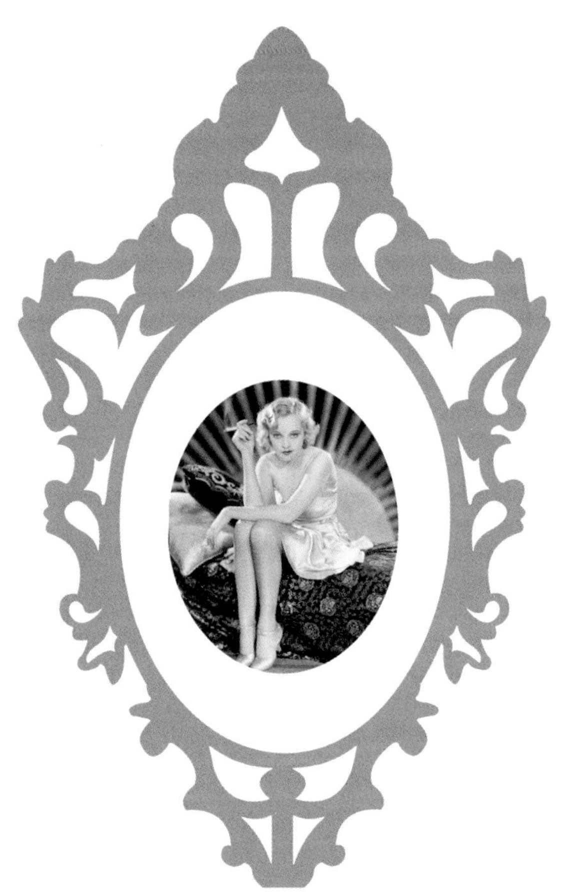

Just a movie list

At age 22

Week-end Marriage (1932), *Jewel Robbery* (1932), *Crooner* (1932), *Two against the World* (1932), *Big City Blues* (1932), *A Scarlet Week-End* (1932), *Three on a Match* (1932), *Scarlet Dawn* (1932), *They Call It Sin* (1932), *You Said a Mouthful* (1932), *I Am a Fugitive from a Chain Gang* (1932), *Haunted Gold* (1932), *20,000 Years in Sing Sing* (1932), *Madame Butterfly* (1932), *The Match King* (1932).

At age 23

Lawyer Man (1933), *Parachute Jumper* (1933), *The Sphinx* (1933), *The Silk Express* (1933), *Private Detective 62* (1933), *The Mayor of Hell* (1933), *The House on 56th Street* (1933), *Convention City* (1933), *Son of a Sailor* (1933).

At age 24

Take the Stand (1934), *Rocky Rhodes* (1934), *When Strangers Meet* (1934), *The Lawless Frontier* (1934), *Neath the Arizona Skies* (1934).

At age 25

A Scream in the Night (1935), *Rescue Squad* (1935), *Social Error* (1935), *Society Fever* (1935), *Bars of Hate* (1935).

At age 26

Murder on a Bridle Path (1936), *Special Investigator* (1936), *Go-Get-'Em, Haines* (1936), *Fury Below* (1936), *A Girl's Best Years* (1936).

At age 27

Hit the Saddle (1937), *Sky Racket* (1937).

At age 28

I Demand Payment (1938).

At age 47

Nothing more, she dies.

Simone Simon

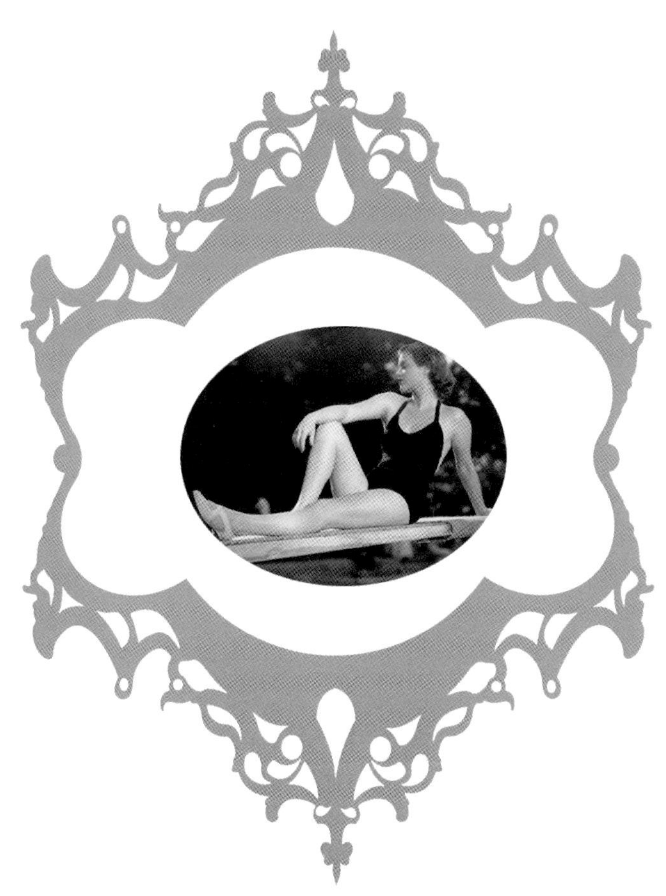

The gold key lady

France
Simon's debut is in *The Unknown Singer*
at age 21, and *Ladies' Lake* (1933) brings her,
at age 26, to Hollywood with a remarkable
publicity campaign.

Hollywood
She works with 20th Century Fox and co-stars
with James Stewart, Constance Bennett, and
Loretta Young.
These films are only moderately successful.

The scandal
Simon's personality is under the flash:
with her triangular face and gamine
figure she attracts men and she loves it.
She is involved in a scandal. She accuses
her secretary of stealing money and the
defense uses her private life, showing Simon's
indulgence with her lovers: very expensive
gifts and gold keys to her boudoir, engraved
with the initials of any man she is intrigued by,
such as composer George Gershwin.
"Above anything else in the relationship,
Gershwin and I shared a common interest
in music," Simon assures later.

France again
At age 28 Renoir rescues her career with
The Human Beast (1938) opposite Jean Gabin.

Hollywood again
At age 31 she achieves her greatest success
with *The Devil and Daniel Webster* (1941) but
the two following horror films are a flop.
Untill the end of the war she plays in low
profile movies.

France again and again and framed
At age 35 she returns but her film roles are
very few.
Simon spends 94 years in an independent life
without any marriages or children.

two
Some Calls

Ann Sheridan

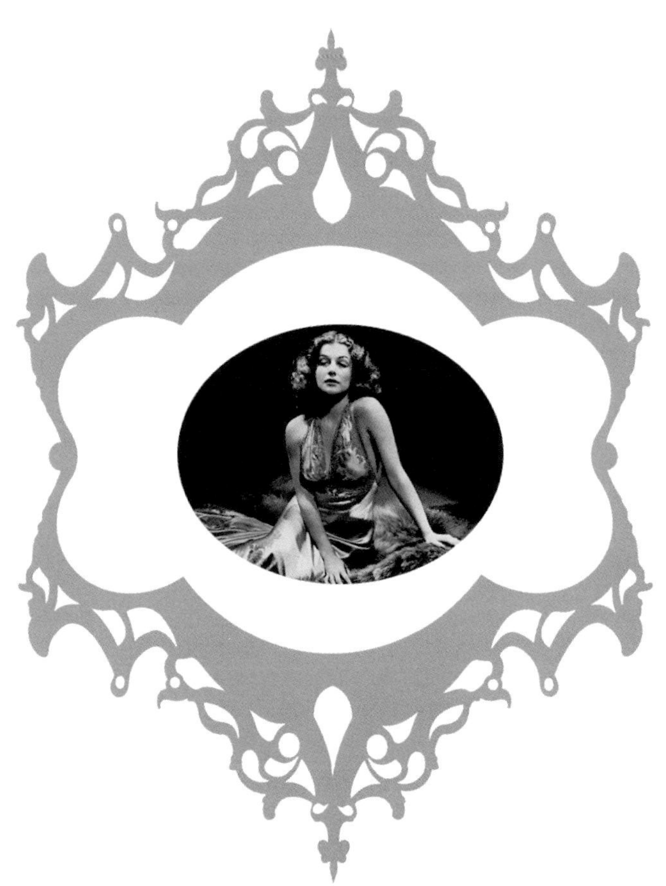

Oomph Girl

Oomph Girl
"They nicknamed me 'The Oomph Girl,'
and I loathe that nickname! Just being known
by a nickname indicates that you're not
thought of as a true actress . . . It's just crap!
If you call an actress by her looks or a reaction,
then that's all she'll ever be thought of as."

Oomph Girl definition
"In the 1930–1940s: a physically or sexually
attractive young woman. Actress Ann
Sheridan. She later becomes the inspiration
for the brand of women's house-slippers
called 'Oomphies.'"

Oomph is the winner of Search for Beauty.
She signs a contract with Paramount at age 19
and soon afterwards with Warner Bros.
The red-haired beauty would soon become
Warner's top sex symbol.
Oomph receives as many as 250 marriage
proposals from fans in a single week.
Oomph, at the beginning of the 1940s, starts
acting in important films like *Angels with
Dirty Faces* (1938) with James Cagney and
Humphrey Bogart as partners, *Dodge City*
(1939) with Errol Flynn, *They Drive by Night*
(1940) with Bogart and George Raft, but her
best moment is in *I Was a Male War Bride*
(1949), at age 34, co-starring Cary Grant.

Oomph at 40 struggles to find work
and her film roles are very sporadic.
Oomph appears in the television soap opera
Another World during the mid-1960s.
Oomph is a chain smoker and ages prematurely.
Oomph dies from cancer of the oesophagus
and of the stomach at age 51.

**Smoking in that historical period is not
penalized nor is it penalizing**
If you think product placement is a recent
phenomenon in Hollywood, take notice.
Seven and six decades ago stars such as
Gary Cooper, Bette Davis, Clark Gable,
Joan Crawford, and Spencer Tracy were taking
the equivalent of millions of dollars in today's
money for glamorizing cigarettes.

The tips:
- Gary Cooper $10,000 ($146,583)
- Joan Crawford $10,000 ($146,583)
- Henry Fonda $3,000 ($43,975)
- Edward G. Robinson $3,000 ($43,975)
- Clark Gable $10,000 ($146,583)

Anne Francis

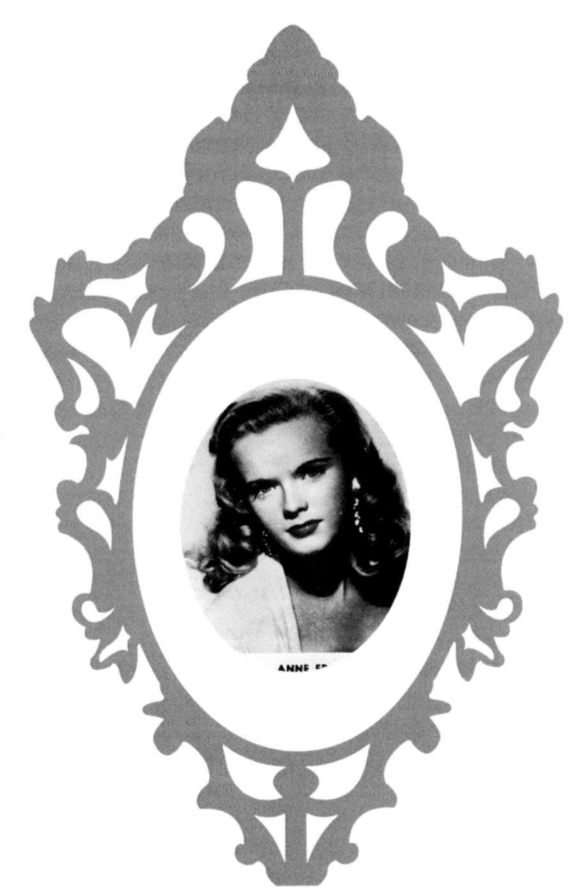

So nice . . .

From the Anne Francis home page
NewsLetters

Dear Friends,
Due to health issues, I'm unable to process
my fan mail in a timely manner.
For this reason, I am temporarily disabling
the collectibles page. For those of you who've
previously sent me fan mail and autograph
requests, I'll try to process them when
I am able to do so.

Thank you for your patience
and understanding.

Sincerely,
Anne Francis

So sweet to be so nice and polite
at age 80 and have fans mailing you.
This means that the tall beautiful girl
with the sexy mole-lip is unforgettable like
her most well-known success:
Forbidden Planet (1956), the science fiction
film in CinemaScope and Metrocolor
directed by Fred M. Wilcox.
At age 30, Anne finds a comfortable
niche on a 1960s television series, where she
combines glamour and a sexy *verve*.
She returns to films only on occasion.
At age 40, in 1970, she adopts
a girl as a single mother, one of the first
adoptions granted to a single parent
in California.
She is still involved in charitable
programs like Direct Relief, Angel View,
and the Desert AIDS Project,
among others.

Constance Campbell Bennett

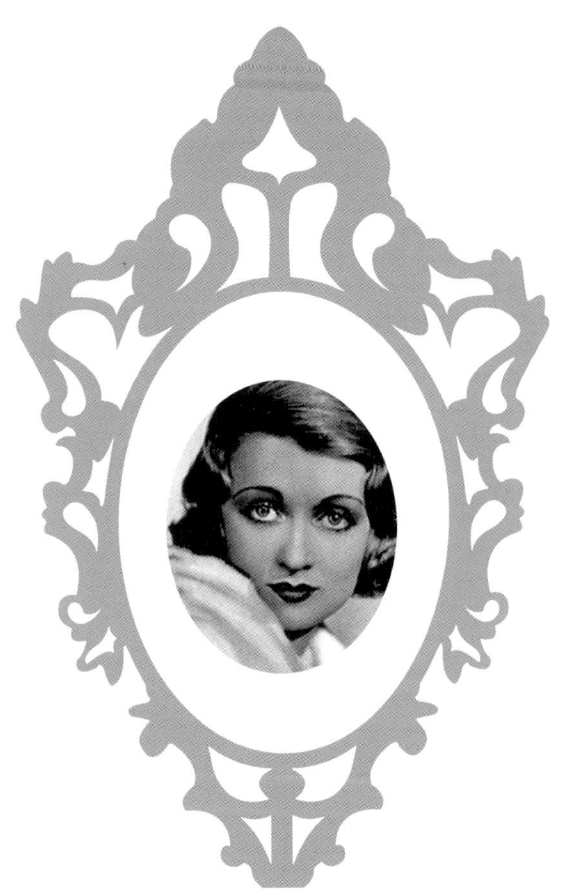

The poker player lady of Hollywood

Has a brief career

Constance Bennett, the first of the Bennett sisters to enter films, appears in New York-produced silent films before a chance meeting with Samuel Goldwyn, America's greatest independent film producer, leads to her Hollywood debut in *Cytherea* (1924) at age 20.

She abandons a burgeoning career in silent films to marry Philip Plant in 1925; after their divorce, she achieves stardom in talkies from 1929.

Her classy blonde looks, husky voice, and unerring fashion sense give her a distinctive style. At age 28 her 1931 contract with Warner Bros., $300,000 for two films, makes her the highest-paid film actor up to that time and reportedly inspired tax legislation aimed at the film industry.

By the 1940s, at age 40, Bennett works less in film but is in demand in both radio and theatre. She founds a cosmetics and clothing company.

She is a frequent winner

Constance adores poker and she is considered, with Kay Francis, one of the best poker players in Hollywood. She also earns a permanent place at the card table of high-stakes gamblers, Goldwyn.

Every Sunday at Samuel Goldwyn's house and on Thursdays at Irving Thalberg's. Film industry giants Darryl Zanuck, Jack Warner, David O. Selznick, Cecille B. DeMille, and Hollywood reporter publisher Billy Wilkerson are among the regulars. Known as "the heaviest game in town," chip denominations reach $20,000 and at least one player reported losing over a million dollars in a year! The games frequently lasted for twenty-four hours straight, or even longer. In the early morning hours, Constance likes to make coffee and scrambled eggs for the bleary-eyed holdouts.

Frequently, Constance is the winner, a real winner and her secret is her inscrutable expression. No expression.

Maybe one of the reasons being a successful card player is that she is the only actor or actress at the table!

Still young looking, she dies suddenly at the age of 60.

Diana Lynn

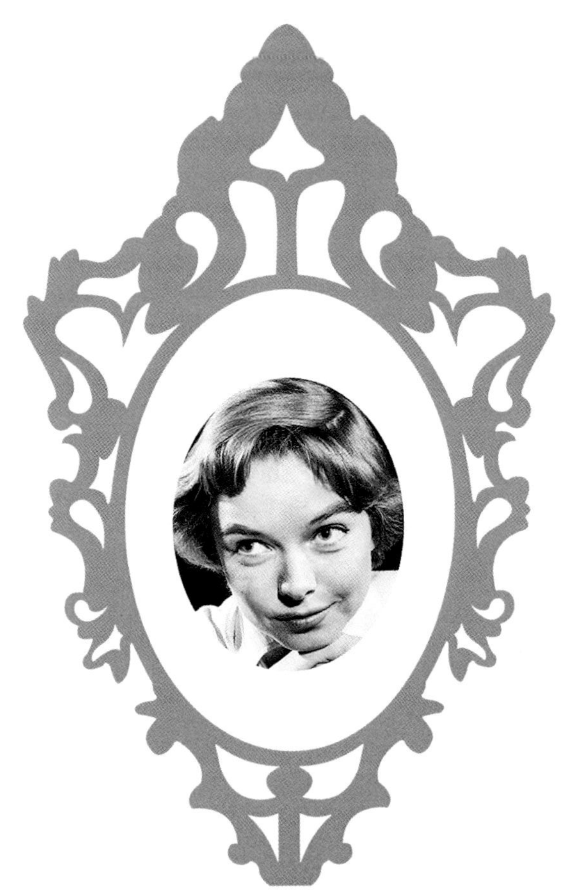

Used and exploited

"Acting was my own decision,
a kind of rebellion.
I loathed playing piano for people,
and I always have.
I was so young when I started;
I was used and exploited,
and I didn't have the courage
or the brains to say "no" to the use
of whatever talents I had."

At age 6 she starts to take piano lessons.
At age 10 she is a child prodigy.
At age 13 she is one of the children
in *They Shall Have Music* (1939).
At age 15 she plays in *There's Magic
in Music* (1941).
At age 16 she signs a long-term
contract with Paramount who changes
her name to Diana Lynn.
At age 18 she plays in *The Miracle
of Morgan's Creek* (1944) and *Our Hearts
Were Young, and Gay* (1944).

Then she matures: just fewer roles in film.
Has a nice career on television shows. Semi-
retired, at age 45, Paramount offers her the
role of Anthony Perkins's wife in *Play It As
It Lays* (1972). She returns to Los Angeles in
preparation for her role.
She dies at the age of 45, due to a fatal
stroke before filming.

Jane Powell

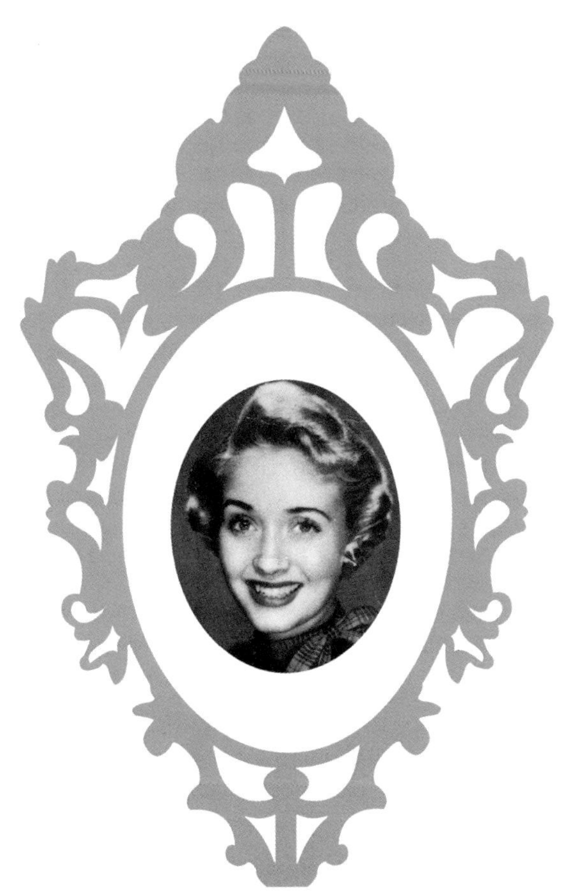

The girl next door and how she grew

"The only thing I knew was MGM, where I had worked since I was 14. Unions were not even a part of my vocabulary. SAG meant a gravity problem. Equity meant owning a house."

You appreciate Jane Powell's candor yet are shocked at the kind of childhood she endures. Clearly, Jane learns to like performing, but she pays a big price for her parents' ultimate decision to support themselves on her talents. They hope she becomes another Shirley Temple, just like in Luchino Visconti's *Bellissima* (1951), where Tina Apicella plays Anna Magnani's 8-year-old daugther. Maria Cecconi is a poor ugly little girl and she starts crying like crazy at the first screen test. She is fired in a violent way. Jane becomes a star, Tina does not want to be in film again, even if she is a real *enfant prodige*. Both of them are little children.

At age 9 she learns and loves to cook. At age 12 she is selected "Oregon Victory Girl." At age 13 she starts her career singing on the radio. She is a *coloratura soprano*, with an extraordinarily wide-ranging operatic singing voice. At age 15 she takes dancing and acting lessons, then makes her film debut in *Song of the Open Road*. At age 16 after her contract at Universal lapses, Powell is signed by MGM, initially promoted as a younger version of Kathryn Grayson. She is cast as the *ingénue* in several of the studio's top musicals. At age 20, along with other Hollywood stars, she performs at the Inauguration Ball for President Harry S. Truman.

"I didn't quit movies. They quit me." Her career in film ends, as she outgrows her innocent girl-next-door image. At age 22 Jane replaces June Allyson and Judy Garland for the part in *Royal Wedding* (1951) (June is pregnant and Judy is ill). At age 25, her best-known film *Seven Brides for Seven Brothers* (1954) opposite Howard Keel, which gives her the opportunity to play a more mature character than in previous films. At age 29 Powell's film career levels off, ending altogether with a misfire attempt at a dramatic role, complete with dark hair and "native" skin coloring in *Enchanted Island* (1958). She keeps busy thereafter with plenty of television performances, concerts, summer stock, and Broadway. During the 1950s and 1960s Powell appears regularly on television. Her last major television appearance is a guest spot on *Law & Order: Special Victims Unit* in 2002.

Jayne Mansfield

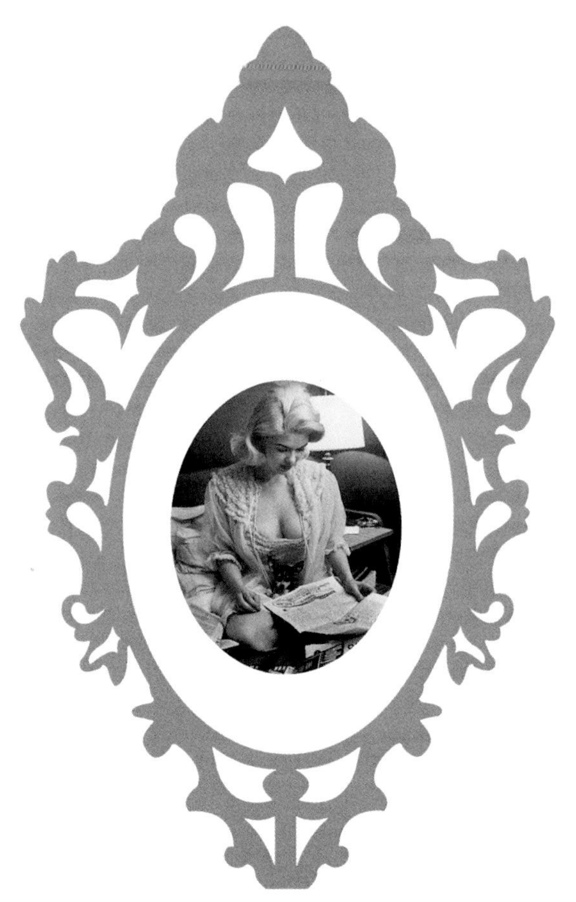

My opposite

She is born a brunette, but she becomes
a blonde bombshell, wearing many
blonde wigs.
She wants to be Marilyn, but her nickname
is "poor man's Marilyn Monroe."
She claims to have an IQ of 163, neverthless
she does not have exceptional grades at school.
She adores to be called "mother"
by her five children, but she likes to generate
negative publicity exposing her breasts
in carefully staged public "accidents."
She is the first American actress to appear
nude in a legitimate major motion picture,
but she is also a pianist and violinist
and can speak five languages.
She wins a Golden Globe as the
Most Promising Female Newcomer,
but she is Playboy Playmate.
She is on the Worst Dressed List in 1961
with Marilyn Monroe, Sophia Loren,
and Shirley MacLaine, and she makes
the list again in 1964.
At age 28 her film career begins to fall
out of favor, nevertheless Jayne's weekly
salary for her nightclub act is $8,000–
$25,000.
She has a serious drinking problem for
most of her adult life, but she goes on with
a wonderful body.
Kiss Them for Me (1957) is the title of a
20th Century Fox motion picture starring
Mansfield and Cary Grant, while *Kiss Them
for Me* (1991) is also a song by English
rock band Siouxsie & the Banshees
regarding her death.
She desires ten more babies and ten
more chihuahuas, but she dies in a crash
car at age 34.

Margaret Lockwood

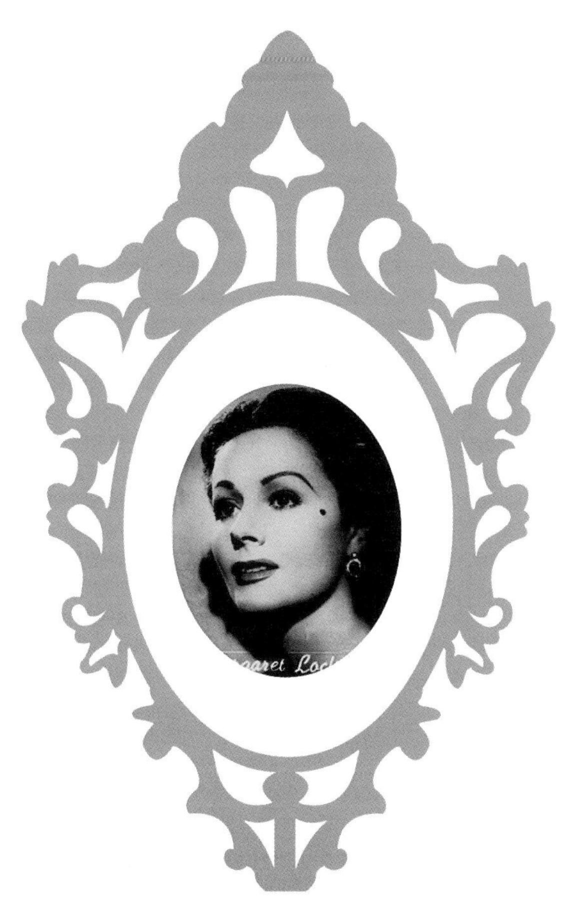

The Gainsborough gothic queen

A British education and CBE
Margaret Mary Lockwood Day is born in
Karachi, British India, now Pakistan to an
English administrator and to a Scottish
mother. When the family returns to the
United Kingdom, Margaret attends Sydenham
High School for girls and a ladies school
in Kensington. She learns acting
at the Royal Academy of Dramatic Arts,
and Margaret's investiture at Buckingham
Palace as Commander of the Order
of the British Empire in 1980 is her last
public appearance.
Margaret, at age 27, stars in her most
successful film, Alfred Hitchcock's
The Lady Vanishes (1938) which gives her
an international status. It's time for Hollywood
but America does not really seem to know
what to do with this British talent. She appears
with Shirley Temple in *Susannah of the
Mounties* (1939) and with Douglas Fairbanks
Jr. in *Rulers of the Sea* (1939). It is not
Margaret's cup of tea and she returns home.

A gothic English queen
where she shifts her image in a spectral black
gothic look and in beautiful and diabolic
stories. She is cast opposite James Mason
in the Gainsborough melodrama *The Man
in Grey* (1943). She plays an amoral woman,
looking for betrayals and murders. It is a huge
hit and the film opens the door to the so-called
series known as *Gainsborough Gothic*. She
goes on with her best success in *The Wicked
Lady* (1945), again opposite Mason where she
plays in a highway robbery murder. Margaret's
breasts are a scandal, but the fans adore her.
At age 35 she wins the Daily Mail First Prize
for most popular British film actress.

Not so wicked anymore
but her roles grow less black-hearted in
the following screenplays. She complains
to the studio and her contract is cancelled.
At age 40 she is no longer the wicked and
bloody minded lady who everybody wants
to see and her popularity declines. Her box
office appeal has waned and she quits
for stage and some TV.

**When she was good she was very very good
and when she was bad she was FANTASTIC!**
(missmatildadreams.blogspot.com/.../
margaret-lockwoods-future.htm)

Miriam Hopkins

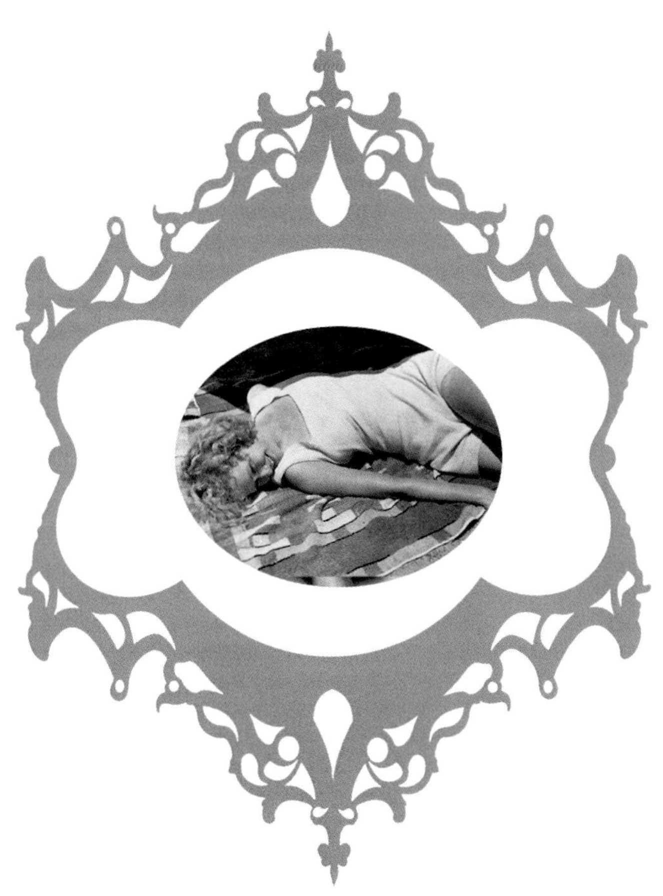

A non-conventional lady

Miriam Hopkins adopts orphanage baby boy

Chicago, May 4 (AP) — Miriam Hopkins, an actress, was aboard a New York-bound train today playing a new role, mother to an adopted baby boy, whom she selected yesterday from The Cradle, an Evanston orphanage. In answering questions necessary to the infant's legal adoption, the screen and stage actress revealed in court that she and her playwright husband, Austin Parker, were divorced. They separated about a year ago. Discovery of her plan to adopt a child and the resulting publicity irked the actress, and after adoption papers were signed she left Judge Edmund K. Jarecki's court, declaring she did not want to talk about it, or anything else for that matter. "I hate all this publicity over a simple thing. I don't have to give any reasons," she said to a reporter who asked why she wanted to adopt a baby. "It is just a fact and we will live wherever I happen to be working." In court she told the judge she would rear the child as her own and had already set aside a trust fund for it. She testified she was unmarried. All that could be learned about the baby was that it was "Boy Wilson." The orphanage operates on a policy of declining to make public information on adoptions. Miss Hopkins came here from Hollywood yesterday.

(from an unsourced newspaper dated May 5, 1932)

Independent

In 1932, at a time when single-parent adoption was illegal in most states, she adopts a baby boy, Michael; he is her own child even if Hopkins marries and divorces four times.

Good family

Born in Beverly Hills in a well-to-do family, but she doesn't get the part of Scarlett O'Hara in *Gone with the Wind* (1939), even if she has an advantage over the other candidates: she is a real native Georgian lady.

Good education

She attends the finest educational institutions including Goddard Seminary in Plainfield, Vermont, and Syracuse University in New York. She begins dancing and is a well-regarded stage performer.

Up to date

At age 28 she is a top Paramount attraction, playing sensual and sexually liberated women in numerous classics.

Difficult

Everybody says she has a difficult personality, and it is not easy to find roles. In fact, when her name comes up in current publications—not infrequently accompanied by the word "bitch." Also her arch-enemy Bette Davis considers her a bitch and admits to enjoying very much a scene in *Old Acquaintance* in 1942 in which she shakes Hopkins hard. On the contrary she is a good friend of actress Kay Francis, playing together in *Trouble in Paradise* (1932).

Hopkins starts to slow down in film work at age 38. She returns to the stage and she is a television pioneer, performing in teleplays in three decades, from the late 1940s through the late 1960s.

Nan Leslie

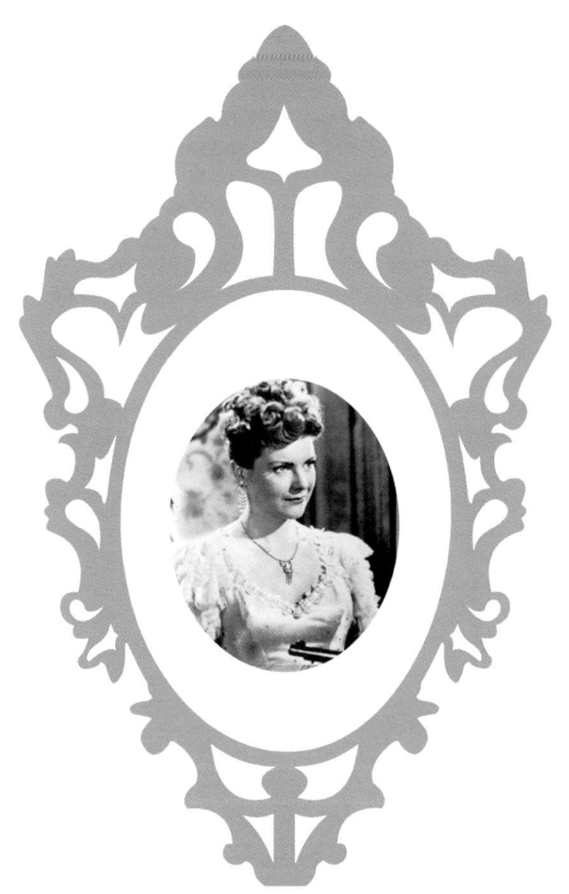

The B-Western lady

Western
Nan Leslie, best known in Hollywood
for her roles in Western films in the 1940s
and 1950s.

B-Western
Nan works steadily in movies most frequently
as the romantic lead in B-Westerns, including
Under the Tonto Rim (1947), *Guns of Hate*
(1948), and *Train to Tombstone* (1950).

Western TV
Westerns are among the first genres to make
the move to television in the late 1940s and
early 1950s, and Nan goes with them and is able
to win her regular roles in television series.

Western lovers
Movie business gossip linked her romantically
to some of her cowboy co-stars, including
Gene Autry and Tim Holt.

Western the end
At age 35 Leslie's career slows
down and her last film is, at age 42,
The Bamboo Saucer (1968), an unusual Cold
War tale about competing US and Soviet
expeditions trying to recover a flying
saucer that crashed in China.

Ruth Hussey

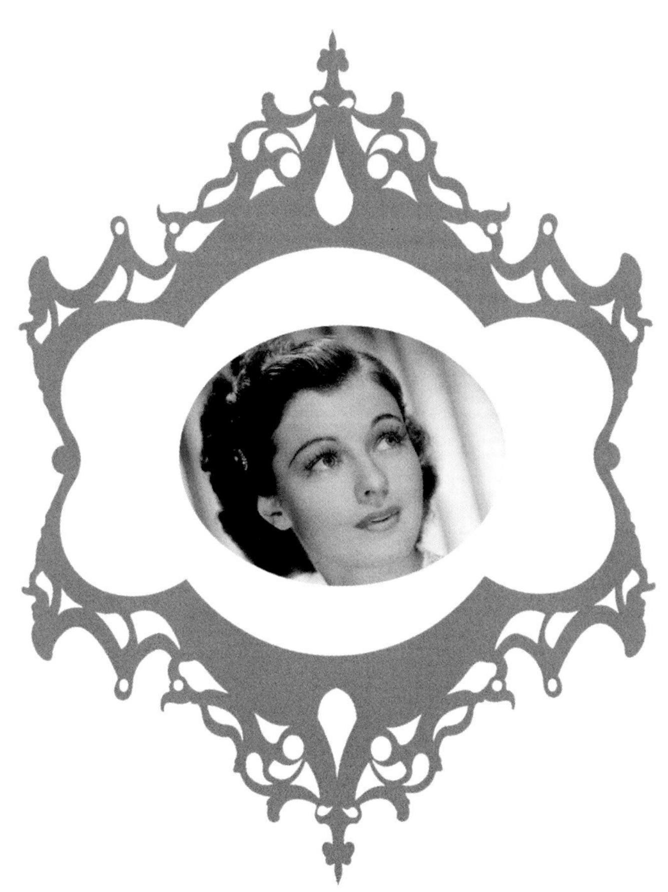

E pluribus una

A graduate of the University of Michigan
School of Drama and then fashion
commentator on a local radio station
and then model by the world-famous
Powers agency, and then some stage roles
with touring companies and then MGM,
her film debut in 1937, at age 26
and then MGM's "B" unit: she usually
plays sophisticated, worldly roles and then
MGM's "A" unit: she is nominated,
at age 29, for an Academy Award as best
supporting role in *The Philadelphia Story*
(1940), playing the cynical magazine
photographer, and then Broadway again
and television drama, and finally
Ruth Hussey dies at age 93.

Ruth Roman

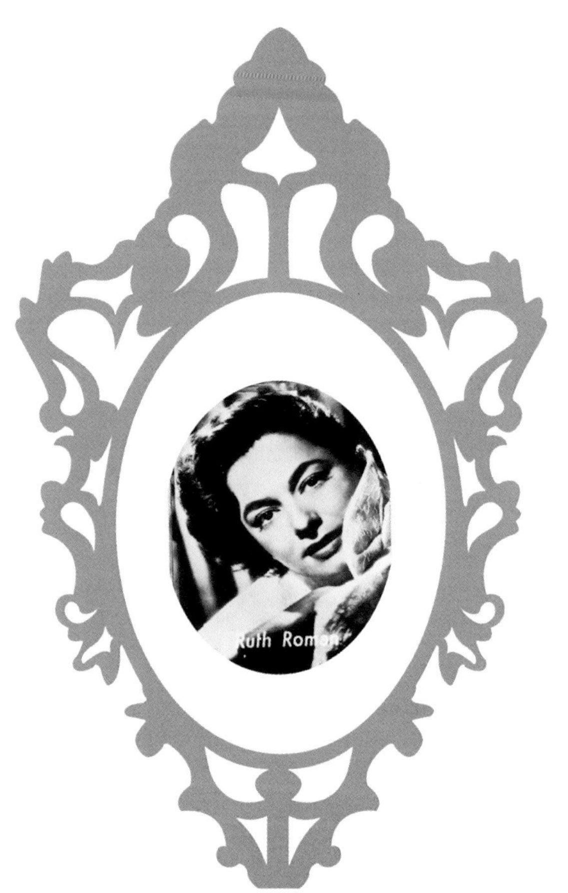

A fighter

From poverty
Roman is the youngest of three daughters of immigrants from Lithuania. Her father dies when she is a child, which forces her mother to work as a waitress, charlady, and laundress. For a while, they move regularly once a month because they cannot pay the rent. Even so, she says that she never feels sorry for herself. She has little formal education.

To Hollywood
In the midst of several difficulties, she works very hard and never gives up her desire to act. Ruth Roman spends six years playing bit parts until she achieves stardom in 1949 and wins a contract with Warner Bros.
In less than three years the studio features her in ten films, but, although she stars opposite some of the top players of the time, including Gary Cooper, Errol Flynn, and James Stewart, Roman is a leading lady rather than a major star, and Hitchcock's *Strangers on a Train* (1951), at age 29, is the only outstanding film she is to make at the studio.

Loved by her collegues, but not loved by directors
She learns from Bette Davis something she never forgets. Once she keeps blowing her lines in one scene with Bette Davis because they are so awful. She finally tells the director and Bette immediately comes to her rescue. "She's right," Bette shouts. "This girl is absolutely right." Later she tells me, "Ruthie, never forget what you did today . . . never be afraid to fight for what you know is right." And she always does. Besides, she is a hard worker, punctual, loved by her collegues. But directors prefer other actresses. Elia Kazan does not want to work with her in *A Streetcar Named Desire* (1951). Warner insists that Hitchcock use Roman in *Strangers on a Train*, and the great director makes it clear that he is unhappy about it.

The actress experiences real-life drama when she is aboard the luxury liner Andrea Doria when it is struck by another ship and wrecked. She is returning home with her son. More than fifty people die, though 760 survive, including Ruth, her son, and Betzy Drake, Grant's wife. Accepts roles on television but never gives up acting Ruth appears on television in the early 1950s and as film roles become scarcer her television work becomes prolific, with guest appearances in over a hundred shows.

Teresa Wright

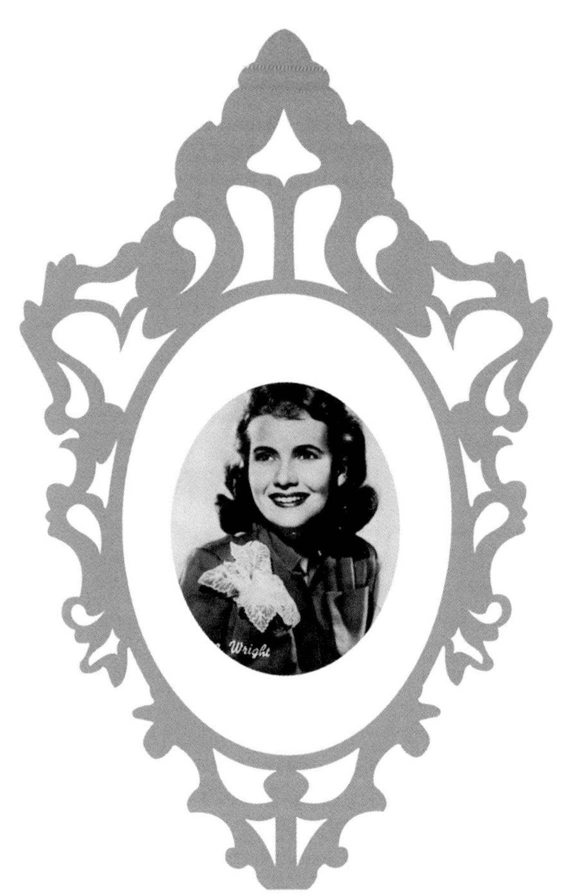

"I only ever wanted to be an actress, not a star."

She is unique in Hollywood, first of all
because she is not a glamour girl.
She has her singular charm, well-behaved,
kind and delicate face, and strong personality.
She is unique because, at 21, she signs with
Samuel Goldwyn a five-year unique contract
by Hollywood standards because
it contains the following clause:

"The aforementioned Teresa Wright
shall not be required to pose for photographs
in a bathing suit unless she is in the water.
Neither may she be photographed running
on the beach with her hair flying in the wind.
Nor may she pose in any of the following
situations: in shorts, playing with a cocker
spaniel; digging in a garden; whipping up a
meal; attired in firecrackers and holding
skyrockets for the Fourth of July; looking
insinuatingly at a turkey for Thanksgiving;
wearing a bunny cap with long ears for Easter;
twinkling on prop snow in a skiing outfit
while a fan blows her scarf; assuming
an athletic stance while pretending to hit
something with a bow and arrow."

She is unique because she is the only
actress to be nominated for an Oscar for
her first three films.
She is unique because she belongs to *the top
elite* nominated for both a supporting
and lead role Academy Award in the same year
for their achievements in two
different movies.

The other are:
Fay Bainter
Barry Fitzgerald
Jessica Lange
Sigourney Weaver
Al Pacino
Emma Thompson
Holly Hunter
Cate Blanchett
Julianne Moore
Jamie Foxx

Nevertheless at age 30 she is fired
by Goldwyn and she rebels against the studio
system of the time. She says: "We have no
privacies which producers cannot invade,
they trade us like cattle, boss us like children."
She has no regret about losing her $5,000
per week contract, and for her following
film Wright chooses a low-paying role in
The Men (1950), co-starring Marlon Brando.
At 34 her high quality film career starts
to suffer but the Golden Age of Television
is her salvation. She works mainly in television
afterwards. She dies at the age of 87.

Virginia Bruce

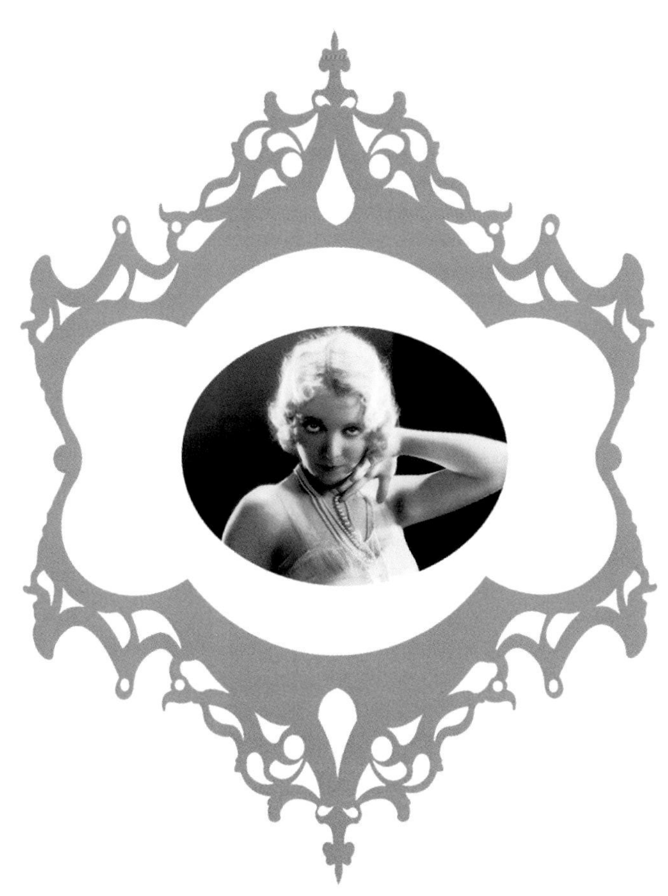

Following love

"My chief purpose in life is to fall in love . . ."
And she does so three times:
The great screen idol, virile and troubled
John Gilbert, who dies at age 37, two years
after their divorce.
The director-producer J. Walter Ruben,
who dies of a heart ailment at age 43.
Virginia's most idyllic love but too short.
The Turkish director and producer Ali Ipar.
They divorce in 1951 when Ipar begins
his Turkish army service: Turkish law forbids
commissions to men married to foreigners.
They marry again the following year, up to
the second divorce in 1964.

". . . I don't know why I want to, but I do."
 "I was absolutely unprepared," Virginia
says later, regarding her film career.
She is not especially a high-flyer and
ambitious, but the number and quality
of her role increases and, at age 24,
she plays her first major lead role in *Jane Eyre*
(1934), co-starring Colin Clive. This version
is criticized but Virginia is well considered
thanks to her stylish beauty, acting ability,
and personality. She plays a super naughty
showgirl in *The Great Ziegfeld* (1936),
but Virginia's promising "A" MGM status
is blemished due to producer Irving Thalberg's
untimely death, at age 37, in 1936.
She has to accept "B" roles and appears
in some Turkish films unseen in America.
That's love!

Virginia Mayo

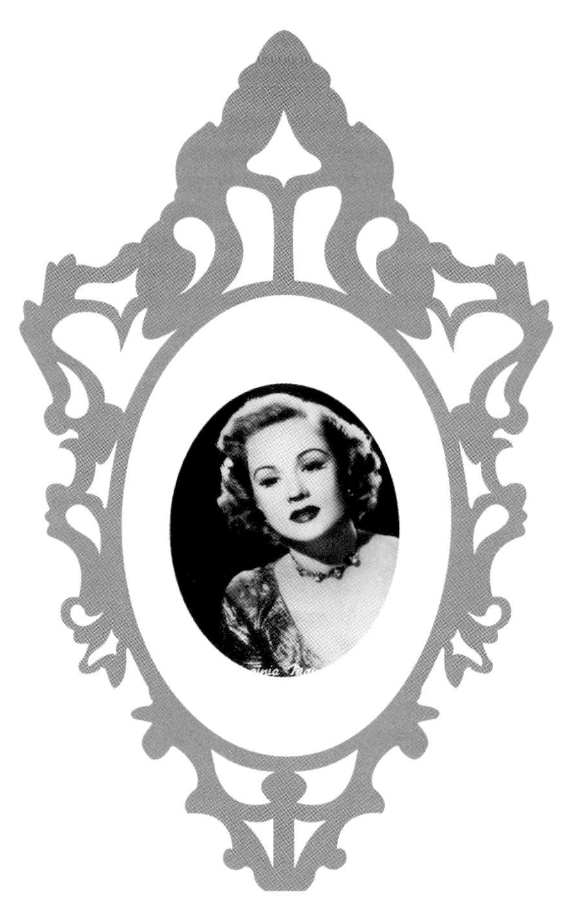

The blonde siren

Virginia Mayo is one of the most beautiful and glamourous screen stars of the 1940s and 1950s: blonde hair, peach skin, green-eyes, and, even if she is slightly cross-eyed and has to be photographed carefully . . . this means *charme*.
"The tangible proof of God's existence," exclaims the Sultan of Marocco during a gala in 1947.

Just one love
"Mike was so tolerant of my working all the time, and he would take care of the house while I had to go to work. And not every man will tolerate that, you know. But he was too clever to let that bother him. He was a great actor . . . I'd do plays with him, and I'd watch him on stage. It was just magnetism. He had a great talent that was never appreciated because he didn't push himself." (About her husband, actor Michael O'Shea; marriage in 1947 to 1973, when O'Shea died.)

But so many important partners
The public adores her and she appears opposite some of the greatest leading men in cinema history such as: Rex Harrison, Paul Newman, Bob Hope, Burt Lancaster, Kirk Douglas, Ronald Reagan, James Cagney, Gregory Peck, Danny Kaye, Louis Armstrong, and . . . this list seems endless!

But it isn't enough
Virginia is one of the best prototypes of a Hollywood victim.
Her career begins to slow down at 40.
B-movies, Westerns, TV, and some theatre in the following decade. No awards at all, not even for a sincere career and professionalism in over thirty years of honest work.

Yvonne De Carlo

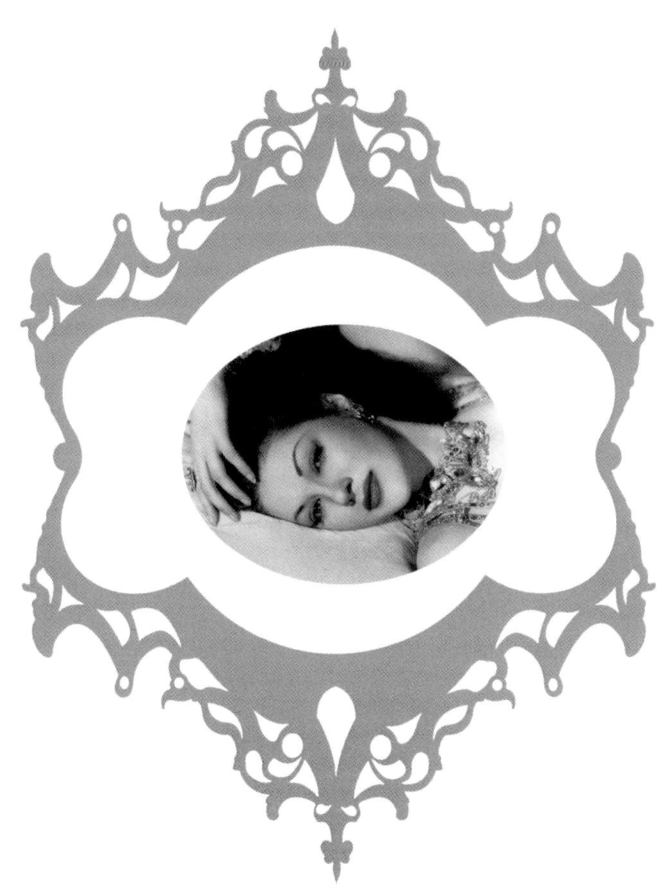

Yvonne vs. Ava . . . just for awhile

"If I could, I'd change a lot of things because I'm not proud of everything I've done in my life. But to those people who helped me, and there were a lot, I say, thank you. They're the reason I wrote this book."

Yvonne was born in 1922, like Ava Gardner. Yvonne, for one period, is Ava's rival both on screen and in the boudoirs of Hollywood; both stars often share the same men, notably Howard Hughes (romantically linked even with Katharine Hepburn, Bette Davis, Olivia de Havilland, Ginger Rogers, and Faith Domergue), Clark Gable, Burt Lancaster, and Robert Taylor.
Yvonne's biography admits about twenty-two loves affairs including Alì Khan, Billy Wilder, Burt Lancaster, Howard Hughes, Robert Stack, Robert Taylor, Clark Gable. Yvonne marries Bob Morgan and has two children.

Yvonne starts her career as a contract player for Paramount at age 20 and her best-known film role, at age 23, is in *Where She Danced* (1945) as Salome. Though not a critical success, it is a box office favorite, and Yvonne is an up-and-coming star. Yvonne's biggest success, at 27, is the female lead opposite Burt Lancaster in *Criss Cross* (1949). She plays a femme fatale, and her career begins to take off. Yvonne's huge success, at 33, is in *The Ten Commandments* (1956), opposite Charlton Heston, in a leading role as Sephora, Moses's wife. She becomes part of a major hit.

Yvonne, at 42, is deeply in debt and her film career comes to a stop. She suffers from depression.
Yvonne, at 46, accepts an offer to reprise her role in a color Munster movie, *Munster, Go Home!* partially in the hopes of renewing interest in the television series. Despite the attempt, *Munster* is canceled after seventy episodes. Yvonne retires to private life after her son's death in 1997.

¿Yvonne de Carlo? ¿Yvonne de Carlo?... ¡Ah! ¡Yvonne de Carlo!
(Manuel Vázquez Montalbán, in *Nueve novísimos poetas españoles*, 1970)

three
Far from Hollywood

Arlene Dahl

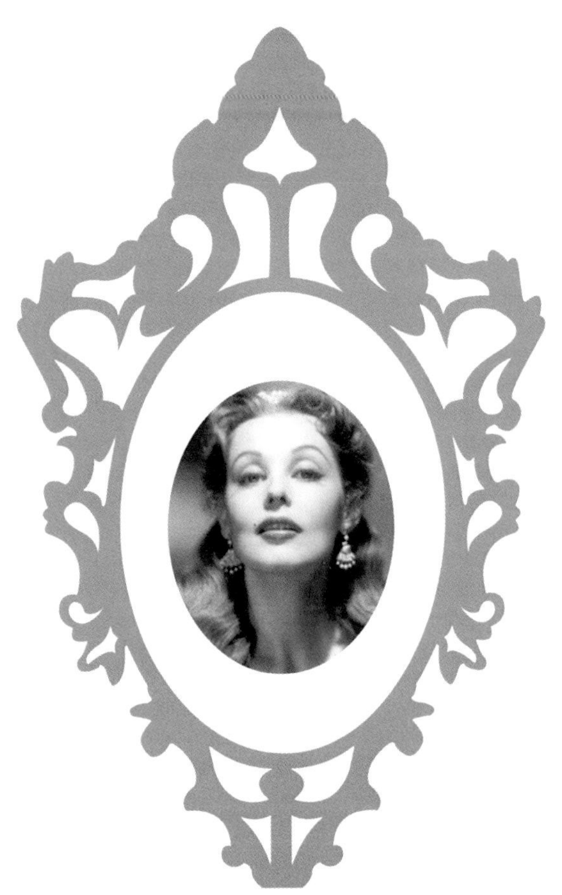

Beauty syndrome

Typecasting syndrome because of her excessive beauty, Arlene Dahl quits Hollywood at age 31 to become a beauty columnist and writer. She later establishes herself as a business woman, founding Arlene Dahl Enterprises, which markets lingerie and cosmetics.

She has several relationships including ones with: Gary Cooper, JFK, Philip Reed, Lex Barker (husband), Howard Hughes, Fernando Lamas (husband), Christian R. Holmes (husband), Alex Lichine, Rounsevelle W. Schaum, Marc Rosen (husband).

The stars say about her . . .
Even-tempered and peace loving, she is not easily ruffled and is rarely given to emotional displays. Arlene Dahl has a calming effect on more high-strung or volatile people, and an emotional steadiness that others find soothing. Though gentle and not easily provoked, Dahl is tremendously stubborn and resists any change that requires an emotional adjustment, such as changes in her home life or marriage.
Arlene Dahl seeks security and loyalty in love relationships, is extremely devoted to her loved ones, and provides a warm, nurturing atmosphere for them. However, Dahl tends to cling to others and prevent them from changing.
A great deal of physical affection, closeness, and touching is crucial to Arlene's wellbeing, and she has a tendency to overindulge in sensual comforts and pleasures.
At times Arlene Dahl substitutes food for emotional comfort and love.
She is quietly devoted and faithful to her loved ones and often becomes subservient to her love partner. Arlene Dahl is more comfortable showing her love by doing or making something for her loved one, or simply being there for him, rather than by making any romantic, soul-stirring declarations. She is timid about expressing too much sentiment or emotion.
Arlene Dahl also underestimates her attractiveness and lovability and doubts her own worthiness of love and appreciation. For Arlene Dahl, caring and affection must be expressed tangibly, and she loves giving and receiving gifts. Arlene greatly values luxury, comfort, and elegance and appreciates beautiful things. She can be self-indulgent and extravagant. Being overly possessive of people she loves and of her belongings is something Arlene Dahl needs to be careful of.
Her romantic relationships tend to be deep, intense, passionate, and highly emotional. It is "all or nothing" with her.
Oftentimes Arlene Dahl is irresistibly attracted to someone and feels that she has very little choice or control over her powerful feelings.
(from an astro profile from topsynergy)

Corinne Calvet

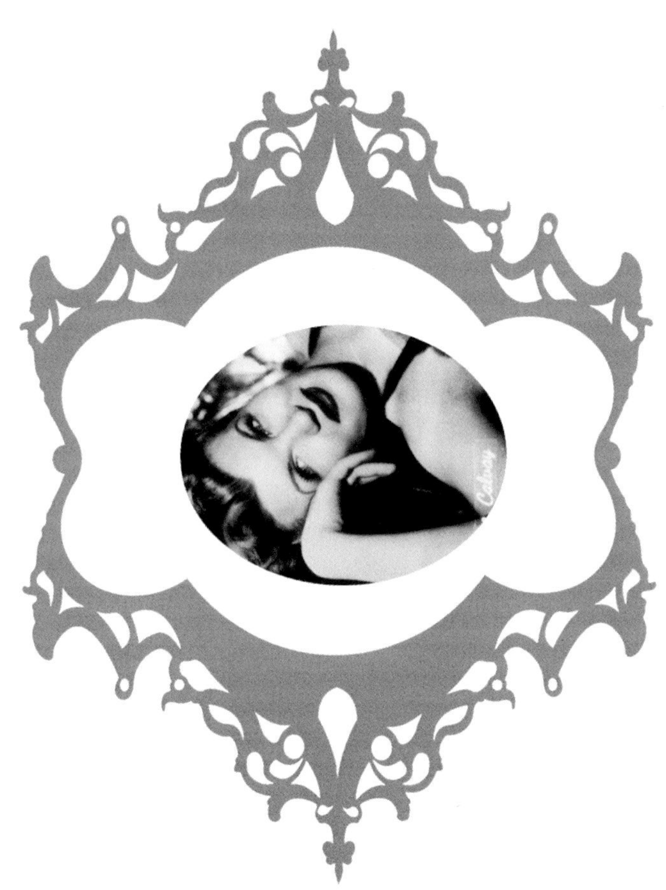

Has Corinne been a good girl?

A hysterically funny book
Readers consider that Corinne Calvet's autobiography (*Has Corinne Been A Good Girl?*) is funny. Corinne Calvet is a French starlet who goes to Hollywood in the early 1950s, she is about 25 years old.
Her dream of stardom never becomes real.

In her view, one of the biggest reasons for this are her conservative upbringing and attitudes, at odds with those towards sex in Hollywood. Corinne Calvet says that her career is seriously hurt by her refusal to have sex with one mogul after another. And as a consequence, she is not allowed to experience a great deal of success in American films.

She is told by the voice of Sarah Bernhardt that she will become a great actress.
She is constantly going on and on about how beautiful and sophisticated she is. According to herself (always according to herself), she is close friends with Cocteau and Sartre. She even refers to Sartre simply as "Jean-Paul." Her art teacher is so impressed with her views that he encourages her to study

Law at the Sorbonne. Law at the Sorbonne! And then there is this episode that the professor takes her into his private study . . . she follows him but of course refuses him sexually . . . everything is so funny for readers.

One reader says that he literally has tears of laughter streaming down his face . . . and he is not the only one. This biography is a must-read for anyone who loves people that will frenetically and with conviction describe themselves as so successful, so good, so beautiful, so everything when in the end they are and do nothing.
Of course anything they do not manage to do is the fault of other people or their inability to evaluate how good they are. For Corinne, this biography must be an epic, and maybe it is, because readers are still laughing.

Corinne Calvet is not abandoned but of course abandons Hollywood to become a therapist.

(Summary of readers reviews available in the web)

Hedy Lamarr

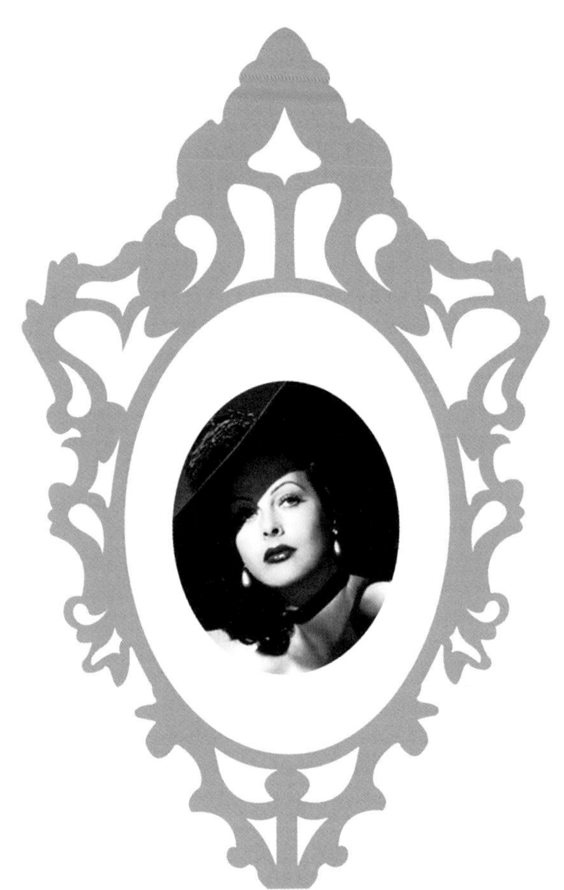

I need a superior man

Hedwig Eva Kiesler simulates orgasms for the first time in the film industry . . .
Born in Vienna, Austria.
Regarded by many as the most beautiful actress ever in Hollywood.
Studies with theater director Max Reinhardt in Berlin.
Begins her career in Czech and German films.

She causes an international sensation thanks to *Ecstasy* (1933). She appears nude. Moreover, she simulates an orgasm.
She receives worldwide attention and is credited for the first nude and the first scene of sex in film history.

. . . and brings Hedy Lamarr into live . . .
As a result she becomes a celebrity and is called to Hollywood. She signs with MGM. The studio changes her name to the more upscale "Hedy Lamarr."

. . . interpreting exotic roles, her career does not last long . . .
She is put in a series of exotic epics such as *Algiers* (1938) and *White Cargo* (1942). She is sometimes considered for non-exotic roles, but often other actresses get the part in the end, like for example the role of Isla Lund in *Casablanca* (1942) in which Ingrid Bergman is cast. Her biggest success is in Cecil B. DeMille's film *Samson and Delilah* (1949) at age 35. Her career declines from that point due to ageing. She leaves the screen in 1957 at age 43.

. . . also her marriages do not last long . . .
She divorces six times:
Lewis J. Boies (1963–1965)
W. Howard Lee (1953–1960)
Teddy Stauffer (1951–1952)
John Loder (1943–1947)
Gene Markey (1939–1941)
Fritz Mandl (1933–1937)

. . . maybe for her being a very intelligent woman and knowing it.
"I must quit marrying men who feel inferior to me. Somewhere there must be a man who could be my husband and not feel inferior. I need a superior inferior man."

Frequency hopping
She is the co-inventor (with George Antheil) of the telecommunications method known as "frequency hopping." This method uses a piano roll to change between frequencies and is intended to create difficulty for the radio-guided torpedoes to be detected by enemies during WWII. US patent number 2,292,387. Since 1942, frequency hopping has been widely used in cellular phones and other modern technology. However the inventors do not profit from this, because their patents have expired. She deservedly receives an award from the Electronic Frontier Foundation in 1997 for her pioneering work. "It's about time," says she.

Irene Dunne

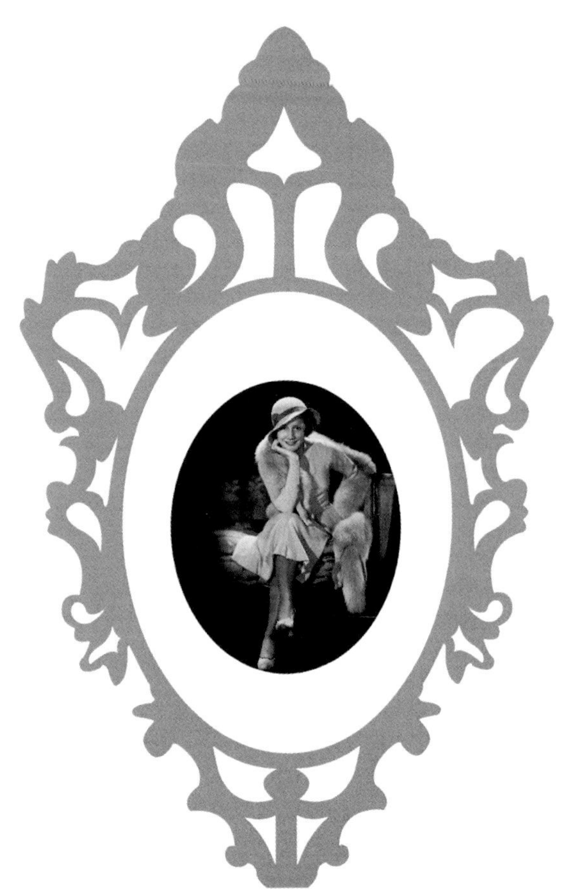

Unconventional Hollywood First Lady

Her way to Hollywood
She is born in Kentucky in 1898. Her father dies when she is eleven. Following a convent upbringing, Dunne has ambitions to become an opera singer, but she fails her audition for the Metropolitan Opera in 1920. Dunne spends her twenties in musical comedies on the stage. She gets a movie contract through one of her tours. Dunne goes to Hollywood. She leaves behind her husband, Dr. Francis Griffin.

Catholic, no scandals, successful marriage
Dunne and Griffin live far away for six years. During this period, Dunne behaves in an impeccable way. She has one of Hollywood's few successful marriages (it lasts until Griffin's death in the 1960s). Dunne is very religious, a Catholic. "God does not read an actresses' press clippings," she says. Later on in her life, she goes to Mass every day.

After five Oscar nominations, she quits to champion several charitable institutions and civic causes
Acutely aware of how Hollywood works, she wisely chooses to leave.
She still appears occasionally on television, but her public appearances turn away from entertainment and move towards service and charity.
In 1957, President Dwight Eisenhower appoints her as special US Delegate to the United Nations, and she quietly champions several charitable organizations and social causes.

Louise Brooks

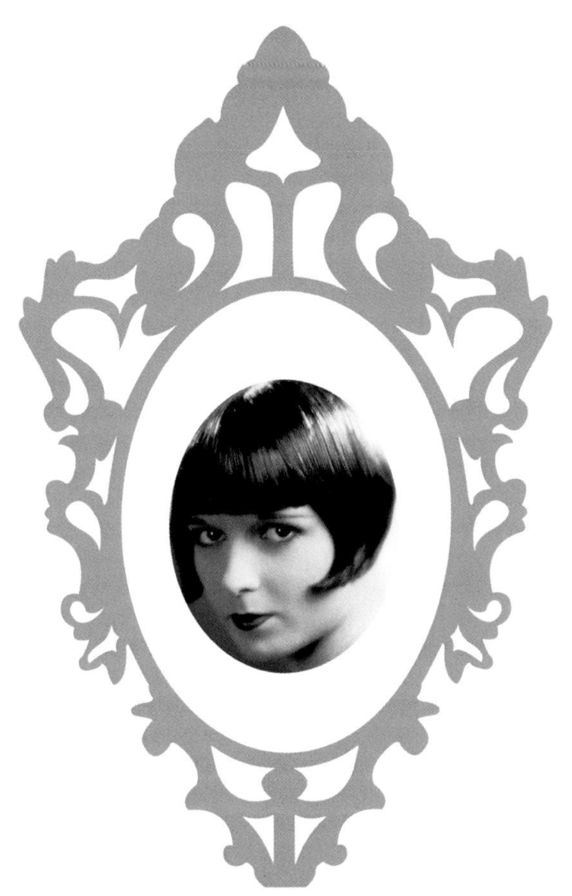

Louise is alive

In the long last years of her life, Louise Brooks, tired of living, ends telephone conversations with the order: "Bring a gun."

Long failure better than short success
Her image remains as sensual and provoking as ever. When she makes her films, in the 1920s, Brooks is at best a second-tier star. Yet she is better known today than Mary Pickford and Gloria Swanson, and many other silent heavyweights. Her failure lasts much longer than their success.

Brief career but resurrection
In the 1920s, she makes fourteen silent films at Paramount, seven of which are now lost. She goes to Europe, where she makes two silent films. When she returns, she is reduced to small parts in early talkies, and two leads in Westerns. Then oblivion.
Her most significant film is Pabst's *Pandora's Box* (1929), where she incarnates Franz Wedekind's Lulu, but it's not appreciated until nearly thirty years after its release.
When she is resurrected, Brooks writes an impressive series of articles about her Hollywood experience.

Molested
She is molested by a man at the age of nine. Louise calls her molester "Mr. Flowers" and sometimes "Mr. Feathers." After that, Brooks always strongly fight against any type of domination.

Freedom above all
Women like Louise Brooks and the 1930s star Frances Farmer are considered martyrs. Farmer's link to Brooks is not only to their being victims, but also Hollywood's misuse of them. Brooks is a woman who knows no law but her own ideas, a real feminist. Dietrich knew everything about the films she was making, while Brooks admits she had no idea while she was making them.

Back to Hollywood
Louise stays in Europe too long. When she returns to Hollywood, there is nothing and nobody waiting for her. She also claims that Paramount blacklisted her, but the exact reason for her downfall is still somewhat obscure. She stays on in Hollywood for most of the 1930s, trying to get work. Even though she is at the height of her beauty and only in her mid-twenties, she only gets insignificant parts.

Poverty
In the mid-1940s, Brooks, around 40 years old, goes to New York, where she works as a salesgirl and call girl, until she is an overweight, alcoholic, middle-aged flop. William Paley, an old friend and lover, comes to her rescue. He gives her money for the rest of her solitary days.

The miracle
Around the mid-1950s, the miracle happens. She is acclaimed for *Pandora's Box* as a neglected titan of the screen. Everything finally falls into place. She is a victim of Hollywood. She becomes a living legend. She writes hard, precise essays that consolidate her reputation. She lives as a recluse and spends the rest of her life in bed with books and booze. She is the one that really links failure to integrity. She is the one who quits Hollywood for freedom.

An aura that influences contemporary culture
Louise Brooks's hair, image, and mainly her charme determine or appear through various aspects of contemporary culture. Individuals model their personas after Brooks. She has a lasting impact on cinema, theatre, literature, comics, fashion, society, and music.

Luise Rainer

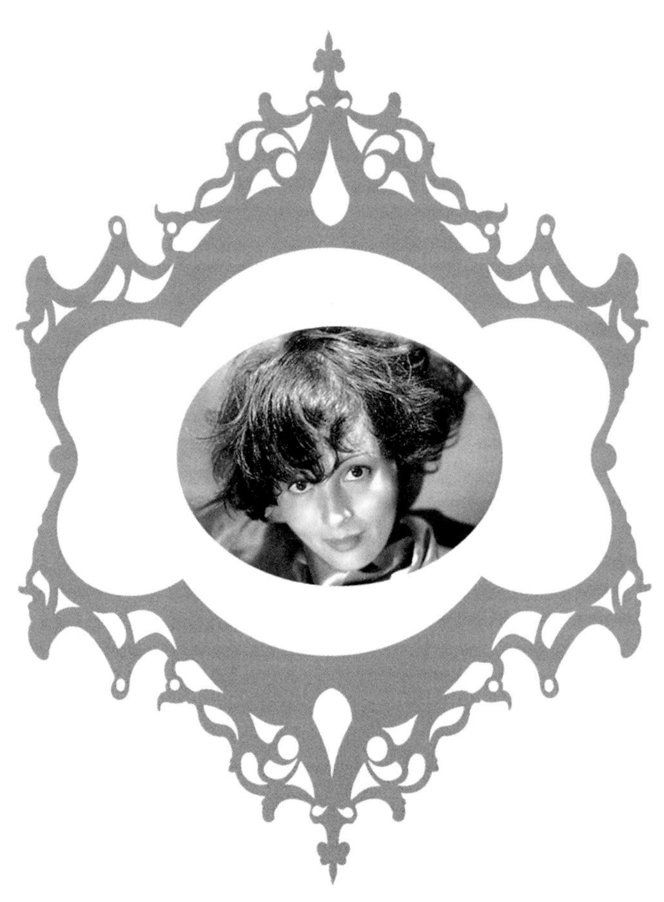

Life is more important than Cinema

"For my second and third pictures I won
Academy Awards. Nothing worse could have
happened to me."

"You are now 60 and I am 20. When I am 40,
the age of a successful actress, you will be dead
and I will live."
(from a dialogue with Mayer)

"It was not the thing that I strived for because,
you see, today's Academy Award is—Oh God!
The thing everyone longs for."

"The Oscar is not a curse. The real curse
is that once you have an Oscar they think you
can do anything."

"I was living in America and was on the stage
there—sporadically. I always lived more than
I worked. Which doesn't mean that I do not
love my profession and every moment I was in
it gave me great satisfaction and happiness."

"To me, it was like a huge hotel with a huge
door, one of those rotunda doors. On one side
people went in, heads high, and very soon they
came out on the other side, heads hanging."

"I couldn't bear this total concentration
and interviews on oneself, oneself, oneself.
I wanted to learn, and to live, to go all over
the world, to learn by seeing things and
experiencing things, and Hollywood seemed
very narrow."

"I just had to get away."

"Soon after I was there in Hollywood, for some
reason I was at a luncheon with Robert Taylor
sitting next to me, and I asked him, "Now,
what are your ideas or what do you want
to do?" and his answer was that he wanted
to have ten good suits to wear, elegant suits
of all kinds, that was his idea. I practically fell
under the table."

"Everybody thanking their mother, their
father, their grandparents, their nurse—it's
crazy, horrible."

"If I don't show up they'll think I'm dead."

Maureen O'Hara

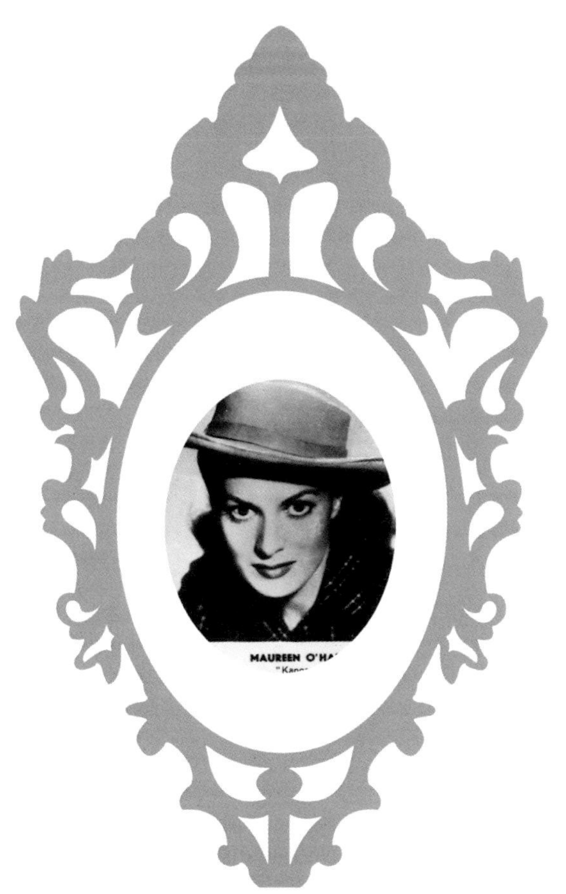

From airlines to autographs

First woman president of a scheduled airline in the US, lives and gives autographs in Ireland

In 1968 Maureen marries Charles Blair. Gen. Blair is a famous aviator. Maureen decides to become a full-time wife. Blair is the real-life version of John Wayne. He is a Brigadier General in the Air Force, a Senior Pilot with Pan American, and holds record-breaking aeronautic achievements. Maureen manages Antilles Airboats, a commuter sea plane service in the Caribbean. She takes trips around the world with her pilot husband.

She owns, writes articles for, and publishes the magazine, *The Virgin Islander*. Tragically, Charles Blair dies in a plane crash in 1978.

Maureen, with memories of ten of the happiest years of her life, keeps going on. She is elected President and CEO of Antilles Airboats. Maureen now lives quite happily in semi-retirement between her home in St. Croix in the Virgin Islands, New York, Los Angeles, and Ireland.

Autograph requests must be sent to Ireland and the rules are:

- Information On Autograph Requests -

RULES FOR OBTAINING AUTOGRAPHS

Anyone wishing to obtain an autograph will now send their request directly to Ireland:

SEND ONE PHOTO ONLY TO:

Maureen O'Hara
c/o Carolyn Murphy
P.O. Box 808
Bantry - County Cork - Ireland

One item only for signing. In consideration of O'Hara's age and volume of photos received you must adhere to this request.

You must indicate the name of the person to whom the autograph is to be directed (make name legible). If no name(s) is given, then no photo will be signed. One photograph can be directed to more than one person.

You must include a self-addressed self-sealing (adhesive flap) envelope, with proper return postage.

Fans from the US may affix American postage to their return envelope. If you live in Ireland, obviously you affix Irish stamps for return. If you cannot provide a photo, there will be a charge of $10 to provide one. This $10 fee will be donated to the Maureen O'Hara Legacy Center. You may send cash, check, or money order payable to the "Maureen O'Hara Legacy Center." Letters with requests not adhering to these requirements will not be returned.

Rosalind Russell

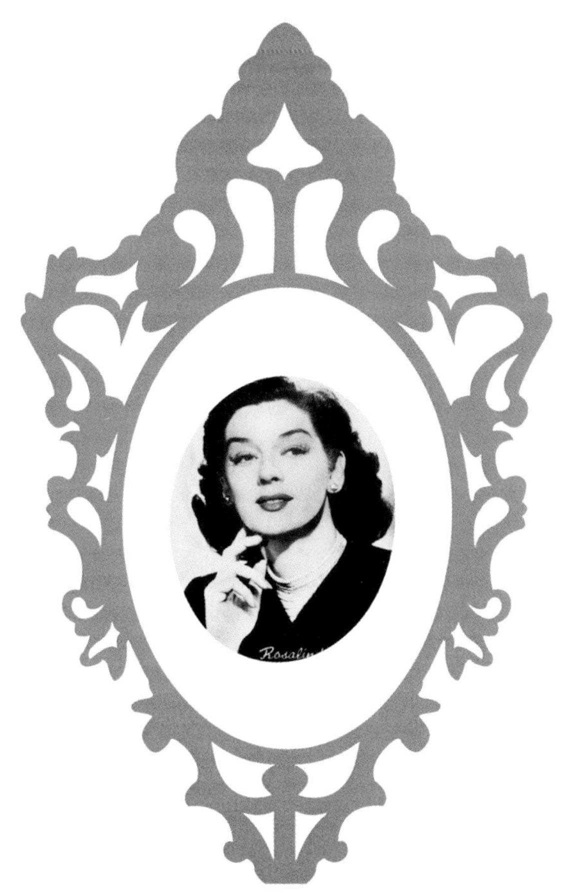

Success in acting boosting charity efforts

From theater to Hollywood and back to theater

Rosalind Russell, elegant and classy, studies at the American Academy of Dramatic Arts, then has her New York debut. Soon after she goes to Hollywood to become a major film star. After four Oscar nominations for *My Sister Eileen* (1942), *Sister Kenny* (1946), *Mourning Becomes Electra* (1947), and *Auntie Mame* (1958), Rosalind Russell decides to return to the stage. Her two major Broadway plays are *Wonderful Town* (1953) and *Auntie Mame* (1956).

Jean Hersholt Humanitarian Award

She receives the Jean Hersholt Humanitarian Award from Frank Sinatra in the 45th edition of the Oscar celebration. The Jean Hersholt Humanitarian Award is given to an operator in the motion picture industry whose humanitarian causes brings solid credit to the industry. As of the last edition of the Oscar celebrations, held in 2009, there have been thirty-three awards presented.

The Rosalind Russell Medical Research Center

"One of her major accomplishments in charity was her work to focus the nation's attention on the seriousness of severe rheumatoid arthritis. In having the courage to publicly share her personal struggle with the disease and by serving on a landmark presidential commission, Rosalind Russell helped pave the way for the major worldwide research effort that continues today."

From the center web site: the United States Congress established the Center at UCSF in 1978 to posthumously honor Rosalind Russell. The Rosalind Russell Medical Research Center for Arthritis at UCSF is a strong international force improving the quality of life for people with the world's number one crippling disease. Countless individuals are living lives with greater mobility and less pain, thanks to research supported by the Center. Specifically, the Center directs contributions from donors to priority investigations conducted by biomedical scientists on the faculty of the UCSF Division of Rheumatology, which is consistently ranked among the top two or three arthritis research groups in the world.

Viveca Lindfors

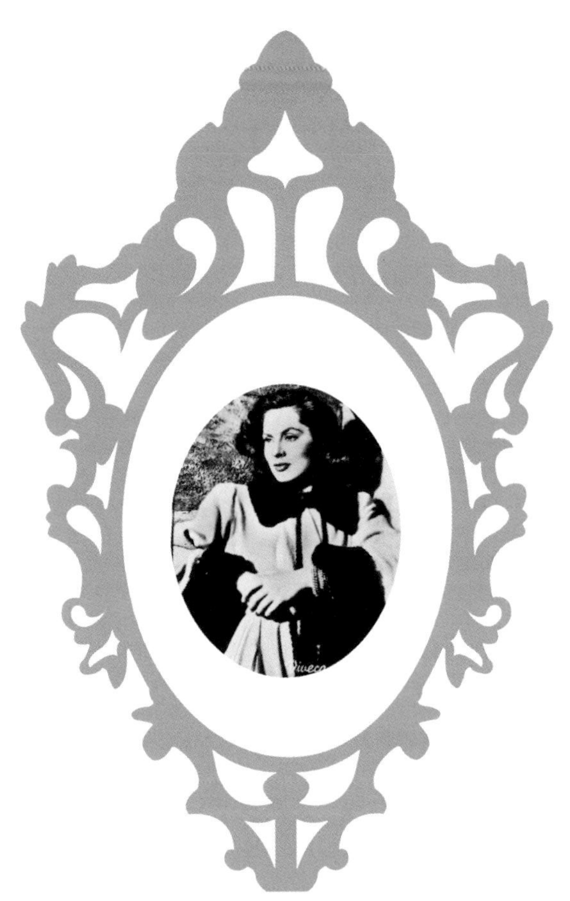

From acting to screen playing and directing

Swedish lady
Viveca Lindfors never achieves superstar status like her Swedish colleagues Greta Garbo and Ingrid Bergman, maybe because she works in movies that are simply unsuited to her, but she has great ability and charisma, and earns awards and builds a reputation around the world.

Cinema and Broadway
When she moves to Hollywood, she signs with Warner Bros. She stars opposite Errol Flynn in *The Adventures of Don Juan* (1948) and appears in *Night Unto Night* (1949), opposite Ronald Reagan in his first starring role. She also debuts in her first French film, *Singoalla* (1949). She makes her first Broadway appearance playing the lead in *Anastasia*. She is a remarkable perfect in *Miss Julie* (1955), *Brecht on Brecht* (1961), and *I Am Woman* (1973).

Beautifully ageing, professionally growing
In her personal life, Lindfors is renowned for her numerous romantic relationships. Her behavior is considered shocking. She is sometimes ironic and claims to have married the first of her four husbands just to prove that a promiscuous woman can indeed marry a decent man.
Lindfors ages gracefully and gains a dignified beauty and even more important roles such as in *Welcome to L.A.* (1976) and Robert Altman's *A Wedding* (1978).
She makes her debut as an excellent and serious screenwriter and director with *Unfinished Business* (1987). Lindfors makes her final film appearance in Henry Jaglom's *Last Summer in the Hamptons* (1995). She dies in October that year from rheumatoid arthritis complications in her hometown of Uppsala.

four
Family, Love, and God

Anne Shirley

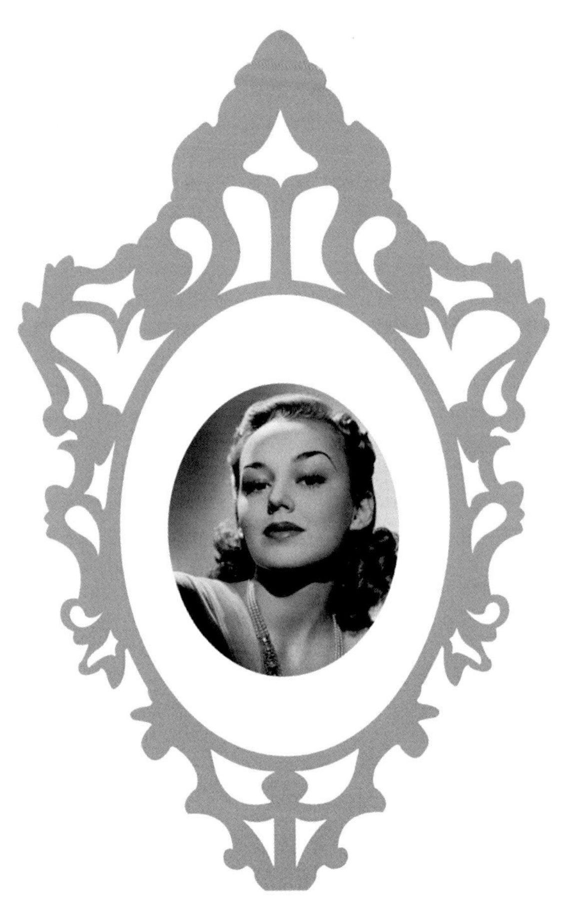

The infant prodige

Daughter of an ambitious stage mother, she becomes a star just to please her mother.
At 14 months she makes her first stage appearance.
She works as a child model.
She is a little child when she is taken to Hollywood.
She appears in children's roles.

She appears in many films when she is a teen.
At age 15, she is given a leading role.
She plays leading roles in more than thirty-five movies before age 26.
For her work in *Stella Dallas* (1937) she receives an Oscar nomination (1938) as best actress in a supporting role.
She retires at age 26.

Carla Del Poggio

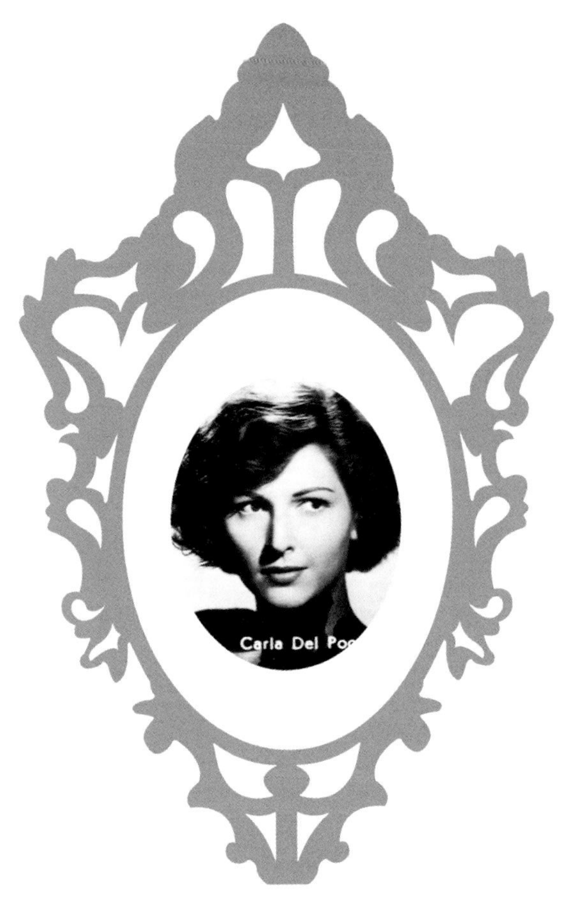

Widow of the director

Director Vittorio De Sica chooses her
for a movie.

Maddalena, zero in condotta (1940).

At 19 she meets her future husband.

The director Alberto Lattuada.

In the 1950s she takes part mainly in theater
plays.

And afterwards some television fictions.

She also takes part in the Fellini's debut movie:

Luci del varietà (1950).

She dedicates her life to her husband
and children.

Cecile Aubry

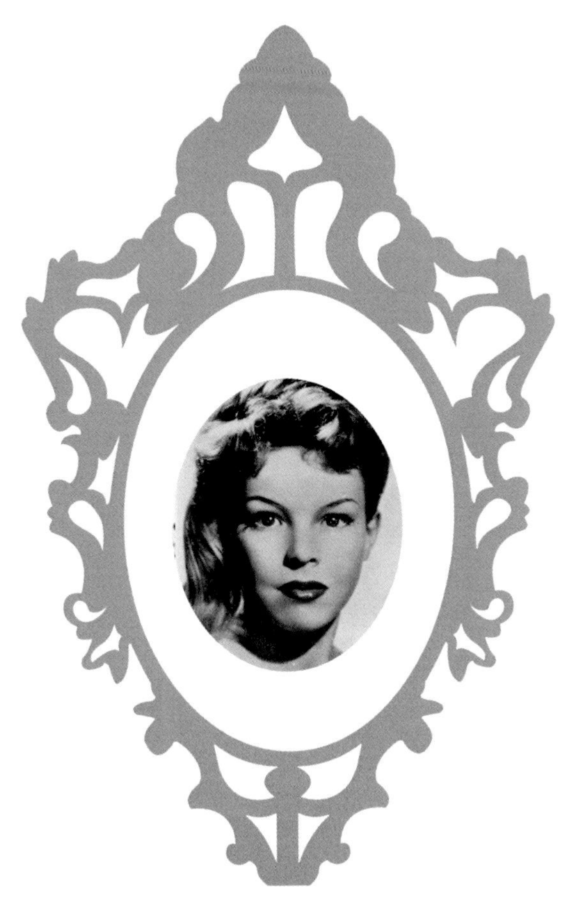

Belle et Sébastien heritage today

Film actress, born in 1928, French.

Author, television screenwriter, director.

British film *The Black Rose* (1950) alongside co-starring Tyrone Power.

Retires after marriage.

Si Brahim El Glaoui, caïd, the husband.

Divorce.

Things vanishes, but . . .

. . . due to one of her books, a heritage today . . .

. . . a band that gives its name on Cecile Aubry children's book:

"Once I went to Andorra. I stayed one night in a sleazy hotel in the middle of the Pyrenees. In this hotel there was a place full of old books for the guests to read. One of them was this original Cecile Aubry's *Belle et Sébastien*. The band took its name from these characters. I didn't even try to get the book, because the Russian guy who was in charge didn't look friendly at all. Buy my friends did it, and gave it to me as a present for my birthday." (Máximo Tuja)

. . . and a French live-action television series in 1965 . . .

. . . and a Japanese anime version nearly two decades later.

Belle et Sébastien is a novel by Cecile Aubry. A 6-year-old boy named Sébastien and his dog Belle. They live in a small French Alps Mountain village on the French side of the border between France and Italy. Sébastien lives with his adopted grandfather, sister, and brother, as his mother dies after giving birth to him while trying to cross the border on Saint Sebastian's day.

Dolores Hart

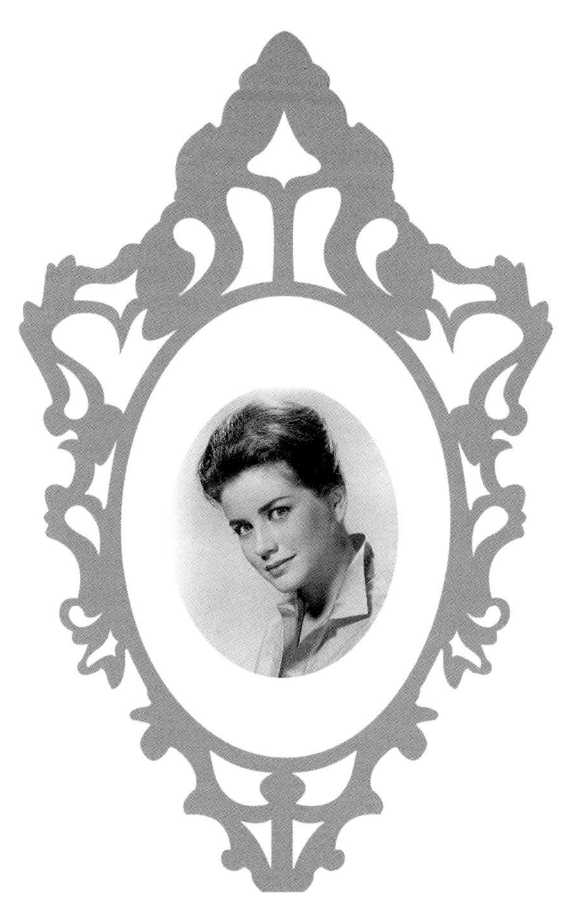

One vocation after another

"It was not a lifelong dream. I did not grow up wanting to be a nun. I wanted to be an actress. If it had ever been suggested I would one day be a nun, it would have been the last thing on my mind. It was a million to one shot I would ever be a nun."

"I have struggled with this call to vocation all my life. I can understand why people have doubts, because who understands God? I don't. When you are dealing with something at this level, you are dealing with mystery."

"I'd done two movies with Elvis Presley. I'd been around Hollywood for a while and saw how needlessly competitive and negative it could be. It never held my interest."

In 1956 she signs as co-star with Elvis Presley in the *Loving You* (1957). She makes two more movies before playing with Presley again in *King Creole* (1958). She denies a relationship with Elvis Presley offscreen.

"What is it like kissing Elvis?" they ask her. "I think the limit for a screen kiss back then was something like 15 seconds. That one has lasted forty years."

A prophetic film for her: *Francis of Assisi* (1961), where she plays Clare.

She plays more films including *The Inspector* (1962) and *Come Fly with Me* (1963). In 1963, she decides to quit and at age 24 she becomes a Roman Catholic nun at the Benedictine Abbey of Regina Laudis in Bethlehem, Connecticut, ultimately becoming the Prioress of the Convent.

In Rome, Hart is St. Francis of Assisi and meets Pope John XXIII. "I am Dolores Hart, the actress playing Clare." The Pontiff says, "No, you are Clara!"

"I will never have to worry again about being an actress because it was all over and behind me." But Lady Abbess says: "I'm sorry, but you're completely wrong. Now you have to take up a role and really work at it."

In 2006, she visits Hollywood after forty-three years to raise awareness for peripheral idiopathic neuropathy disorder, a neurological disorder that afflicts her.

Elisa Cegani

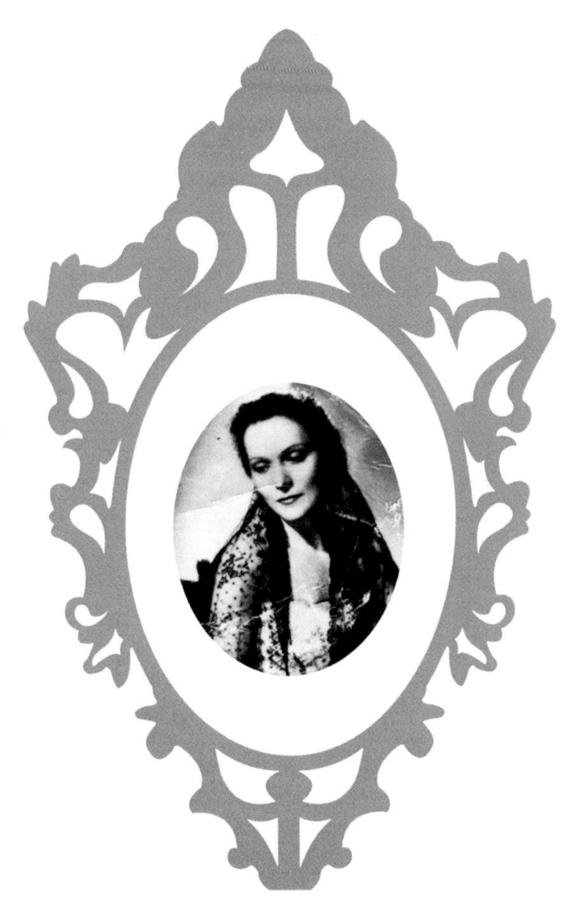

She is Blasetti's wife above all

Aldebaran,
directed by Alessandro Blasetti (1935).

Contessa di Parma,
directed by Alessandro Blasetti (1937).

Retroscena,
directed by Alessandro Blasetti (1939).

La corona di ferro,
directed by Alessandro Blasetti (1941).

La cena delle beffe,
directed by Alessandro Blasetti (1942).

Nessuno torna indietro,
directed by Alessandro Blasetti (1943).

Un giorno nella vita,
directed by Alessandro Blasetti (1946).

Fabiola,
directed by Alessandro Blasetti (1949).

Altri tempi: zibaldone numero 1,
directed by Alessandro Blasetti (1952).

La fiammata,
directed by Alessandro Blasetti (1952).

Tempi nostri: zibaldone numero 2,
directed by Alessandro Blasetti (1954).

La fortuna di essere donna,
directed by Alessandro Blasetti (1955).

Amore e chiacchiere,
directed by Alessandro Blasetti (1957).

Liolà,
directed by Alessandro Blasetti (1963).

Io, io, io ... e gli altri,
directed by Alessandro Blasetti (1966).

Frances Dee

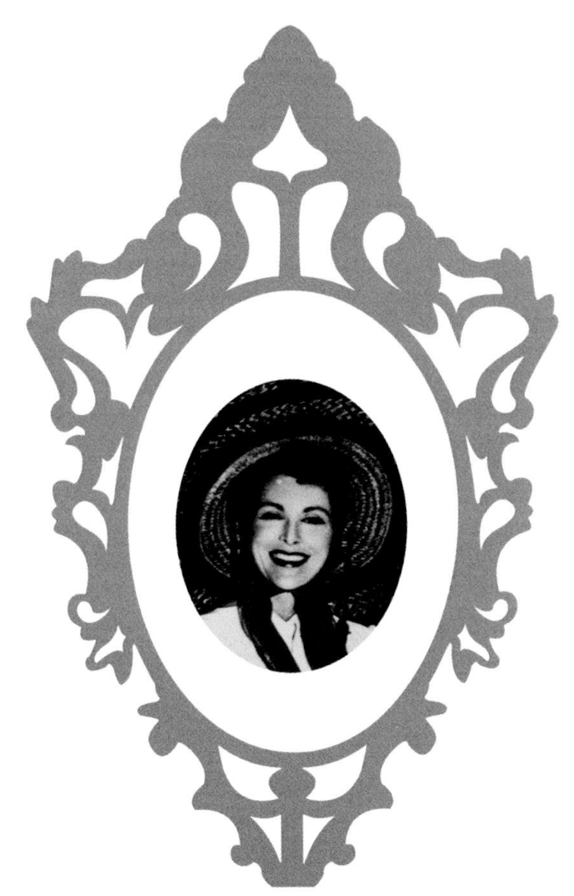

Love story

Frances Dee is in several Selznick films, but due to her beauty Selznick considers not appropriate to cast her as Melanie Wilkes, because he thinks her beauty might overshadow newcomer Vivien Leigh. Olivia de Havilland gets the role, wins an Oscar nomination, and has a highly successful career.

Frances Dee's career works in Hollywood for as long as she wants but never reaches its true potential.

Husband
She meets future husband actor Joel McCrea on the set of *The Silver Cord* (1933) and gets married with him that same year. She retires in 1953 to devote herself to her family.
McCrea retires from films in 1962 while still a star. They cultivate their ranch in Thousand Oaks, California. They donate a couple of hundred acres to the park.
They raise their three children and celebrate their 57th wedding anniversary before his death in 1990. Frances Dee dies at age 94.

June Haver

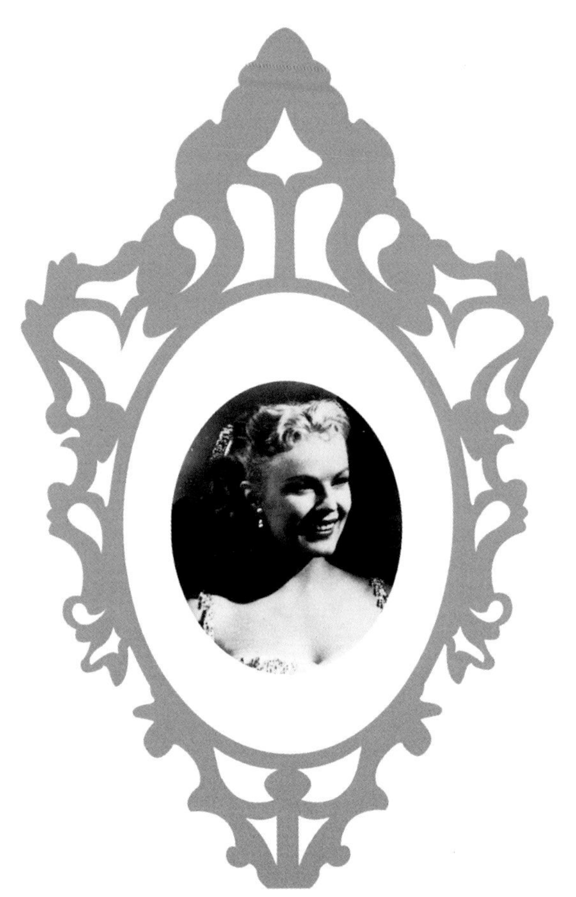

Fast nun

Born in 1926.
Her mother who had been an actress pushes
her into show business when she is very little,
almost an infant.
She is a child prodigy.

"Every time a bandleader came to town,"
she says, "I'd march to his hotel armed with my
scrapbook. I'd tell him that he could get a lot
of publicity if he would let me sing with
his band for his onenight stand in our town."

At age 27, June Haver ends her career
and joins a convent with the intention
of becoming a nun.

The decision is not a true vocation.
It is led by dellusion and sadness: a divorce
in 1948 and the death of her fiancé in 1952.
She stays at the convent for only six months.
After one year, she remarries Fred MacMurray
in 1954 and works as an interior decorator.

Marisa Pavan

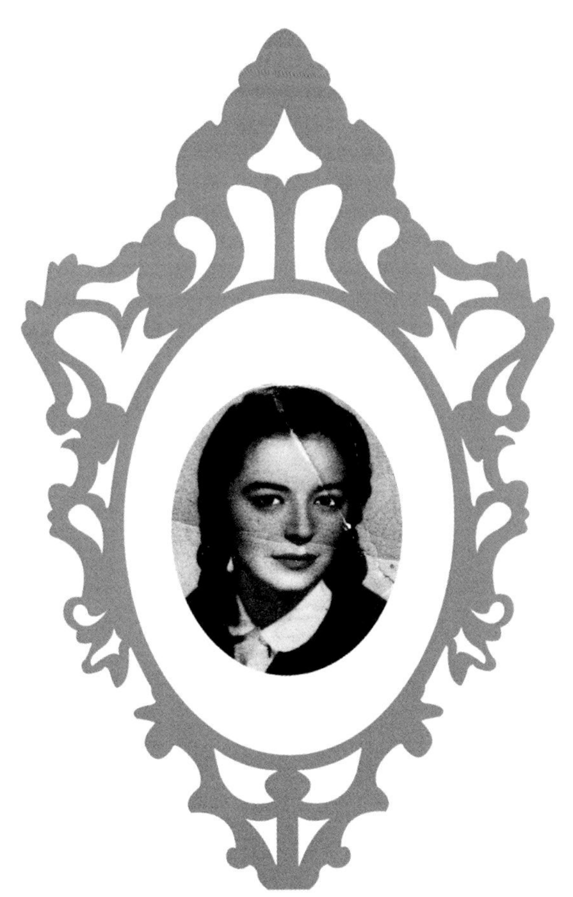

Happy and alive.
Who cares about an Oscar nomination?

Born Marisa Pierangeli
Pier Angeli's twin sister
Sardinian
Alive
Actress
The Rose Tattoo (1955)
Oscar nomination for that
Golden Globe winner also
Love for husband
Or better, total devotion
He sings, she sings
She quits Hollywood for that
A singing wife
Not first class singing tours
Vegas and so
But happy she is
And alive

Nancy Olson

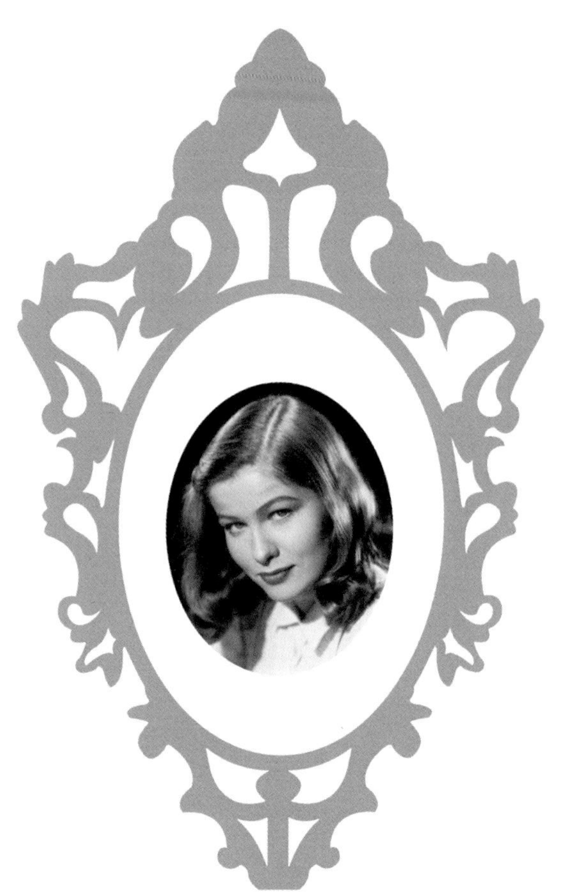

You can be a girl next door just for awhile . . .

Olson is signed by Paramount in 1948 at age 20.

She is given the role of Delilah in Cecil B. DeMille's 1949 film *Samson and Delilah*, but she says she is not suitable for the role. Hedy Lamarr gets the part.

In *Sunset Boulevard* (1950) she plays Betty Schaefer and wins an Oscar nomination as best supporting actress.

Her acting together with William Holden is a success. She appears with him in other films during the 1950s, but none of them has the same success as *Sunset Boulevard*. Other films starring Nancy include *So Big* (1953) and *Battle Cry* (1955).

Nancy Olson is not extremely dedicated to her career mainly because of her family. Therefore her career declines.

She marries the lyricist Alan Jay Lerner, as his third wife, in 1950, has two daughters, Liza and Jennifer, but after seven years they get a divorce.

During the marriage, she almost gives no importance to her career and she never fully recoveres even if she desperatley tries a comeback. It is too late. By the late 1950s at age 30 Nancy is too mature to be playing the girl-next-door type for which she is known.

. . . But you can work for Disney for a long time if you are the right type.

She does make some memorable films for the Walt Disney studio: *The Absentminded Professor* (1961), *Son of Flubber* (1963), *Pollyanna* (1960), and *Snowball Express* (1972). Her last time on screen is a cameo appearance in the *Flubber* (1997) remake.

In 1962 she marries again. He is an important Capitol Records executive, Alan W. Livingston, he is considered one of the best in the business. He is the one who signs Frank Sinatra and The Beatles, among other legends. He dies in 2009; they have a son, Christopher.

Norma Shearer

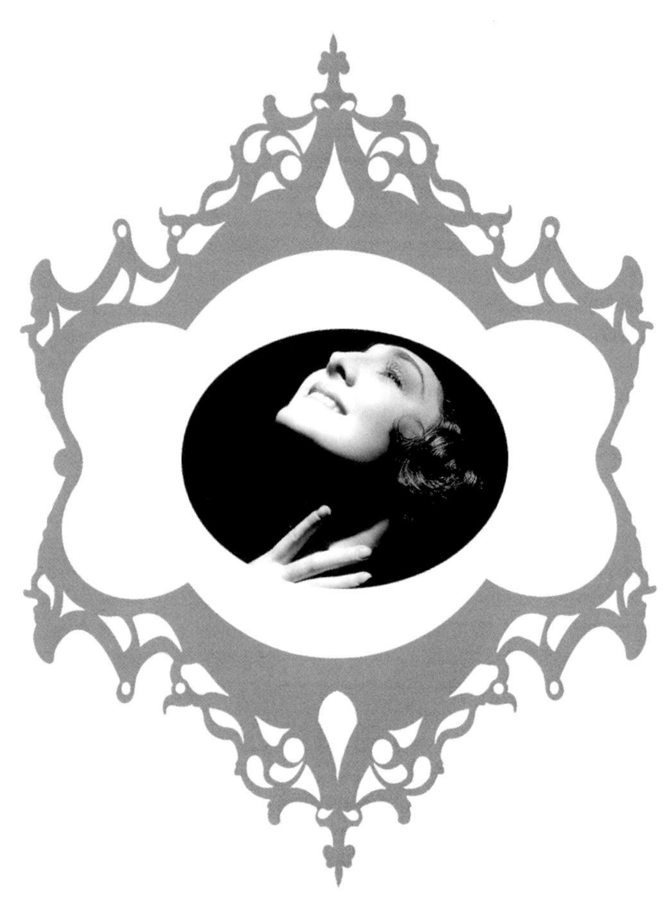

Not less than any Hollywood myth

After an Oscar as best actress in a leading role for *The Divorcee* (1930) and five Oscar nominations as best actress in a leading role for *Their Own Desire* (1929), *A Free Soul* (1930), *The Barretts of Wimpole Street* (1934), *Romeo and Juliet* (1936), *Marie Antoinette* (1938).

There is a long story to tell before the sky instructor

Norma Shearer is born in 1902 in Montreal, Quebec. Norma's mother is quite ambitious for her daughter and pushes her to performances and beauty contests.

When Norma is 18, her mother separates from her husband and moves with her children to New York. Norma does modelling and makes some silent movies, including *Way Down East* (1920) by director D.W. Griffith.

Irving Thalberg is in love

She appears in quite a number of insignificant films. But with the creation of mega-studio Metro-Goldwyn-Mayer in 1924, Norma begins her way to success.

Thalberg becomes the most powerful man in Hollywood with Louis B. Mayer, and he is completely in love with Norma. Totally determined to make her one of the most important stars of Hollywood, he marries her.

Her first sound film works pretty well, and a year later she wins the Academy Award as best actress for her work in *The Divorcee*. Many Oscar nominations are given to her afterwards. Snake-like Joan Crawford says: "How can I compete with her, she sleeps with the boss!" Norma's most famous roles portray sophisticated proper intelligent modern women and this gives her an excellent high profile image.

Norma gives birth to Irving Thalberg, Jr. in 1930. Irving, two weeks after the opening of *Romeo and Juliet*, suffers a fatal heart attack at age 37. Norma is devastated. Many people think that she will quit, but she works on *Marie Antoinette* and wins another Oscar nomination. This film is her biggest success.

In the late 1930s, she has an affair with married George Raft. It is a scandal but with no major consequence.
In the 1940s she makes films of high and not so high quality.

The instructor she is in love with

Shortly after, she quits and goes on a ski holiday with her children. While there she meets a ski instructor several years her junior. They soon get married. She never comes back and devotes the rest of her life to her husband and children. She dies in 1983 at age 81.

Peggy Dow

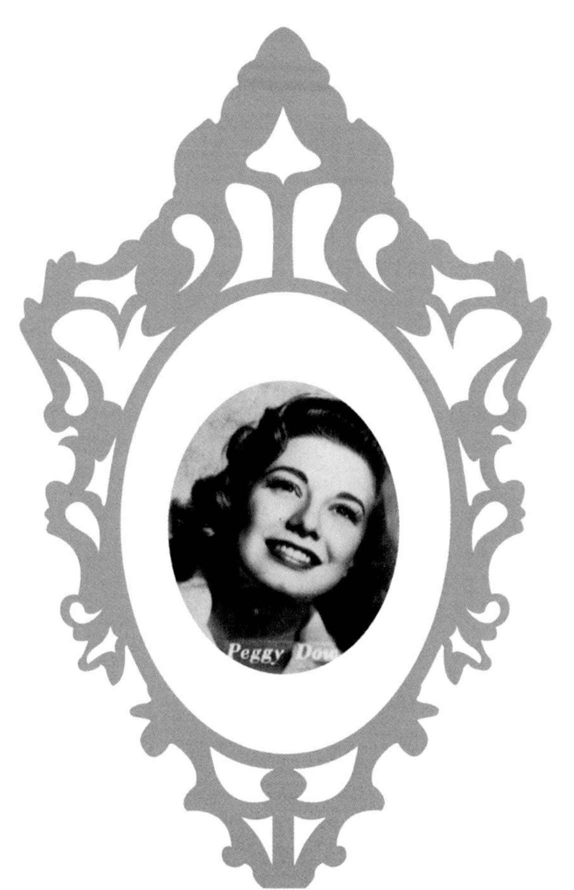

Early voluntary retirement. After only three years

Beautiful. Intelligent. Talented. 1950s Universal
Supposed to go straight to stardom, but she decides to retire for domestic life.

She plays a vacationing schoolteacher who accidentally gets involved in a murder in the thriller *Undertow* (1949).
She also plays in the thriller *Woman in Hiding* (1950), with co-stars Ida Lupino and Stephen McNally.

She proves to be perfect both in comedy and in drama. She is at her top as a lovely nurse in the James Stewart film *Harvey* (1950), and also in the completely different movie, the drama *Bright Victory* (1951), the story of a soldier who after the war has to accept blindness.

At this point, Hollywood knows she is a professional and excellent star.

But she retires
After a couple of pictures, Peggy suddenly retires after a career of only three years at age 23.

She marries Walter Helmerich in 1951.
They relocate to Tulsa, Oklahoma.
She never looks back and raises five sons and devotes herself to charity.

In 1998 she receives an honorary degree from the University of Oklahoma for her dedication to improving health care education and cultural events in Tulsa. She helps establish the Tulsa Library Trust and the Peggy V. Helmerich Distinguished Author Award given each year to writers.

Peggy Ryan

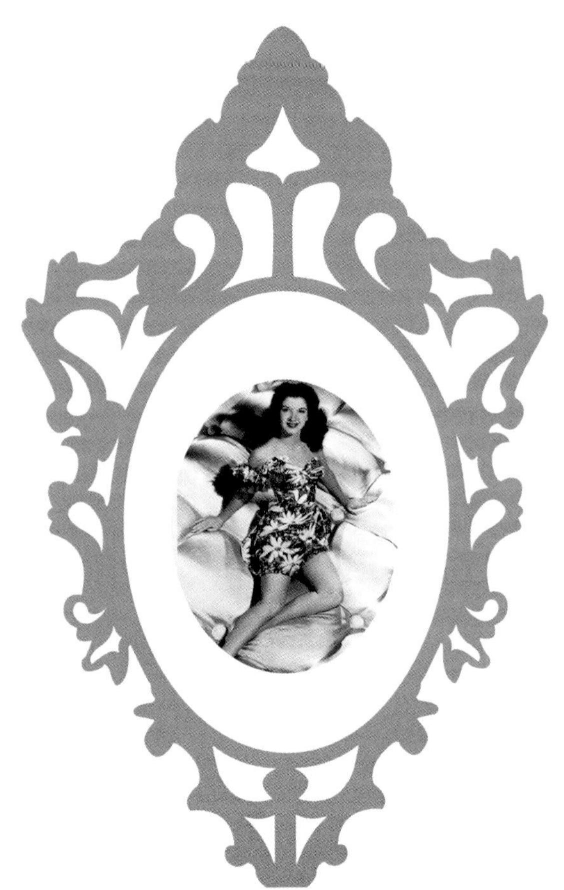

A dancer

Peggy is discovered by George Murphy at age 12.

Peggy dances with Murphy in the Universal musical *Top of the Town* (1937).

She makes a few more films in the following few years, but she is hardly noticed except for some dance scenes.

Universal then casts her opposite Donald O'Connor in *What's Cookin'?* (1942) and she becomes a leading star in youth musicals during World War II.

They team in a series of low budget but famous musicals such as *Private Buckaroo* (1942), *Give Out, Sisters!* (1942), *Get Hep to Love* (1942), *Top Man* (1943), *Mr. Big* (1943), *Chip Off the Old Block* (1944), *This Is the Life* (1944), and *Bowery to Broadway* (1944).

These are not films for intellectuals, but teens have fun with them and they are a huge success. Given the low investment, they are quite profitable for Universal.

Her career slows down after the war. In 1945, she marries songwriter James Cross, and quits acting at age 21. In 1949, she decides to make two musicals, and in 1952 she divorces Cross and meets her second husband, dancer Ray McDonald. She meets him in her supposedly last film appearance, *All Ashore* (1953).

Tragically, McDonald dies in 1957.

Peggy Ryan moves to Honolulu after marrying her third husband. She teaches dance classes at the University of Hawaii. In 1969, she surprisingly goes back to acting on a long-running show, *Hawaii Five-O*. She plays the role for seven years.

Peggy Ryan eventually relocates with her husband to Las Vegas, where for the last few years, she teaches tap dancing.

Priscilla Lane

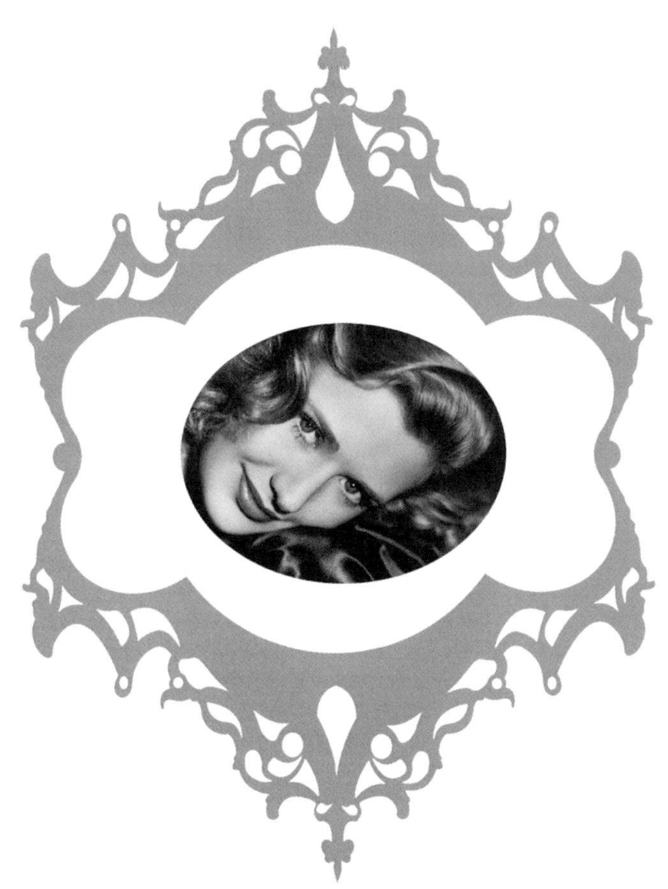

Family first

Priscilla Lane retires to domestic life. During her brief Hollywood career she becomes the leader in terms of receiving mails in the 1940s. The public loves her.

Priscilla Lane's most notable films are:
Four Daughters (1938), with John Garfield. Bette Davis had turned down the role.
The Roaring Twenties (1939) with James Cagney. Alfred Hitchcock's *Saboteur* (1942). Hitchcock is unable to get Barbara Stanwyck.
Arsenic and Old Lace (1944) with Cary Grant.

She marries twice
The first weeding lasts only one day, Priscilla leaves him after one day. He is an assistant director and screen writer. The marriage is annulled.
The second weeding is during World War II. She starts to give less and less importance to her Hollywood career. She has four children: Joseph Lawrence (1945), Hannah (1950), Judith (1953), and James (1955).

She quits acting completely in 1948 to raise her family, at age 33.
After her retirement, she follows her Air Force husband, often singing at camp shows.
Priscilla Lane returns to show business as the host in a television program just for a while in 1958.

Susan Fleming

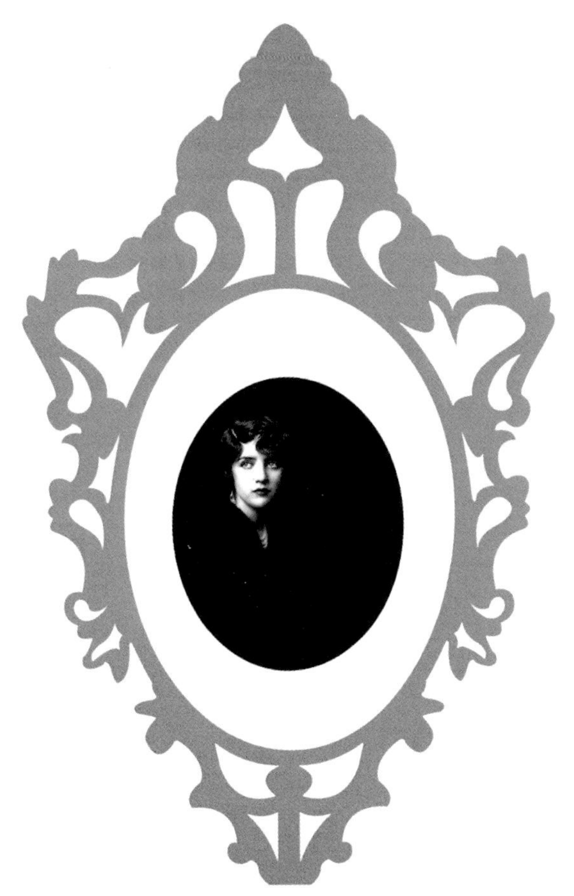

Long life for a good lady

Fleming is very happy to leave acting
She dedicates herself to Harpo Marx and
to raising their four adopted children.
Harpo Marx starts painting.
Susan helps him make sophisticated frames
for his works.
Susan paints as well. They are also collectors.
Their collection is donated to charity after
his death.

After the last film of the Marx Brothers, *Love
Happy* (1949), they move to Palm Springs,
California.
In Palm Springs, Susan Fleming becomes
an avid charity and philanthropy supporter.
Marx dies at age 75. They stayed together
for over twenty-five years.

Following his death, Fleming becomes even
more involved in community activities.

Fleming outlives Marx by almost forty years
during which time she is an artist and activist
in the Palm Springs area.
She dies at age 94 in 2002 of a heart attack.
She is survived by four adopted children, five
grandchildren, and two great-grandchildren.

Susan Kohner

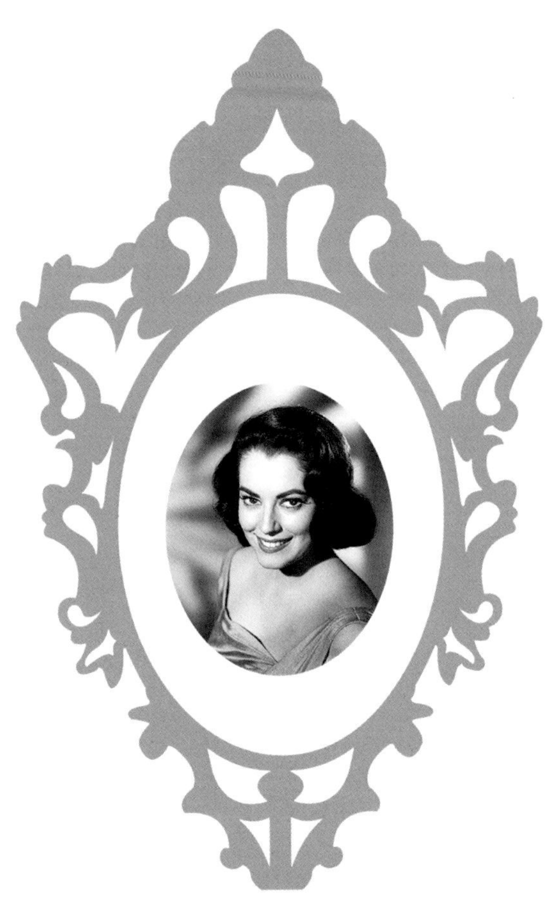

Are you black? No.
Are you black? What difference does it make?

In 1959

At age 23

She interprets the famous role of Sarah Jane

In the color remake of *Imitation of Life*.

Imitation of Life is a box office hit.

Susan Kohner wins the Oscar

And Golden Globe nominations

In the supporting actress categories.

But in 1964 at age 28, she retires

And marries German novelist and fashion
designer John Weitz.

It is up to their children

Chris and Paul Weitz

To keep the tradition

And become successful film directors
in Hollywood.

Virginia Cherrill

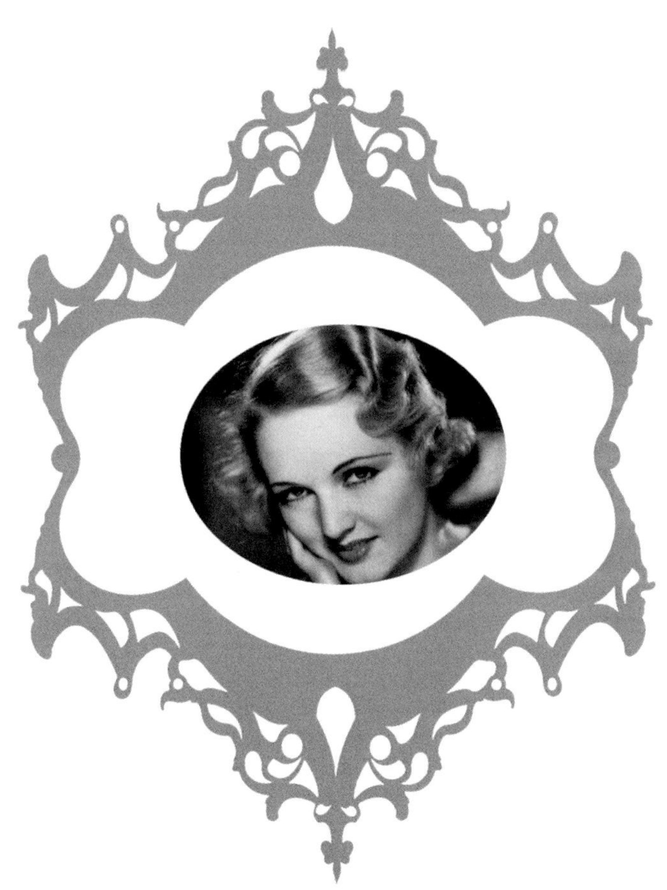

From the blind flower seller to Countess, through Cary Grant

Charlie Chaplin
City Lights (1931) introduces Charlie Chaplin's new female star to the world. The film is a nightmare to make. Chaplin's insistence on controlling every detail of the movie, both on screen and on set, means it takes more than two years to complete the movie.

And despite his having plucked Virginia from obscurity to stardom in the movie, Chaplin and his protégée do not get on, so much so that she is the only leading lady of his silent films with whom he never has a sexual relationship. Things gets so bad that after making her shoot 1 scene a record 342 times, he fires her, only to have to beg her to come back to film the ending.

When *City Lights* is released the critics go wild for Virginia. She is the toast of Hollywood and the girl everyone wants to meet, including Cary Grant.

Cary Grant
The couple meet in 1932 during a party at actor Randolph Scott's place. The first out of five of Cary Grant's weddings lasts not even a year because Virginia seeks divorce blaming him for being an hot-tempered alcoholic. Paramount, in order to defend the image of its star, is obliged to work out a Freudian counter-campaign, revealing the hypersensitiveness of little Cary and his sorrow for having been abandoned by his mother and his great childhood friend.

The 9th Earl of Jersey and the English aristocracy
In Britain, Virginia's beauty and adventurous nature sees her become the toast of a fast, aristocratic set for whom traditional ideas of morality do not seem to apply. When she goes to Britain, she is, let's say, a little promiscuous.

The actress and the Earl marry in 1937. Virginia takes the title of Countess of the Isle of Jersey and the couple embarks on a marriage that was, in its own way, every bit as bizarre as that with Grant. "He was a very strange man," Virginia says of the Earl. "He had his bedroom, I had mine. I slept with the dogs."

She also sleeps with a succession of wealthy men, including the Maharajah of Jaipur, Sawai Man Singh, a dashing champion polo player whom she meets on a tour of India shortly after her marriage.

"Marriage to Jersey seems to have been on the understanding that they could both lead their private lives," says her biographer. "She would allow him to carry on with other women and he made it absolutely clear that he didn't mind about her being with the Maharajah."

During the war their home in Oxfordshire is requisitioned as a convalescent home for Polish airmen and so begins the last leap between worlds for Virginia.

The Polish flying ace
For it is there she meet her last husband Florian Martini, a Polish flying ace. She and the Earl divorce after the war in 1946 and the following year she marries Martini. They move back to America where they start a small avocado farm in California. She withdraws from the public eye. Virginia and Florian remain married until her death in 1996.

five
Beyond Fiction

Barbara Bates

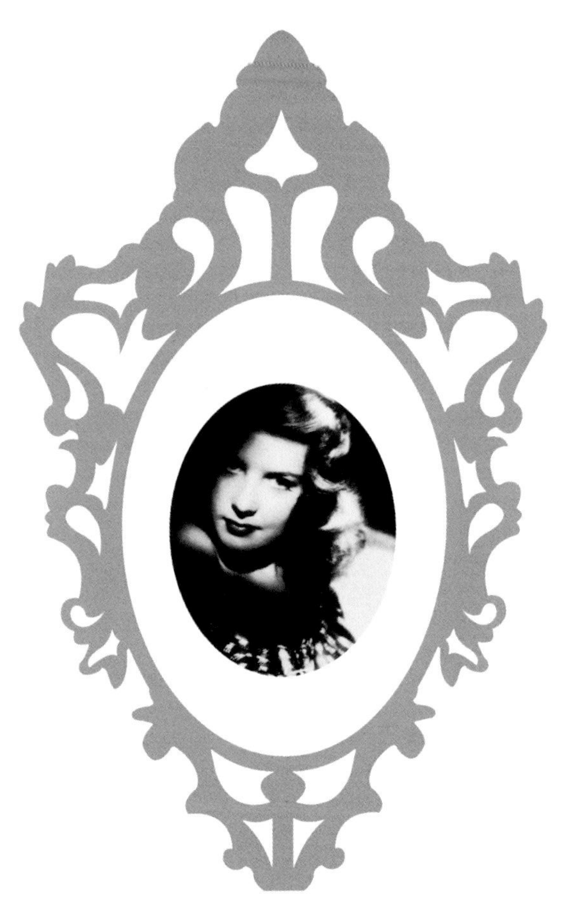

It is for these few seconds she will always be remembered

All about Eve

All about Eve
The one role Barbara Bates will always
be identified with is also the smallest part she
has during her brief career as leading actress.
She plays Phoebe in the very last scene
of *All about Eve* (1950).
Phoebe is a schoolgirl wannabe actress,
who has a promising future. In the last scene
of the movie, she poses in front of a three-way
mirror while holding Anne Baxter's award
who has just stolen Bette Davis's role, and who
from being a predator of Bette Davis in the
movie will become a victim of Phoebe.

Useless *All about Eve*
In 1951, experts in Movieland say the
"fifteen finest" newcomers who seem destined
for fame include Marilyn Monroe,
Debra Paget, Mitzi Gaynor, Jeff Chandler,
Jane Powell, Howard Keel, Mario Lanza,
Mala Powers, Marlon Brando, Gordon
MacRae, Frank Lovejoy, Patrice Wymore,
Dean Martin and Jerry Lewis, Judy Holliday
and . . . Barbara Bates.
When asked about her movie prospects
following her performance in *All about Eve* she
says: "I thought great things were going
to happen. So far, nothing. They keep casting
me as a 16-year-old; I can't seem
to get up to 20."
Barbara suffers serious psychological problems
that lead her to extreme mood swings,
insecurity, ill health, and chronic depression.
She is taken off two important movies during
filming. Before turning 30, she is completely
forgotten by Hollywood.

Her personal life in a paragraph
Born in 1925. Meets Cecil Coan in 1944. In
1949, she is offered a career at Columbia on
the condition she divorce Coan; she refuses
and signs with Fox.
In 1951 Coan is diagnosed with cancer, and
she never leaves his side. He dies in 1967,
and she's at his bedside. In 1968 she marries
sportscaster William Reed, whom she has
known since childhood.
In 1969 at age 44 she commits suicide, death
from carbon monoxide poisoning. She was
supposedly pregnant.

Betsy Drake

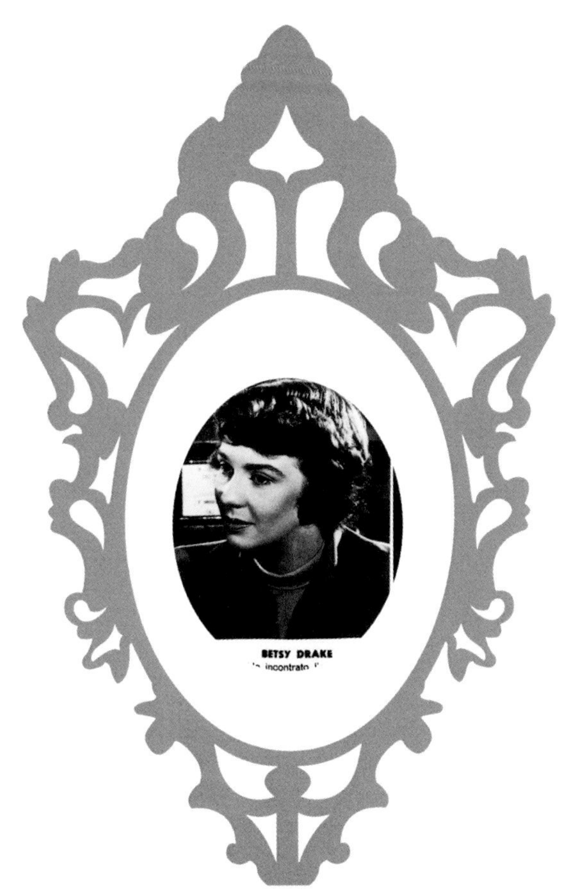

Her life is . . . Cary Grant

Betsy is the wife of Cary Grant. Their wedding lasts for twelve years and it is his longest wedding, but the least important.

She is not his strongest passion

That is Sophia Loren, as he admits several times. He has an affair with Sophia while still married to Betsy. He is destroyed when she marries Carlo Ponti.

She is not the woman that gives him his only child

That is Dyan Cannon. He does everything he can to convince Dyan Cannon not to get a divorce. He is completely obsessed with his little daughter.

She is not the woman close to him until his death

That is Barbara Harris. She is not the first wife. That is Virgina Cherrill.

She is not the one that brings him a child from a previous wedding

That is the millionaire Barbara Hutton. Grant does not need her money, and he does not seek, or receive, any money from Barbara in their divorce. He loves her son and is devastated by his early death.

Betsy's major influence on Grant is the worst of all: his use of LSD

Betsy and Grant meet in 1947, and have an instant relationship.
Betsy appears in her first film *Every Girl Should Be Married* (1948), opposite Grant. They get married in 1949 and participate in other movies together.
On her way back from Spain in 1956 Betsy survives the sinking of the Andrea Doria. She went to Spain to visit Grant. During his stay in Spain, he is passionately involved with Sophia Loren. Grant and Drake separate in 1958 and divorce in 1962.
Betsy uses LSD and introduces Grant to it. Cary uses LSD for almost all his life. He claims to achieve mental equilibrium thanks to the drug. Drake keeps taking LSD as a way to recover from their divorce.

She gives up acting in order to focus on writing and earn a degree from Harvard University. She works as a practicing psychotherapist. She is still alive. Her most recent screen appearance is in a 2004 documentary: *Cary Grant: A Class Apart*, in which she reflects on their time as a couple.

Dorothy Comingore

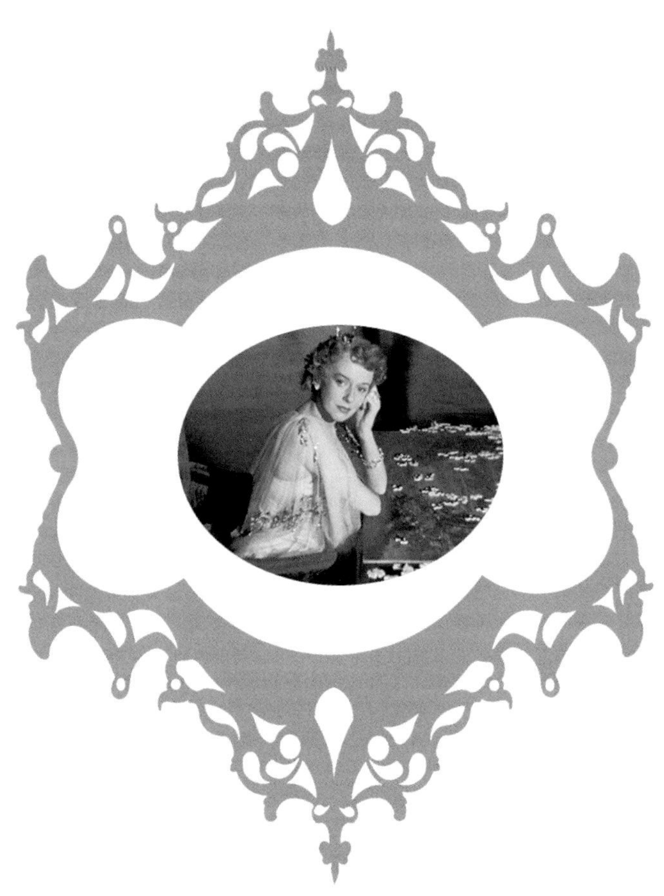

A blacklisted star

Discovered by Charles Chaplin.
After starring in Orson Welles's *Citizen Kane* (1941) at age 28, Dorothy Comingore is destined to become a star.
However, she only makes three more films.
Dorothy is washed out in Hollywood.

She is blacklisted
The Hollywood blacklist includes several US entertainment professionals who are denied employment because of their political beliefs. Sometimes these beliefs are real, but most of the time they are not, which means no sympathetic attitude towards the American Communist Party exists. The blacklist is not divulged at that time, but causes direct damage to careers and lives.
Her husband, screenwriter Richard Collins, after a brief period on the blacklist, becomes a witness and dumps her because she refuses to give names. Divorcing Comingore, Collins manages to gain custody over their child.
Before the House Un-American Activities Committee, she declines on constitutional grounds to answer questions regarding political affiliation.
Dorothy develops paranoiac behavior. She is convinced of being harassed, and as a consequence, keeps moving to avoid detection. She succumbs to alcoholism and dies of a pulmonary disease at the age of 58.

Frances Farmer

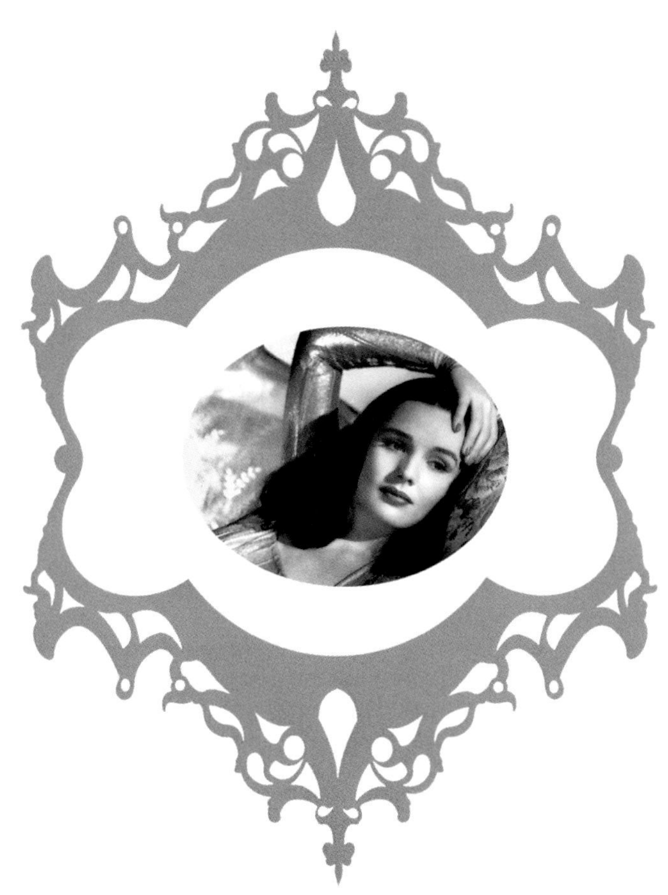

Frances Farmer will have her revenge on Seattle

It's so relieving to know that you're leaving as
soon as you get paid
It's so relaxing to hear you're asking wherever
you get your way
It's so soothing to know that you'll sue me,
This is starting to sound the same
I miss the comfort in being sad

In her false witness, we hope you're still with us,
To see if they float or drown
Our favourite patient, a display of patience,
Disease–covered Puget Sound
She'll come back as fire, to burn all the liars,
And leave a blanket of ash on the ground
I miss the comfort in being sad
(Nirvana, 1993)

Born in Seattle
Frances Farmer, a rebel for then-standards,
refuses studio attempts to make her life an
homologated one. She refuses to attend parties,
she refuses to date other stars, she refuses to
dress and look like a star. Farmer loves theatre;
her contract with Paramount allows her nine
months a year to dedicate to theatre! But she
soon quits Broadway. She works on films.
Her performance in the film *Son of Fury* (1942)
is mostly admired by the critics. In 1942,
however, Paramount cancels her contract due to
bad behavior, and her first marriage ends.

Starting on October 19, 1942: The arrest
Farmer is arrested by the Santa Monica police
for hazardous driving. She is jailed overnight.
Farmer is fined $500 and given a 180-day
suspended sentence. She immediately pays
$250 and is put on probation. She fails to pay
the rest, plus a studio hairdresser accuses her of
attacking him. Her arrest on these charges leads
to her being placed in a private institution in
southern California, the LA General Hospital.

The hospital
There she is diagnosed with "manic depressive
psychosis." She is given insulin shock therapy.

Farmer is no longer able to concentrate or
remember her lines. Her family later claims
they did not give their consent to the treatment.
After about nine months, Farmer walks away
and goes to her half-sister's house.

The mother
Lillian Farmer travels to California and begins a
legal battle to have guardianship of her daughter.
Although several psychiatrists testify that Farmer
needs further treatment, her mother wins.
They leave Los Angeles together. Farmer moves
back in with her parents. She and her mother
fight and Farmer physically attacks her. Lillian
secretly has Frances committed to Western State
Hospital at Steilacoom, Washington.

The hospital again
There, Farmer sometimes receives electro-
convulsive shock treatment (ECT). Three
months later, during the summer of 1944, she is
declared "completely cured" and is then released.

**The second arrest, the mother again,
and the hospital again and again**
Farmer is again arrested for vagrancy in
California. At her mother's request, at age
32, Farmer is recommitted to Western State
Hospital and remains there almost five years,
with the exception of a brief period in 1946.

The end
Frances is released in 1950 and takes
a hotel laundry job in Seattle to help support
her parents. In 1954, she marries a utility
worker, but quickly leaves him and moves
secretly to Eureka, California, where
she works anonymously for several years
in a photo studio.
In 1957, she is discovered by a talent agent who
promotes her and is able to revive her career.
By 1958, she successfully hosts a movie
interview program, *Frances Farmer Presents*.
By 1964, she is fired due to her alcoholism. She
dies from oesophageal cancer at age 57.

Gene Tierney

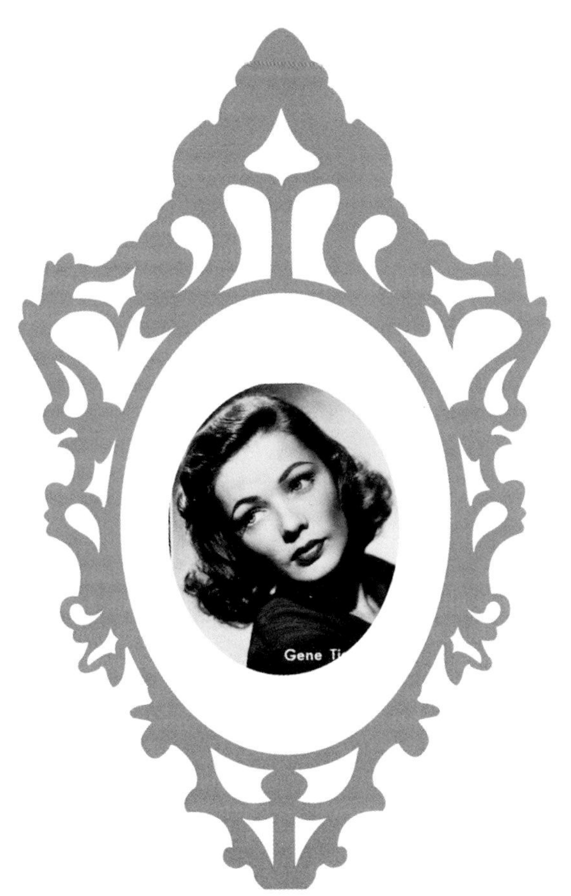

"Undeniably the most beautiful actress in movie history."

(Darryl F. Zanuck)

Academy award-nominee
Beautiful and bipolar
C*hina girl*
Depression from daughter
Emphysema
Fluent French
Greenwood cemetery
Howard Hughes and Howard Lee
Irish descent
Jealous *Femme Fatale*
Kennedy
Laura
Menninger clinic

Newyorkese
Oleg Cassini
Prince Aly Khan
Quality
Richard Nixon
Suicide attempt
Tyrone Power
Upscale
Variety, Vogue, Vanity Fair
Walk of Fame
X large cheekbones
Young widow
Zanuck

Gloria Grahame

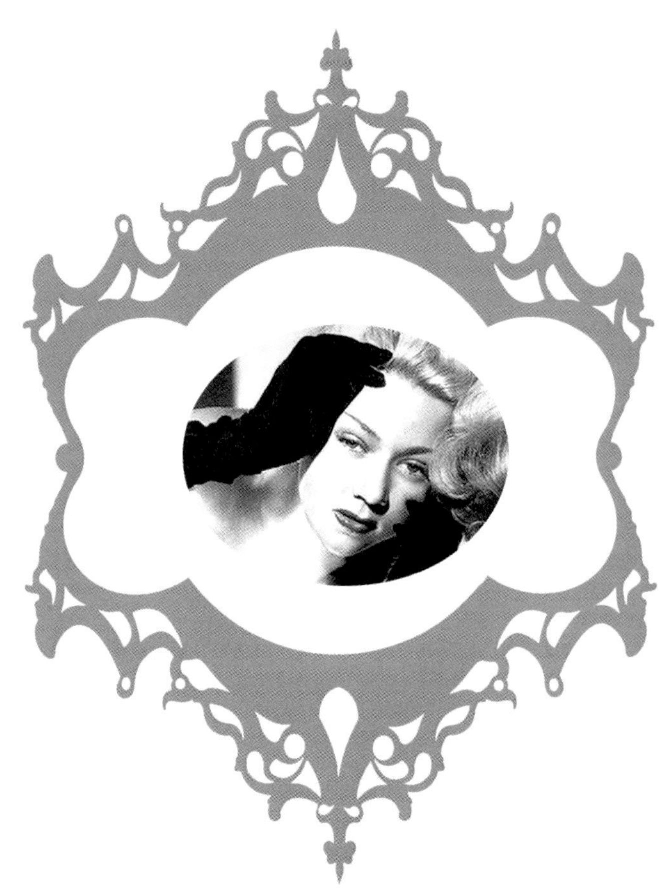

Marrying both father and son

Gloria is the Hollywood stereotype
of the bad girl that participates in noir films:
"It wasn't the way I looked at a man, it was
the thought behind it," says Gloria.
She is very concerned with her body and face.
She lifts weights and has plastic surgery.

**She has four husbands, but two of them
have the same last name: Ray**
She marries Nicholas Ray in 1948 at 24
and marries his son Anthony in 1960 at 36.
The marriage with Nicholas lasts less than
four years. One afternoon Nicholas comes
home early from work and finds Gloria
in bed with his then 13-year-old son,
Tony Ray. Tony is his son from his first

marriage to journalist Jean Evans.
Soon thereafter Nicholas divorces Gloria.
Between Nicholas and Ray, there is another
husband, Cy Howard.
In 1960 in Tijuana, Mexico, to the shock
of all in the entertainment business, Gloria
marries her former step-son, Tony.
She makes him the new stepfather of his
brother Timothy Ray, a child from her
marriage with Nicholas.
When Nicholas Ray learns about it,
he cannot believe and accept it.
Gloria has four children and two of them
belong to Tony Ray.
This whole situation totally damages her
reputation in the industry.

Jean Seberg

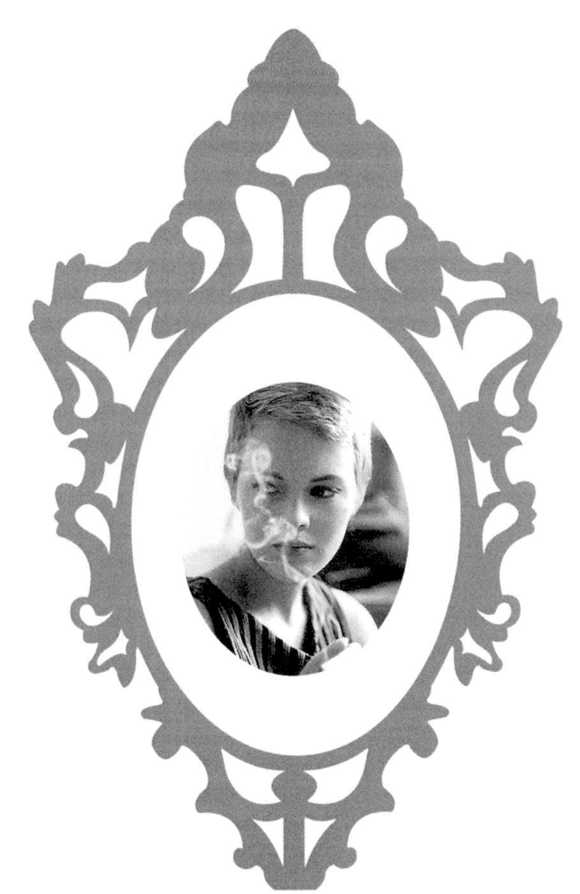

The fair panther

"In my long and difficult and mature life,
I have come to learn that the less I know about
acting and the more I know about everything
else, the better I'll be at both acting and living."

JS the icon
From her appearance age 20 in Preminger's
Saint Joan (1958) to a cultural icon in France,
influencing even the fashion. Thin like a
mannequin, she is gorgeous with her short
hair à la garçonne. She is often compared
to Louise Brooks for the intelligence and
personality that she puts into her roles. She is
one of the Nouvelle Vague's icons.

JS the actress
A movie career full of ups and downs doesn't
help Jean.
Jean-Luc Godard's *Breathless* (1960) brings
her renewed international attention. She plays
a great schizophrenic in *Lilith* (1964). Some
years later she moves to America playing *Paint
Your Wagon* (1969) and, at age 32, the colossal
melodrama *Airport* (1970) about a bomber on
board an airplane and various personal problems
of the people involved. It is a huge box office hit
which earns over $100,000,000 with 1 Oscar
winner, another 5 wins and 17 nominations.

JS the panther
She supports the Black Panthers, a radical black
nationalist movement founded in 1966 and
dissolved around 1976. Jean's faith in the BP is
noted with particular attention by the FBI.
She is a movie star, having an influence over the
public opinion, so that's why she is dangerous.
She is framed by the FBI, who spreads
rumours about her pregnancy in 1970,
insinuating that Raymond Hewt, a Black
Panther movement leader, is the father
of the little girl, who dies at birth.
Jean shows to the press the white body
of her dead daughter. The father
is the writer Romain Gary.

**"Forgive me. I can no longer live with
my nerves."**

The dramatic incident, the negative press,
and personal problems contribute
to Jean's blue funk over the years and
the end of her career.
At age 40 her frozen stiff body is discovered
after 11 days from her death in a car back
seat in a working class neighborhood in Paris.
Jean's death is still a mystery.

Jennifer Jones

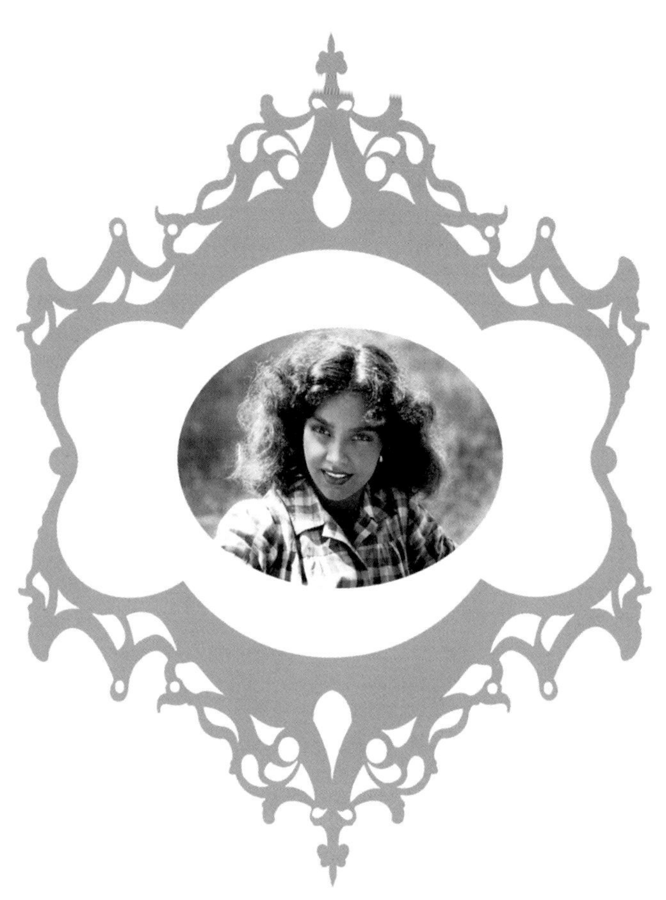

From Bernadette to Mrs. Norton

Jennifer Jones, chairwoman of the Norton Simon Museum in Pasadena, California, dies of natural causes in 2009 at age 90. She is the widow of the industrialist and art patron Norton Simon. She hates public appearances and interviews, but is always under the spotlight for:

The Song of Bernadette
Selznick gets her the role of Bernadette in *The Song of Bernadette* (1943), which is a huge hit. She receives an Oscar as best actress in a leading role.

The first husband crisis and death
She is the wife of the young actor Robert Walker and the mother of two small boys. They separate in 1943. Jennifer Jones is involved with Selznick. Walker then has huge success as the villain in Alfred Hitchcock's *Strangers on a Train* (1951). He dies at 32 in 1951 after years of emotional problems and drinking, which he attributes to his loss of her.

The influence of Selznick on her career
Jennifer Jones and Selznick are married from 1949 until his death in 1965. He makes almost all the decisions in her career. She receives Oscar nominations as best actress for *Since You Went Away* (1944), *Love Letters* (1945), *Duel in the Sun* (1946), and *Love Is a Many-Splendored Thing* (1955). After Selznick's mastermind death in 1965, her film career declines and she then only makes a couple of films including *The Towering Inferno* (1974).

Attempted suicide
In 1967 she swallows a bottle of sleeping pills and is discovered near death, lying in the surf at Malibu.

Daughter's suicide
In 1976, her 21-year-old daughter, Mary Jennifer Selznick, commits suicide by jumping off a building in West Los Angeles.

The wedding with Norton Simon
She marries Norton Simon, a multimillionaire industrialist and art collector. He has one of the country's greatest private art collections, housed at the Norton Simon Museum. After serious health problems, Simon is succeeded by Jennifer Jones as President and Chairwoman of the museum. She manages a gallery renovation by the architect Frank O. Gehry.

Joan Bennett

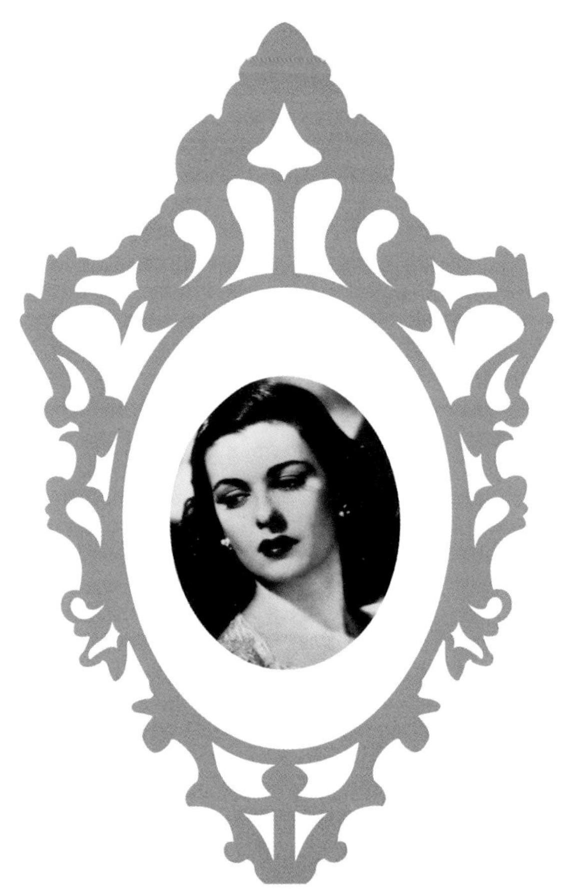

Always moving

She moves from silent movie to sound era.
She moves from being an innocent blonde girl
to a sensuous brunette femme fatale.
She moves from movies like *Little Women*
(1933) to film noir in the 1940s.
She moves from scandals to being family
oriented:both grandmother and pregnant
at age 39.
She moves from stardom to "no more calls."
Her third husband shot and injured her agent.
He thought was Bennett's lover.
The scandal damages her career.
She moves from "no more calls" to a successful
theater and television career.

Her strength
If you watch one of her films, you can feel it,
she is a very strong lady.
And it is not a matter of life and death to be
or not to be an actress.
She is as happy as usual before and after
the scandal.
She is not disappointed with losses,
nor excited by successes in her career.
Joan Bennett dies at the age of 80 and is
survived by four daughters and thirteen
grandchildren.

In one phrase, she states her own career:
"I'm aware of the priceless privilege of having
been born into the theater. Although it was
a career I rejected at first, the profession
has given me an incredibly varied life
and more than my fair share of success,
failure, love, laughter, and despair.
I've not a single regret for any of it."

Loretta Young

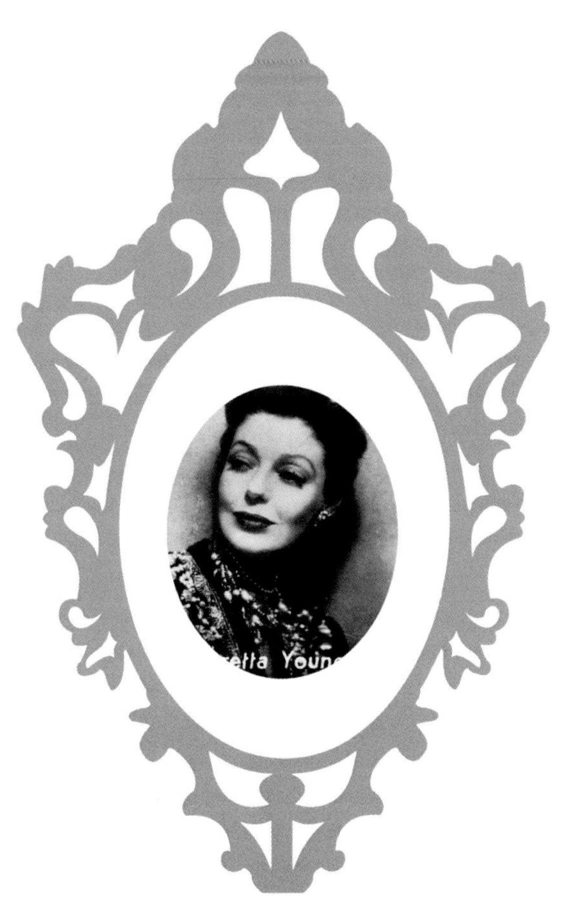

Was it worthwhile to hide her motherhood for almost her entire life?

In Hollywood in the 1930s giving birth outside of marriage is not acceptable.
Clark Gable is married to his second wife Maria Franklin Gable. But they have an affair during the filming of *The Call of the Wild* (1935). Loretta gets pregnant at age 22.

She knows that having a child out of wedlock would ruin her career. She postpones all film commitments, claiming she is ill. She hides away until the birth of her daughter, Judy. Clark Gable announces his divorce. Loretta declines his request to see the child. But some time after, she decides to let Gable visit his daughter. He finds her sleeping in a bureau draw. He gives Loretta Young a few hundreds dollars and says: "The least you can do is buy her a decent bed."
Several months later, Judy is sent to the St. Elizabeth's Infant Hospital in San Francisco, where she remains for five months.

After that, Young "adopts" her. Young says she has adopted two daughters, three-year-old Jane and Judy. However, the Jane part is not true, and soon after Loretta announces that Jane's birth mother wants her child back. Young's story deceives very few in Hollywood. Judy has her father's ears.
Judy meets Gable without knowing he is her birth father. Then Gable gives her a kiss on the forehead. They never meet again. Judy later finds out all the truth about her birth mother that Hollywood already knew. Judy moves on and achieves success, as her mother's career declines. Judy quits acting to become a therapist.

Young dies in 2000. That year, *Forever Young*, her authorized biography, says that Judy is a lovechild of her and Gable and that she covers up the scandal.
Gable's family refuses to recognize Judy. Judy does not care.

Lupe Vélez

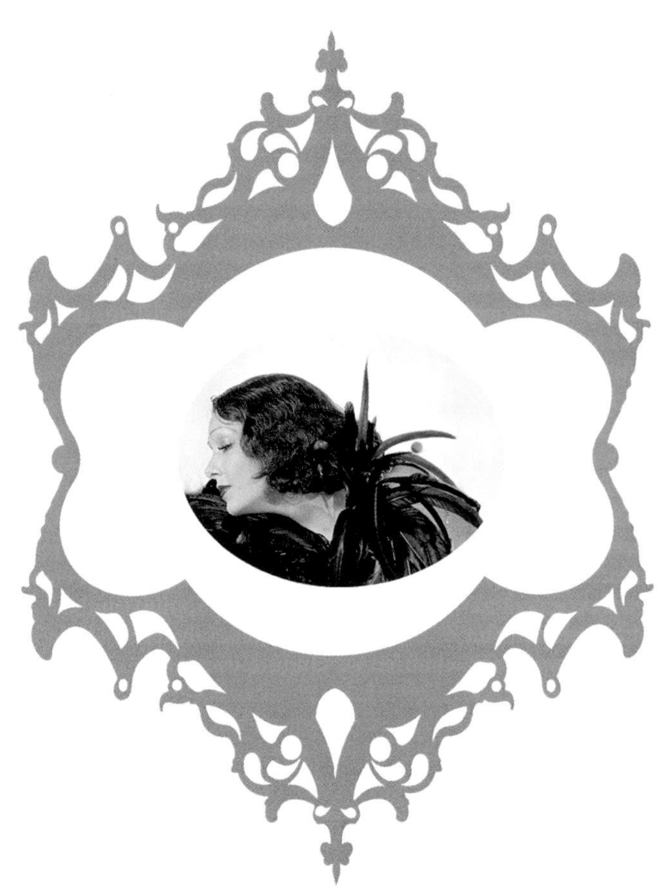

The most beautiful suicide ever

Lupe (1965), an Andy Warhol film. *Lupe* was based on Lupe Vélez, the "Mexican Spitfire who lived in a Mexican-style palazzo in Hollywood." Lupe commits "the most beautiful" suicide ever, "complete with an altar and burning candles. So she set it all up and then took poison and lay down to wait for this beautiful death to overtake her, but then at the last minute she started to vomit and died with her head wrapped around the toilet bowl."

Lupe's personality
Lupe says: "To what do I attribute my success? I think, simply, I'm different. I'm not beautiful, but I have lovely eyes and I know exactly what to do with them. Even though the public thinks I'm a pretty wild girl. I'm really not. I'm just me, Lupe Vélez, a simple and natural Lupe. If I'm happy, I dance and sing. And if something angers me, I scream and sob, and I feel a little better. Someone named that 'personality.' If I tried to look like Norma Talmadge or like the aristocrat Dolores del Río or sweet Mary Pickford, I would be nothing more than an imitation. That's what I only want to be me, Lupe Vélez."
She is also fragile. Jimmy Durante says: "This little girl was a female Pagliacci. She seemed so happy, so full of life that you didn't think she ever had a care in the world. But they used to tell me at the time of *Strike Me Pink* (1936) that she used to go to the bar at Frankie and Johnny's place and sit there all alone. Well, who can see into another person's soul?"

Career
Lupe starts out in Mexico and then moves to the US. She works in a comedy with Stan Laurel and Oliver Hardy, in the film *The Gaucho* (1928) with Mary Pickford, and in *Palooka* (1934). She plays Carmelita in *The Mexican Spitfire*'s movie series. At age 30, her career starts to decline.

Love affairs
Lupe's affairs includes Clark Gable and Charlie Chaplin. Lupe marries Tarzan star Johnny Weissmuller. Lupe bites and beats him during discussions that end up in a divorce after five years. Lupe has a three-year relationship with Gary Cooper.

And the famous and gorgeous suicide
At age 36, on December 13, 1944, Lupe commits suicide. She is pregnant with Harald Maresch's child. She says just before her death: "It is my son. I could never kill him and live in peace with myself. I'd rather kill myself." Is it the shame of bearing an illegitimate child that leads Vélez to suicide? Perhaps Lupe suffers from bipolar disorder. Lupe Vélez does not care about moral convention, so it seems unlikely that an illegitimate child is the reason for her suicide.
Lupe plans all the details of the suicide: gardenias and tuberoses. Lit candles. Coiffed. Manicured. Glamorously dressed. Make-up. Body position. A suicide note. She swallows seventy-five illegal Seconals. The plan is ruined: during the night, she wakes up, walks to the washroom, slips, breaks her neck, and drowns in the toilet. Another report says she falls knocking her head into the toilet and then drowning. Her secretary Kinder reports finding Vélez asleep in her bed.

Mabel Normand

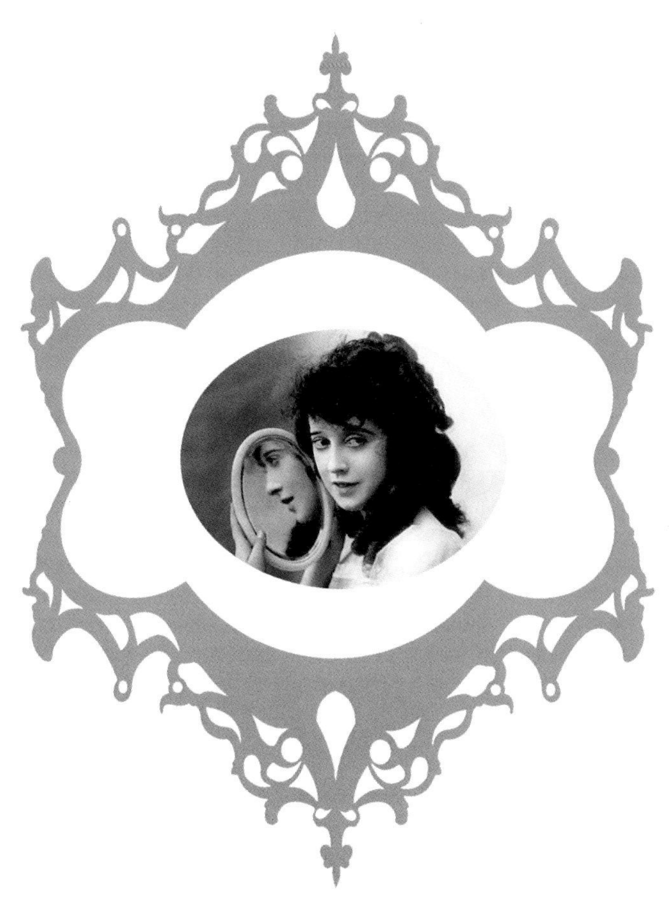

Waisted talent

Mabel Normand is one of the most gifted comic actors of the silent era and one of the first female film directors. She often works with Charlie Chaplin.

The murder of William Desmond Taylor, then Paramount director, destroys her career. She admits to have seen Taylor before the murder. The negative publicity from the case makes the public censor her films. A second scandal follows: her chauffeur shoots a wealthy friend of hers. After that, the vast majority of people decide to boycott her films and stage plays. Her career could not survive the second scandal, yet with another death, the public no longer accepts her. She carries on her partying as her health declines, enters a sanatorium, and dies of tuberculosis at age 34 in 1930.

Los Angeles, February 3, 1922 (The United Press): Mabel Normand today told the United Press of her visit to the home of William Desmond Taylor on the night he was murdered. Miss Normand is near collapse from the tragedy. Tears stood in her eyes as she spoke:
"I have known Mr. Taylor for years," the comedienne said. "There was never any love affair existing between us, never! I loved Mr. Taylor simply as a good comrade, a pal with whom I could discuss subjects in which we were mutually interested. For instance, I have been studying French. Mr. Taylor, who spoke French fluently, helped me tremendously. I am somewhat interested in philosophy and metaphysics. Again, in those subjects he was an invaluable teacher. I seldom saw Mr. Taylor except at a gathering of friends. It's true. But I frequently conversed with him over the telephone. As a general rule, this was merely to ask certain questions regarding the subjects in which I am interested."

Then the star of *Mickey* (1918) and *Molly O* (1921) told of her visit to Westlake Terrace Court on the fatal night: "Wednesday was the first time I had ever called upon Mr. Taylor alone," she said, speaking in a low tone.

"Then I stopped in for a few moments on my way home in response to a message from Mr. Taylor left with my secretary. The message stated that Mr. Taylor had already sent one book I wanted to the house and had purchased another—one I wanted particularly—and had it at his home. It was for this book that I stopped at the Terraces on my way home."
(Newspaper men ascertained that this book was one of Freud's recent works on sex psychoanalysis.)

"I arrived at Mr. Taylor's home about 7 o'clock Wednesday evening and left at 7:45," Miss Normand said.

"He accompanied me to my car at the curb of Alvarado Street and chatted for a few moments. He laughingly criticized my literary taste; there was a copy of the *Police Gazette* in the car and he thought it didn't fit in very well with Nietzsche and Freud. After he had said good night and promised to phone me within an hour, I directed William, my chauffeur, to drive me home. Being tired and having a studio call for 7:30 Thursday morning, I retired to my room. In a few moments I was in bed, where I had dinner served to me."

"That was about 8:15. Then I dropped off to sleep and slept until Edna Purviance phoned me yesterday morning about the news of Mr. Taylor's death."

Miss Purviance is a leading lady with Charles Chaplin. She has a court bungalow near Taylor's.

"Did I know that Mr. Taylor was married?" Miss Normand repeated an interviewer's question.

"No, I didn't. People had told me, but I didn't know if it was true. Mr. Taylor had never discussed his private affairs; there was no reason for his doing so."

Mary Astor

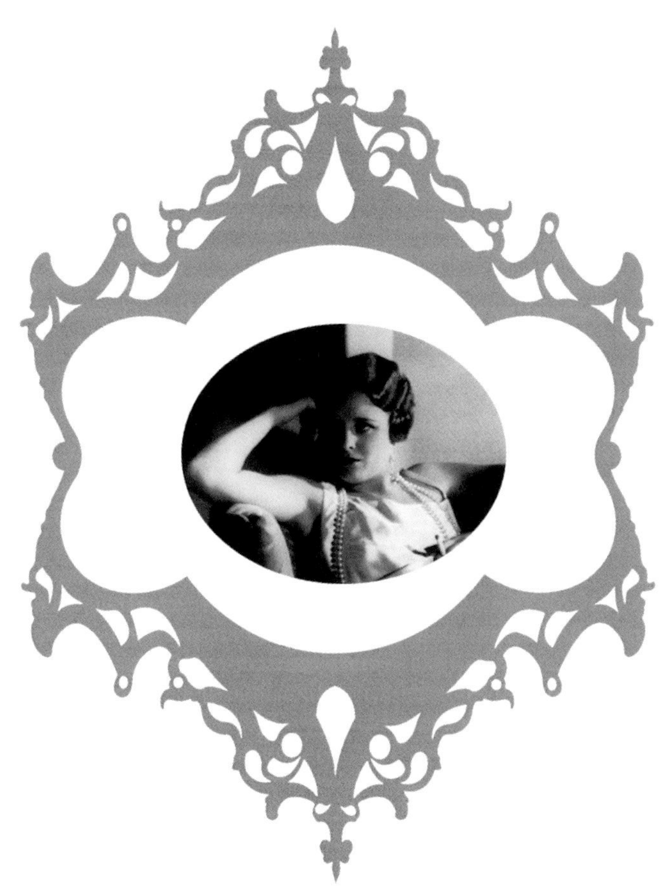

"There are five stages in the life of an actor: Who's Mary Astor? Get me Mary Astor. Get me a Mary Astor type. Get me a young Mary Astor. Who's Mary Astor?" says Mary

Who's Mary Astor?
Mary Astor is one of the few exceptions . . .
the older she gets, the more the public seems
to love her. Pressured by ambitious parents,
Mary Astor becomes a silent film star
before she is 17.
She is not to be a victim of the sound revolution;
she perfects her vocal technique superbly.

Get me Mary Astor
Astor's ex-husband tries to gain custody
of their daughter by making public her diary
in which Mary Astor discusses her affair
with playwright George Kaufman.
The scandal does not ruin her career. Astor's
then employer, Sam Goldwyn, stands by her.
People are touched by Astor's fight for
the custody of her child and willing to forget
her mistakes.
"I played secretaries, princesses, crooks,
the wife of, the girlfriend of," she writes.
She has a fear of too much responsibility
and repeatedly turns down contracts where
she is given star billing; sometimes she has
a large role but is actually billed behind
character actors.

Get me a Mary Astor type
The public loves her, but she is getting old,
so they have to find a younger replacement
for her.

Get me a young Mary Astor
In *The Maltese Falcon* (1941) starring
opposite Humphrey Bogart and *The Great Lie*
(1941) in which she wins an Academy Award
starring opposite Bette Davis, they use
many tricks to make Astor looks younger
than she really is.

Who's Mary Astor?
She is becoming a better actress as she
gets older, but health problems, alcoholism,
aging, and attempted suicide damage
her life and career.
She retires at 60. She has serious health
and financial problems. She spends
her last years in a small bungalow on the
grounds of the Motion Picture Country House
and Hospital. She dies alone at age 81.
Astor writes two insightful books on her
career, *My Story* and *A Life on Film*, maybe
with the desire not to be completely forgotten.

Patrice Wymore

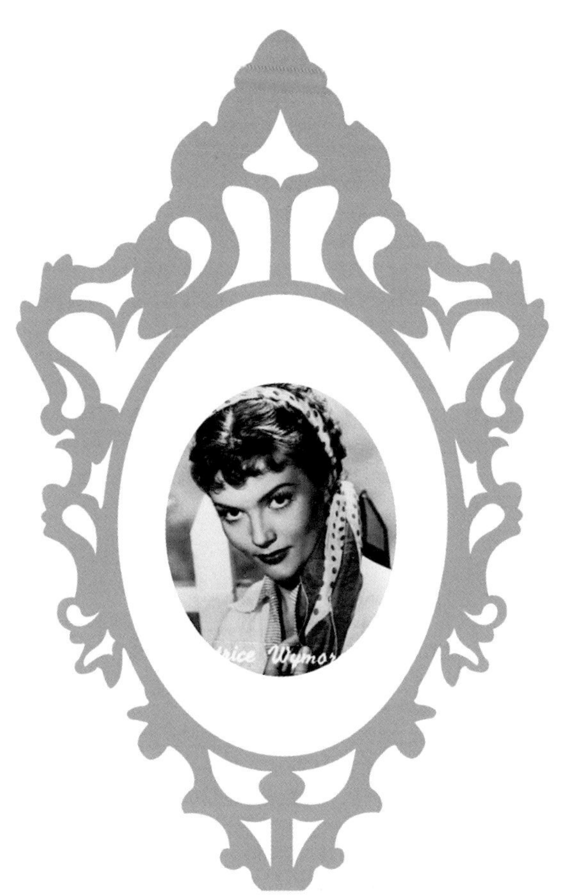

Portland's love story

"Patrice Wymore Flynn has two great loves: her late husband, the actor Errol Flynn, and her adopted home, Portland. This evening, the American actress who shunned the limelight for over four decades, dons her dancing shoes for both. The former leading lady from Miltonvale, Kansas, is patron of a centennial ball in her husband's honor, to be held at the Ken Wright Pier, located at the Errol Flynn Marina in Port Antonio. Minister of Tourism Ed Bartlett and the Jamaica Tourist Board are putting on the event to point to Errol Flynn's contribution to tourism. 'I'll open the dance floor with a waltz,' said the 83-year-old Patrice Flynn. Proceeds of the charity event will go to the Port Antonio Marching Band."
(Saturday | November 14, 2009, Brian Bonitto, Jamaica Editor - Overseas Publications)

From hell to heaven
Patrice Wymore does it all to convince her husband to give up alcohol. She is desperate to save her family. She quits Hollywood to try to support him and properly raise their daughter. He has a strong addiction to drugs and alcohol and her efforts are useless. She is unable to save him and decides to separate, hoping that the separation would be a good thing for him. But he then lives with another lady. He dies at age 50. Patrice never remarries.

After his death, she tries a comeback in Hollywood but it does not work. She begins working in a nightclub in Las Vegas and in stock musicals. She is cast for a soap opera, and appears in minor roles. After a hard and unsuccessful try, she then decides to retire again and returns with her daughter to Jamaica to the mansion Flynn built and bequeathed to her along with a cattle ranch and a 2,000-acre coconut plantation. She also goes into business. She operates a boutique and a furniture manufacturing plant. To date she continues to attend tributes and dedications to her husband.

Susan Hayward

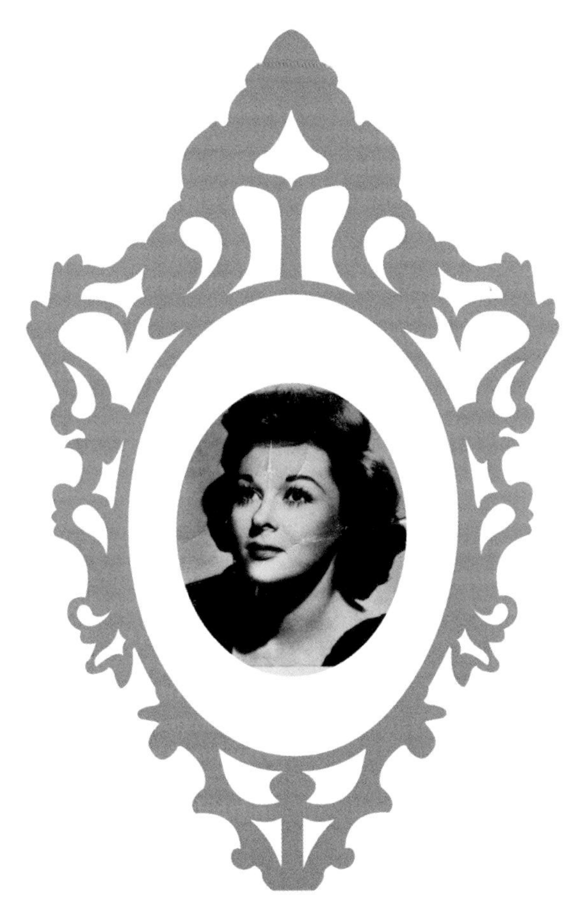

The Conqueror, the killer

Her performance in *I Want To Live!* (1958) is considered the best performance of the cinema era by many. Susan is considered very professional and talented. She receives several awards including: Oscar as best actress in a leading role for *I Want To Live!*. Four Oscar nominations as best actress in a Leading Role for *I'll Cry Tomorrow* (1955), *With a Song in My Heart* (1952), *My Foolish Heart* (1949), and *Smash-Up: The Story of a Woman* (1947). Cannes Film Festival best actress for *I'll Cry Tomorrow*. Golden Globe best motion picture actress – Drama for: *I Want To Live!*. Golden Globe best motion picture actress – Musical/Comedy for: *With a Song in My Heart*.

Atomic testing area
She dies of brain cancer at age 57, diagnosed with twenty brain tumours, which is the result of exposure to dangerous radioactive toxins on location in Utah while making *The Conqueror* (1956) together with:
John Wayne: dies at age 72 from lung and stomach cancer;
Agnes Moorehead: dies at age 74 from uterine cancer;
Pedro Armendáriz: dies at age 51, self–inflicted gunshot suicide to avoid impending slow death from cancer;
Dick Powell: dies at age 59 from lymph gland cancer.
The case is still a scandal. The location of the filming is St. George, Utah. The area receives radiation due to its downwind position close to atomic testing areas in Nevada. Many actors and a great percentage of the local population contract various forms of cancer.

Thelma Todd

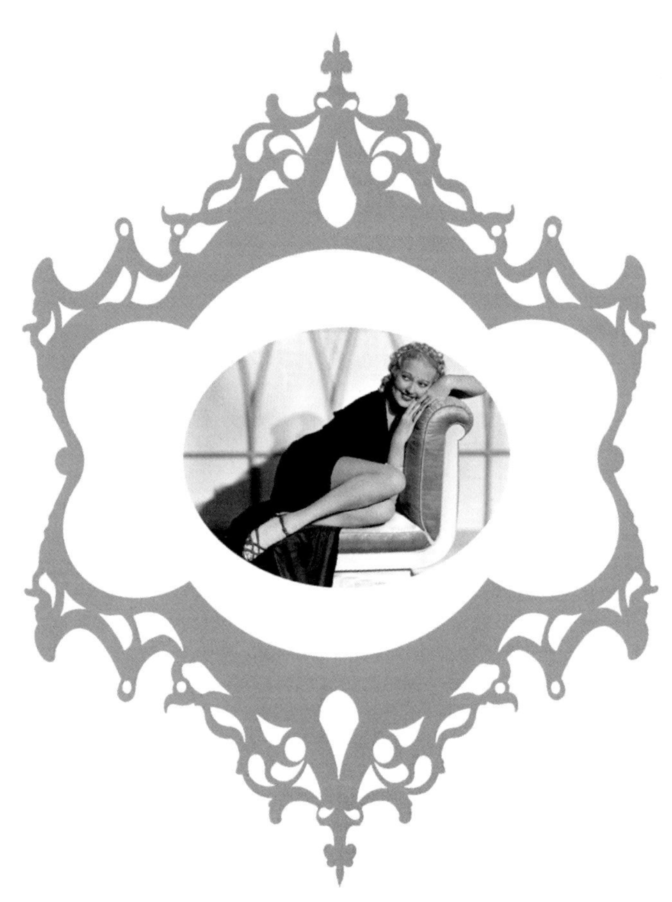

A lot of dreams. No one

"I want to be as good an actress as Bette Davis, and I'd like to be a great singer."
Fine acting talent with a strong singing voice,
tall and glamorous. She signs with Warner
Bros. and she wants to be an actress. She
appears in successful films in the early 1940s,
usually as the second female lead. She starts
a relationship with the president of 20th
Century Fox, Darryl F. Zanuck, and, when
the affair ends, her contract with Fox is
canceled and she is just in B-movies.
She is an ardent feminist and a liberated
woman and this does not help her a lot.
She plays her last two films in England.
Warm-hearted Carole puts in all her energy
during World War II, visiting troops overseas,
but she contracts amoebic dysentery
and malaria.

"But more than that I'd like to be happily married and have some children."
Landis has five husbands from 1934
to her death in 1948. Failed marriages
and failed lovers.
She desperately wants to become a mother
but no way: she suffers from endometriosis.
She is plagued by depression her entire life.
She has a poor health.
Her career is definitely in decline and her last
marriage is collapsing.
She falls in love with married actor Rex
Harrison, who refuses to divorce his wife
Lilli Palmer for her.
Unable to cope any longer, she commits
suicide by taking an overdose of Seconal.
Harrison discovers her body.
She is 29 years old.

"I know how Lupe Vélez felt. You fight just
so long and then you begin to worry about
being washed up. You fear there's one way
to go and that's down."
(on Lupe's suicide, four years before her own)

Clara Bow

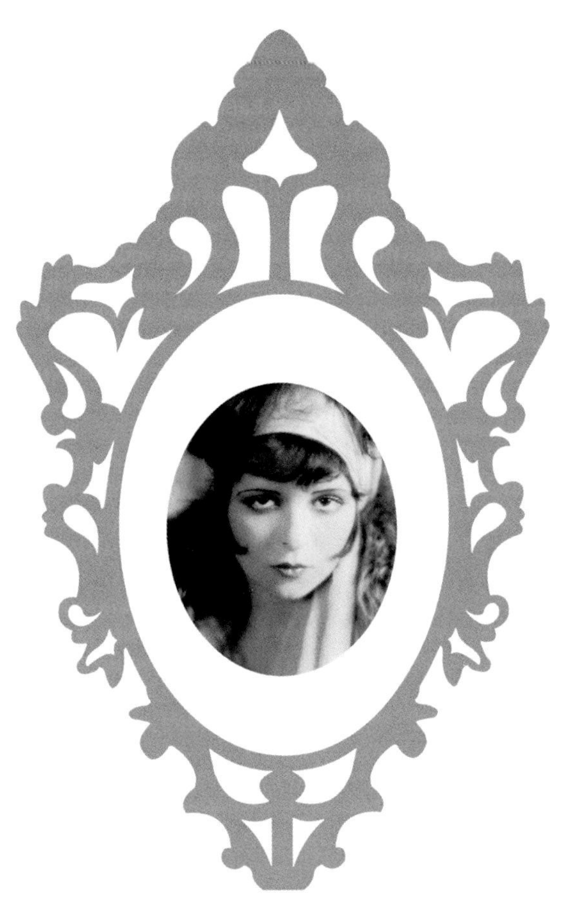

"The real thing,
someone to stir every pulse in the nation."

(F. Scott Fitzgerald)

Born July 29, 1905, Brooklyn, NY
Clara is born into madness and poverty.
Clara's mother is an occasional prostitute who
suffers from mental illness and epilepsy.
She has frequent public affairs with local
firemen. She tries to kill Clara in her sleep.
Clara's father is verbally and physically violent
and he abuses both wife and daughter. He
rapes Clara when she is 15 or 16 years old.
However, later Clara tries to do her best to
help him, but no way. He is a drinker and sex
addicted who tries to pick up young girls by
telling them his daughter is . . . Clara Bow!

Dies September 27, 1965, Los Angeles, CA
Clara dies, at age 60, from a heart attack
by watching a Gary Cooper film, one of her
ex-lovers.

US film actress
At age 16 she wins a magazine contest
that gives her a bit part in a film. Hired by
Paramount Pictures in 1925, she plays bigger
roles in silent films such as *Mantrap* (1926)
and *Kid Boots* (1926).
Clara is both a heroine and a victim of silence.
She is the new breed of woman, with her
sexy and liberated style. She inspires Max
Fleischer's cartoon character Betty Boop.
After her starring role as a flapper in the
popular film *It* (1927), Bow becomes known
as "the It girl," with "It" being understood
as the appeal of a liberated young woman.
"It girl" is difficult to define: a combination
of raw animal magnetism and an
unselfconscious indifference to this same
ability to attract members of both sexes;
"It girl" first sex symbol and most popular
female icon of the wildly modern, jazz, gin,
sex- and cinema-filled decade of the 1920s;
"It girl" in 1928, at age 23, she becomes
the highest paid movie star, receiving $35,000
per week;

"It girl" Clara is shunned by Hollywood
high society, who takes care to omit her name
from the guest lists. She is a low-life
from Brooklyn, vulgar, immoral, cheeky,
and rude.

But scandals . . .
Clara can embarrass even the most "modern"
of hosts: she likes dirty jokes, she drinks
immoderately, she is a drug addict, and she
has no manners at all.
Clara has a turbulent love affair with actor
Bela Lugosi and many others including
Victor Fleming, Gary Cooper, and Gilbert
Roland. This behavior horrifies her peers,
and eventually she is driven out
of Hollywood.

**. . . and nervous breakdowns
undermine her career**
Clara's popularity starts to fade
because of:
the advent of sound;
the Depression's unfavorable attitude
towards jazz-age extravagances;
gambling debts;
weight problem;
mental instability;
unpaid taxes;
several sensational public court battles
involving alienation of affections and
embezzlement (by her secretary).

At age 26 Clara marries cowboy
star Rex Bell.
At age 28 Clara retires from the screen.
She never makes another film.
Clara is confined to a sanitarium from time
to time, without any access to her loving sons.
At age 44 she is diagnosed with schizophrenia
and is given shock treatment. Later Rex Bell
moves her to one of the top mental
institutions in the nation.

Dolores Costello

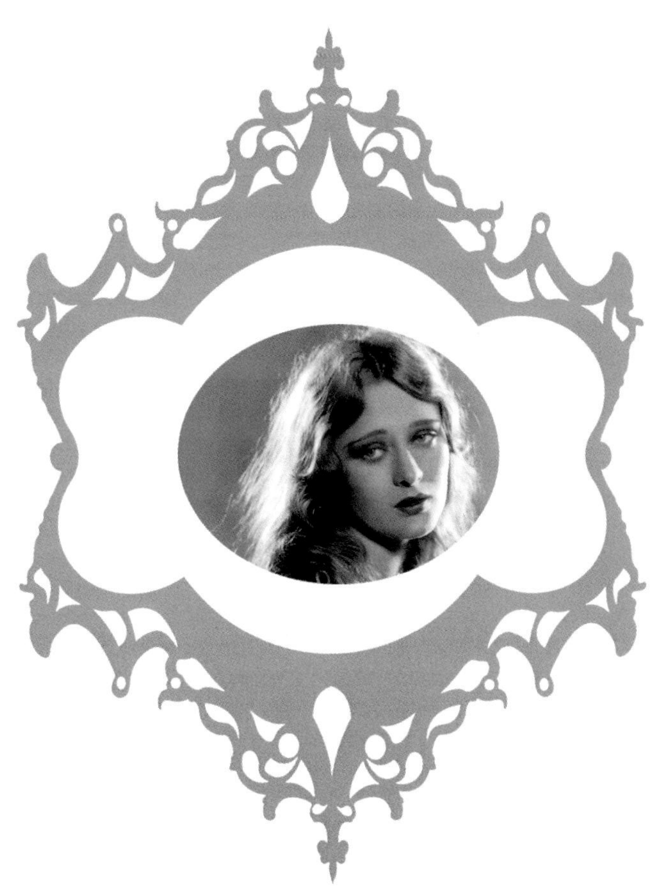

Take care of your skin

So beautiful . . .

"The most beautiful creature I have ever seen."
John Barrymore falls in love with the wampas
baby during the filming of *The Sea Beast*
(1926). They have a long and legendary kiss
scene. They marry in 1928 and divorce seven
years later. Dolores has to fight with John's
alcohol addiction and they have two children.
John begins drinking even more and Dolores
marries again and returns to star in *Little Lord
Fauntleroy* (1936).

. . . and so devastating

However, the lovely Dolores develops a severe
reaction to the harsh make-up used in her
movies. The studios are not happy at all.
The skin on her cheeks gets worse and worse
and artists find her condition impossible
to hide. She achieves some success such as
The Magnificent Ambersons, Orson Welles's
best film in 1942, and her final film is *This
Is the Army* in 1943. She is forced to quit,
reluctant to be seen in public. She is only 40.

Looking after your skin in your twenties

Your twenties is a great time for your skin!
You've left behind adolescent acne and your
skin has a radiant, youthful glow and the
epidermis is well toned. However: No mid-day
sun, or cover-up. Penetrating UVA rays will
start to damage collagen fibers and elastin
coils in your skin. No smoking.

Looking after your skin in your thirties

Skin cell turnover has slowed down and
first wrinkles may start to appear. Yes, daily
skincare regime that involves exfoliating (2/3
times a week), cleansing, moisturising. Yes,
sun protection. Yes, a balanced diet of fresh
fruit, vegetables, grains, and fish, which are
high in antioxidants. Yes, drinking plenty
of water every day and alcohol in moderation.

Looking after your skin in your forties

Collagen fibers decrease in number, stiffen,
break apart, and become a shapeless, matted
tangle. You must use a rich nourishing night
crème exfoliant regularly, a facial scrub
(2/3 times a week).

Looking after your skin in your fifties

After menopause, skin loses its plumpness
and tone, and it may be dry, itchy, and more
sensitive to allergens. Mature skin is more
fragile, prone to injury and infection.
Extra care of your skin's health and remember
a face that has a lived-in look is much more
attractive than a Botox face,
and character is much more beauty!
(Doctor Danny Siegenthaler's advises)

Gia Scala

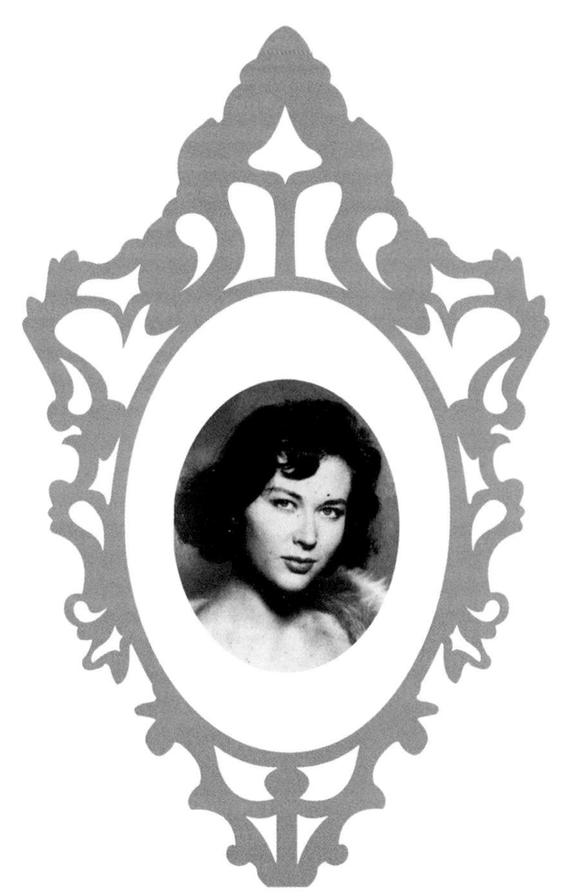

Too less oxygen

**"I don't know what I was doing.
I wasn't myself."**
Gia is the very well-known Anna, the Greek
resistance fighter, in the classic all-star epic
film *The Guns of Navarone* (1961) opposite
Gregory Peck, David Niven, Anthony Quinn,
and Irene Papas. She is 27.

At age 19 she signs contracts with Universal
Studios and Columbia. She makes her debut
with Glenn Ford, Robert Mitchum, and
Wernher von Braun. Gia's successful start
begins to deteriorate quite soon because
of alcohol dependency and lack of self-
confidence. She moves to England in an
unsuccessful attempt to revive her film career.
Her marriage ends in divorce after eleven
years. At age 36 she decides to return
to Hollywood, but her problems continue
to follow her.

Female jail
At age 23 in 1957 Gia is booked
for driving under the influence of alcohol.
Police say she fails the test. "I just had a couple
of glasses of champagne with a doctor who is
treating my mother." Her mother has cancer
and is given only a few months to live.

Waterloo Bridge. First attempted suicide
At age 24 in 1958 Gia makes an unsuccessful
attempt at suicide by throwing herself off
Waterloo Bridge.
"I don't know what I was doing. I wasn't
myself. A few months ago my mother died.
We were very close—always together."

State hospital
At age 37 in 1971 a judge sends her
to a state hospital for psychiatric examination
after she collapses in a drunk driving
condition. Later she is released for two mouths
into the custody of actress Anna Kashfi,
Marlon Brando's ex-wife. Some months later
she returns to Camarillo State Hospital for
psychiatric observation.

Crash car
At age 37 in 1971 she is injured
when her car overturns. She is driving
alone and apparently loses control. It takes
a fire crew to take her off and bring her to
Hollywood Receiving Hospital for lacerations
and multiple bruises.

Stop harassing
At age 37 in 1971 Los Angeles Superior Court
orders her to stop harassing her former
husband, Don Burnett.
He enjoins her from "molesting, striking,
harassing, or otherwise disturbing the peace."

Death
At age 38 in 1972 autopsy: death from an
overdose of drugs and alcohol. Accidental?
The Los Angeles County coroner rules her
death accidental. She takes medication for
her drinking problem and she suffers from a
coronary condition. The coroner states she
died from advanced arteriosclerosis. This
opinion could explain her bizarre behavior
during almost all her life: her brain was simply
not getting enough oxygen.

Jean Arthur

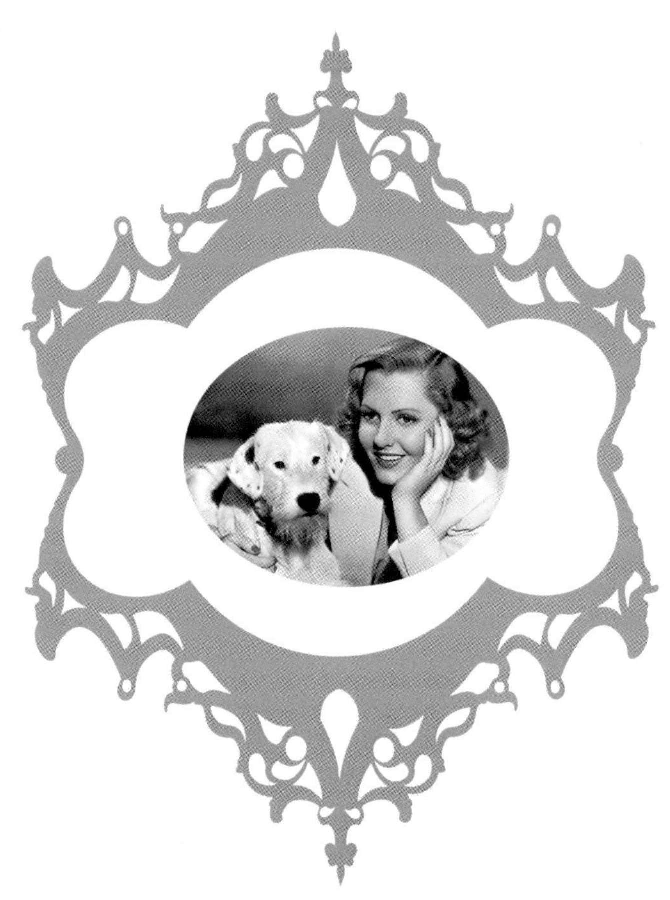

So painful

Your mouth is so dry, you smack your lips without control and you even change the tone of your voice
In 1943 Jean Arthur, for her performance in George Stevens's *The More the Merrier* (1943), receives a best actress Academy Award nomination, but the award goes to Jennifer Jones in *The Song of Bernadette* (1943).

Your body and your hands start shaking and your heart, too, and you feel like dying
In 1944 her career begins to fade and she is replaced by Rita Hayworth as Columbia Pictures' top female star. Later she appears in only two more films, for Oscar-winning directors Billy Wilder *A Foreign Affair* (1948) and *George Stevens Shane* (1953).

Your knees knock together and you feel like falling down
In 1946 she moves to Broadway in the play *Born Yesterday* but, once again, her nerves and insecurity get the better of her and she leaves the production, opening the door for the newcomer Judy Holliday.

You are terribly nervous both before and after filming a scene
In 1950 Jean returns to the stage, most notably to play her favorite character, Peter Pan, but her chronic insecurity becomes crippling. The contract is cancelled at the last minute with "illnesses."

You become hysterical when besieged by fans and non-responsive to reporters
In 1975 at age 75, Jean tries again: she is the first female Supreme Court justice in the play *First Monday in October*, but once again she succumbs to extreme stage fright and quits.
For the most part, she lives quietly in her home in California, seeing a few friends and taking care of her beloved pets.

Kay Francis

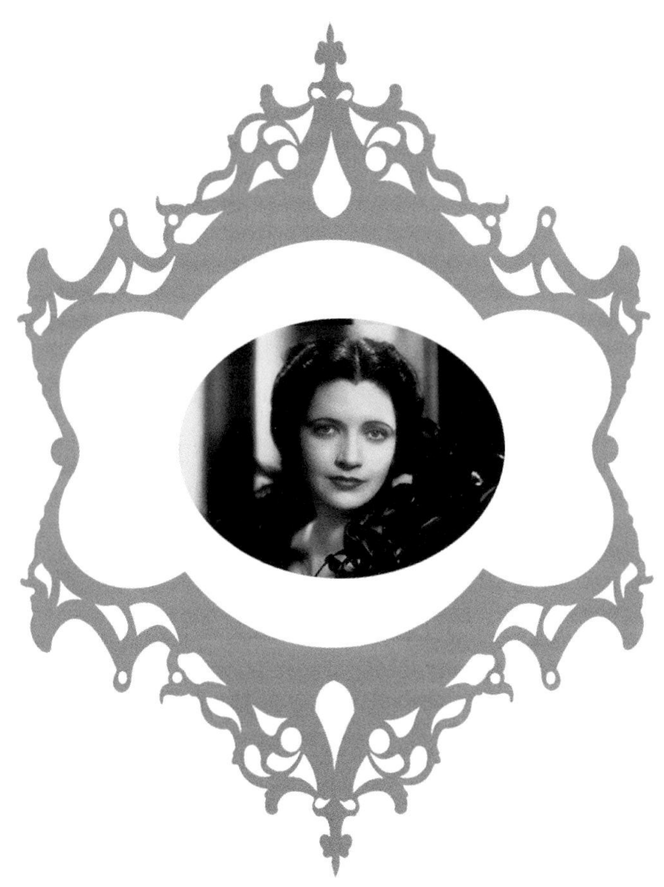

She is made for . . .

She is made for life
A passionate, liberated, outgoing, free-spirited woman, generous and deprived. Kay's nature gives a great contribution to the army forces during World War II and writes a private "scandalous" diary, surely "not to be forgotten." The best tennis and poker player in Hollywood, with her pal Constance Bennett.

She is made for fashion
Her ability and sophisticated personality to wear clothes makes her an icon of the 1930s. She is 1.77 meters tall and she moves in wonderful creations by Adrian, Travis Banton, or Orry Kelly haute couture, wearing hats that hide half of her face. In 1937 she is elected the most elegant woman in America, but she doesn't care.

She is made for turbulent relationships
"I'm not a star, I'm a woman, and I want to get fucked." Five marriages and divorces, many love affaires, maybe bi-sexual, no children.

She is made for the camera
Sleepy slow eyes set wide apart, throaty voice, a large mouth, black hair, beautiful skin, blue eyes. She is clever.

She is made for mystery
There is speculation and doubts about her birth. 1905, or anywhere between 1899–1908? Studio records reflect the year of birth as 1899 but her listing in the US Census is in April 1910, when she is living at a convent school. To add another detail: people say she is half-blood with some Afro-American descendants.

She is made for money
Kay hit top between 1930 and 1936. Kay's best film is Ernst Lubitsch's *Troubles in Paradise* (1932) with Herbert Marshall and Miriam Hopkins. To remember *Girls about Town* (1931), *One Way Passage* (1932), and *Confession* (1937). Kay is the best-paid actress in Hollywood but, in 1937, at age 32, her film scripts get worse and worse. Warner is looking for another star, less beautiful and charming and the name is . . . Bette Davis! Kay is humiliated, however her salary is still greater than $5000 a week!
She loves money.

She is made for Warner Bros.
Warner has always placed Kay in roles "of inferior quality." She wants a change in her contract. Nothing happens and Kay suddenly changes her mind: to stay at the studio and fight for her $5,200 weekly salary and to finish out her contract in B pictures. She is still a movie glamour queen and she proves it with the movie *In Name Only* (1939).

She is not made for a happy ending
Kay spends her days on stage, touring in various productions. In 1948, at age 43 (who knows?!) she has a fatal accident in which she badly burns her legs on a radiator (allegedly under the influence of prescription drugs). Her stage career loses momentum and she quits. She drinks night and day.

She is made for hearted charity
In 1966 Kay dies from breast cancer. She has no immediate descendents. She leaves over $1,000,000 to an organization, Seeing Eye, Inc., that trains guide dogs for the blind.

Linda Darnell

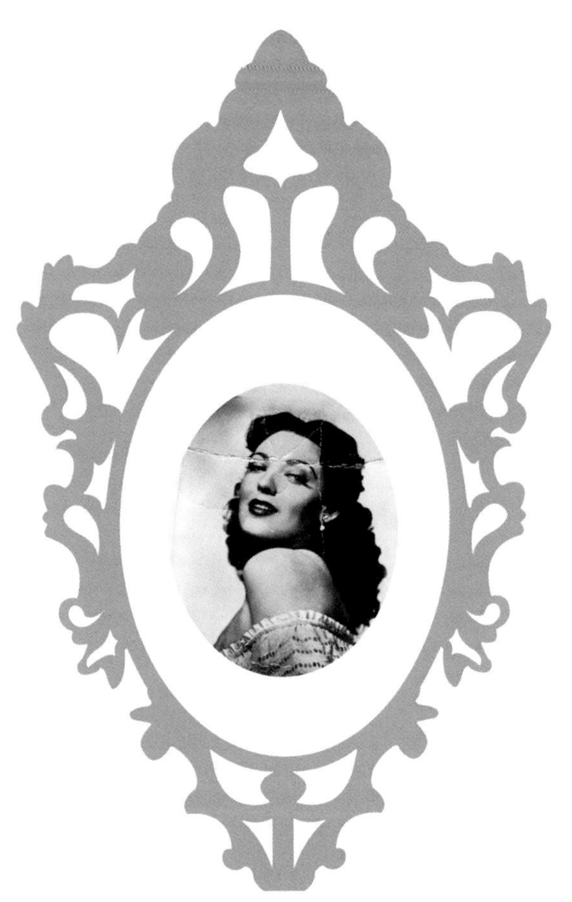

Don't play with fire!

Too young
Chaotic home, absent father, Linda is manipulated and driven by a stage-struck mother who runs her life without any pity for her. She is so beautiful and young and she has to become rich and famous. At 13 Linda's first talent scouts. She goes to California but when the studio finds out how young she really is, she is sent home. She will be back at 15. The mother doesn't give up and she goes on.

Too adult
Linda is put into adult roles immediately and the studio prepares special make-up tricks to make her look older. Linda is a leading lady in such notable Hollywood films as *The Mark of Zorro* (1940), *Blood and Sand* (1941), *Hangover Square* (1945), *My Darling Clementine* (1946), *A Letter to Three Wives* (1949), *No Way Out* (1950), as well as the notorious *Forever Amber* (1947).

Too breakable and naive
Linda is unable to cope with tough Hollywood. Her naive expectations and lack of education lead her in a downward spiral of alcoholism, failed marriages, and love affairs, including a devastating relationship with Joseph Mankiewicz. She has one adopted daughter, Linda's only child.

Too sorry
At age 26, she is one of the three wives in the comedy/drama *A Letter to Three Wives* (1949) and she is quite close to winning an Academy Award.
It doesn't happen, and her career is on the wane.

Too much . . . fire
She dies in a tragic house fire in Chicago, after suffering burns on ninety percent of her body. She is only 41. Before the fire she was watching *Star Dust* (1940) on television, one of her first films. Amber St. Clair, the character she plays in *Forever Amber*, survives the London fire. Tuptim, the character she plays in *Anna and the King of Siam* (1944), doesn't survive the torture by fire.

Maria Montez

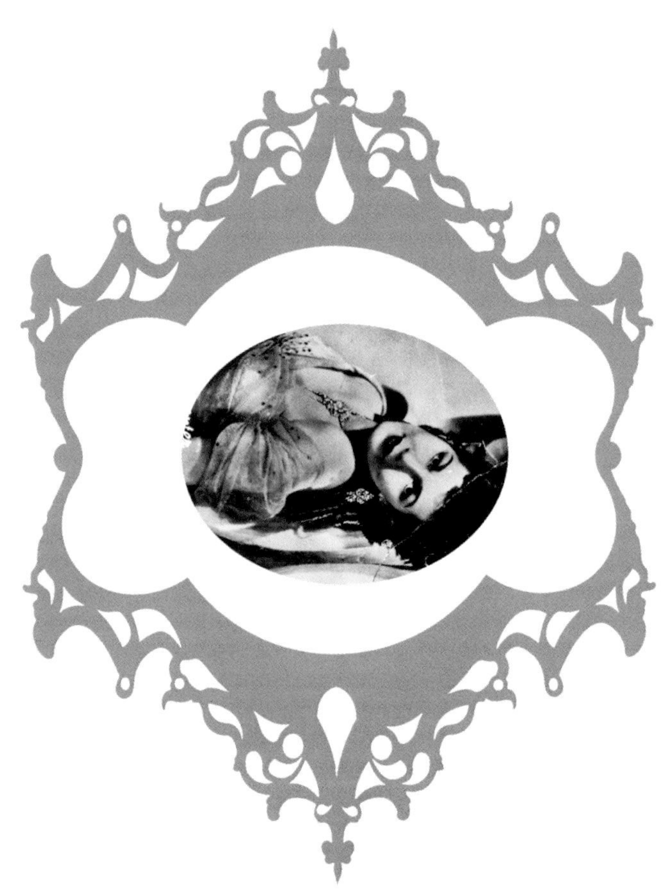

The exotic star against depression and war

**"When I look at myself, I am so beautiful
I scream with joy!"**
She is Dominican, the second daughter
of ten children and, ever since childhood,
Maria dreams of becoming a movie star.
She tries unsuccessfully with the stage; she
models but it isn't enough.

**A perfect Hollywood gift against Depression
and War**
America is still trying to get out from
under the Great Depression and World War II
is spreading throughout Europe and Asia.
Hollywood turns to fantasy movies
for the public. Maria is the perfect actress
for this moment. Maria has exotic looks,
exotic beauty, and an exotic accent
and the studio does not lose time in pairing
her with other "exotics," such as Sabu and
Turhan Bey. Low-budget stories located in
nowhere lands with fantasy costumes and
Maria . . . becomes immensely popular,
a tempestuous Latin leading lady, also known
as The Caribbean Ciclone. She plays star
night and day and she always does her best
to attract attention at nightclubs or at
social events.

**But as the Depression eases and the
War ends . . .**
Fans are bored with her films. Maria is
"no longer called" and, with her second
husband Jean-Pierre Aumont, she moves to
Europe. She appears in a number of German,
French, and Italian productions.
She is discovered dead from a heart attack
at her home in Paris. Her sisters find her
drowned in the bath tub. The accident
could have been provoked by two different
situations: heart attack due to a shock, because
the water is too hot (45 degrees C) or the hot
water makes her faint and she drowns.
No autopsy. She is only 39.

Still loved
Maria's legacy lives on. In 1997 the new
international airport at Barahona, her
hometown in the Dominican Republic,
is named the Maria Montez International
Airport and . . . someone adds: "I hope some
day in the Dominican Republic, it will be a
museum dedicated to the actress where we
could dream today and tomorrow with that
gorgeous and exotic lady who was so close
to us." (Angel Feliz, a fan)

Marie McDonald

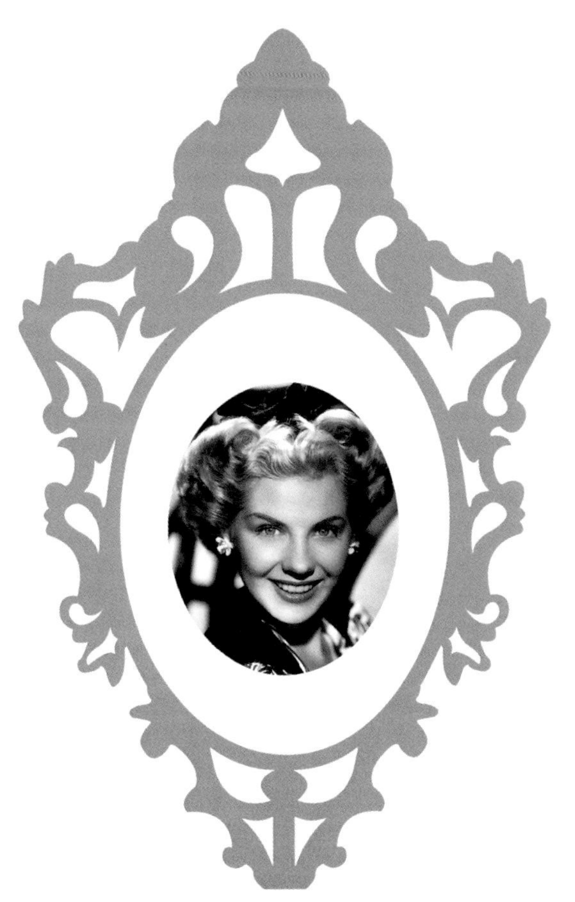

Husbands are easier to find than good agents

"Husbands are easier to find . . ."
Six husbands and seven marriages
in a short life: the first one at age 17,
the last one at age 40.

Donald F. Taylor: from 1963 to 1965
Edward F. Callahan: from 1962 to 1963
Louis Bass: from 1959 to 1960
Henry Karl: from from 1947 to 1954
and from 1955 to 1958
Victor M. Orsetti: from 1943 to 1947
Richard Allord: from 1940 to 1940

Marie has three children, two of them adopted.
In 1965 Marie is up and happy and goes
to bed. The next morning her last husband,
Donald Taylor, finds Marie slumped over
a dressing table in their bedroom. Marie
dies of a drug overdose. There is air in the
needle that she injected into herself.
She is 42 and she commits suicide.
Donald is devastated after Marie's death
and he is charged with murder. About three
months after Marie's death, Donald,
age 47, kills himself with an overdose
of barbituates in the same bedroom
where Marie dies.
Harry Karl, the father of her three children,
does not want the children after Marie's death.
His wife at the time, Debbie Reynolds,
insists on having the children at home to take
care of them, and she wins.

". . . than good agents."
A beautiful body and notorious scandals
make Marie a star. At the height of her
popularity Marie receives 100,000 fan letters
a year. Press agents nickname Marie
"The Body," but "This body isn't ready
for an autopsy yet," Marie says regarding
her frequent illnesses.
Too many sex scandals, alcoholism, drugs,
frequent skirmishes with the law, and nervous
breakdowns do not help her career even with
a good agent. Marie's last effective role is
in the Jerry Lewis film *The Geisha Boy* (1958)
at age 35. She replaces Mamie Van Doren in
the movie *Promises! Promises!* (1963) at age
40 and during the shooting she fights with the
other bombshell star Jayne Mansfield.
She marries the producer of the movie,
Donald F. Taylor, her last suicide husband.

Paula Raymond

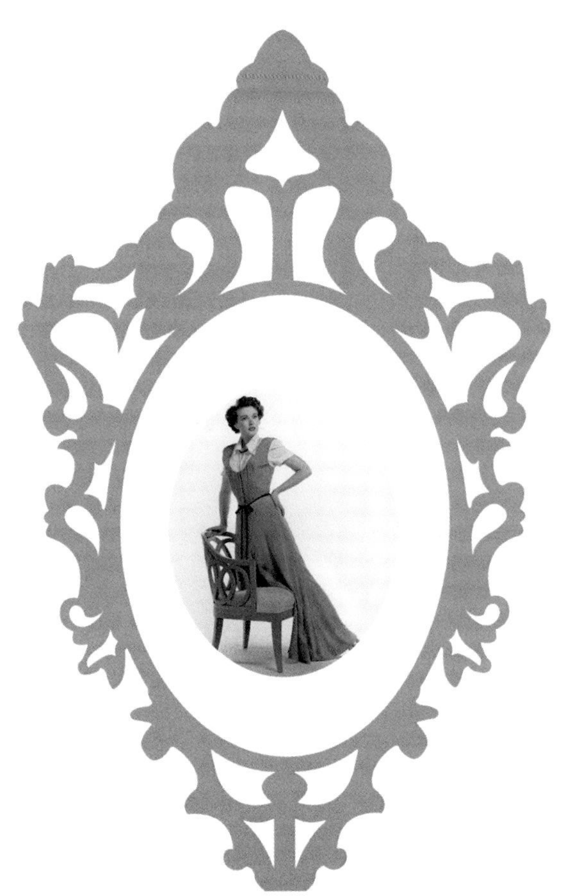

A working woman

"I was just filling space. I was not given many acting roles. I didn't want to work, but I had a daughter to support. I became an actress because it was the only way I knew to earn a living. I wasn't trying to be a glamour movie star."

She is a working student
A lawyer's important daughter and a good education: she studies ballet, voice, music, and piano, singing coloratura roles in junior opera productions, Hollywood High School, and University Law in San Francisco.

She is a working actress
At age 20 she marries a marine captain but divorces two years later just after the birth of their daughter. She moves to Hollywood looking for a job: model, Columbia in five "B" pictures, television appearances, and then her contract with MGM in 1950. She plays opposite leading men like Cary Grant and Dick Powell. Despite her prominent roles, Paula does not attract a strong following, and the studio gives her minor roles. She fires her agent and leaves MGM to freelance.

She is the space heroine
At age 29 she goes straight into her most remembered film, Lourié's *The Beast from 20,000 Fathoms* (1953), about a rhedosaurus which wreaks havoc after being thawed from its Arctic home by atomic tests. She is the paleontologist's assistant. *Fathoms*, with its innovative stop-motion special effects, is a huge hit and becomes an important cult film, the first in which nuclear energy frees a monster that embarks on mass destruction.

She is a working mother and a working actress
At age 31, Paula leaves movies: "I had a daughter to support. So, I looked in the classified ads." She works as a receptionist, a bookkeeper, and an insurance clerk. She quits, finds a new agent, and plays on television until 1962.

She is a crash-miracle woman
At age 38 in 1962, Paula and her friend Gloria Beutel drive on Sunset Boulevard. Gloria loses control of the car and hits a tree. The car overturns several times and Paula is pulled out of it just before it explodes. The rear view mirror crushes and takes her nose off completely. She is pronounced dead at the hospital, but later she is revived by a neurologist. She has a skull fracture and her nose cut off and a plastic surgeon works all night on her. He does a wonderful job. Her beauty miraculously recovers but a slight disfigurement remains.

She is a strong-willed woman until she dies
Just one year after the tragic accident, Paula returns to television and makes three more movies. She works in business, her daughter dies, she breaks her ankle, she breaks both hips, she breaks her shoulder. Anyway she spends the rest of her life writing poetry, music, and fan mail.

Phyllis Thaxter

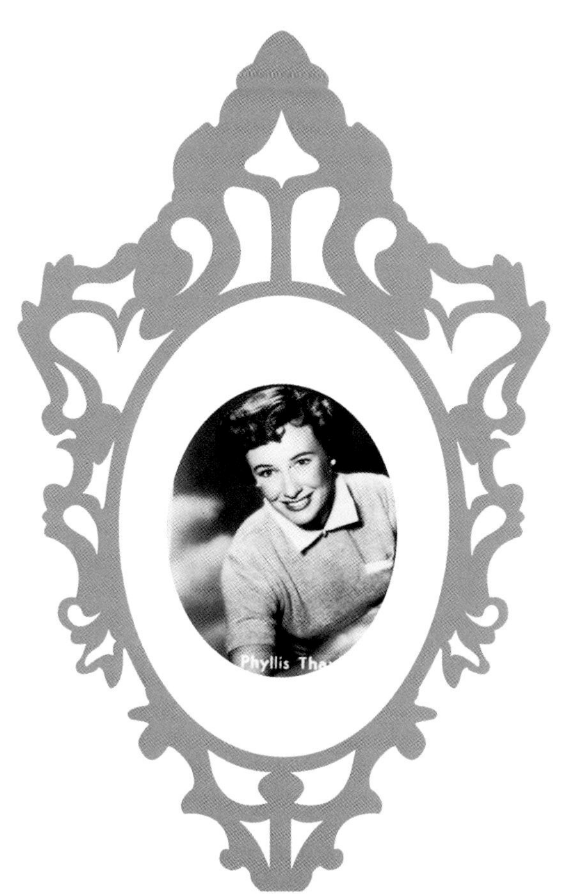

An outstanding survivor

She is a warm and sensitive talent that graces
too few Hollywood films during the Golden Age.
She is very natural and not glamourous, quite
similar to June Allyson and Teresa Wright.
She is depended on as a stabilizing factor
in melodramas and war pictures.
She is the girlfriend or the daughter waiting
on the home or the ever-patient wife
to a number of leading men, including
Robert Ryan in Fred Zinnemann's *Act
of Violence* (1948), one of her best
performances.
She moves from Warner to Paramount,
but again and again she plays the ever-patient
wife to some top actors including John
Garfield, Gig Young, and Gary Cooper.

At age 31 her career is suddenly cut off by
illness. She contracts a form of infantile
paralysis. She recovers quickly, she survives
but she has awful problems with her legs.
Film roles are few and far between after this.
At age 32 she starts a new life
and a new career: the birth of her son
and a slow television comeback in character
parts, frequently accepting roles that would
challenge her physical limitations.

**Some important celebrities who survive
the infectious disease poliomyelitis**
Lionel Barrymore contracts polio at age
30, in the mid-1930s, which leaves him
in a wheelchair.
Mia Farrow collapses at age 9.
She spends eight months in the hospital.
Mel Ferrer's career is stalled when he contracts
polio in the early 1940s.
Ida Lupino catches polio at age 17.
Donald Sutherland contracts polio as a
child and develops a love of reading while
bedridden.
Francis Ford Coppola: "When I was 9 I was
confined to a room for over a year with polio,
and because polio is a child's illness, they kept
every other kid away from me. I remember
being pinned to this bed, and longing for
friends and company."
Renata Tebaldi contracts polio at age 3,
which is the cause of her difficulty to walk.
During this experience she discovers music.
Neil Young gets polio at age 5, during
the epidemic of 1951.
Frida Kahlo catches polio at age 6 and spends
several months in bed. Kahlo is left with a
deformed and shortened right leg all her life.

Anna Maria Pierangeli

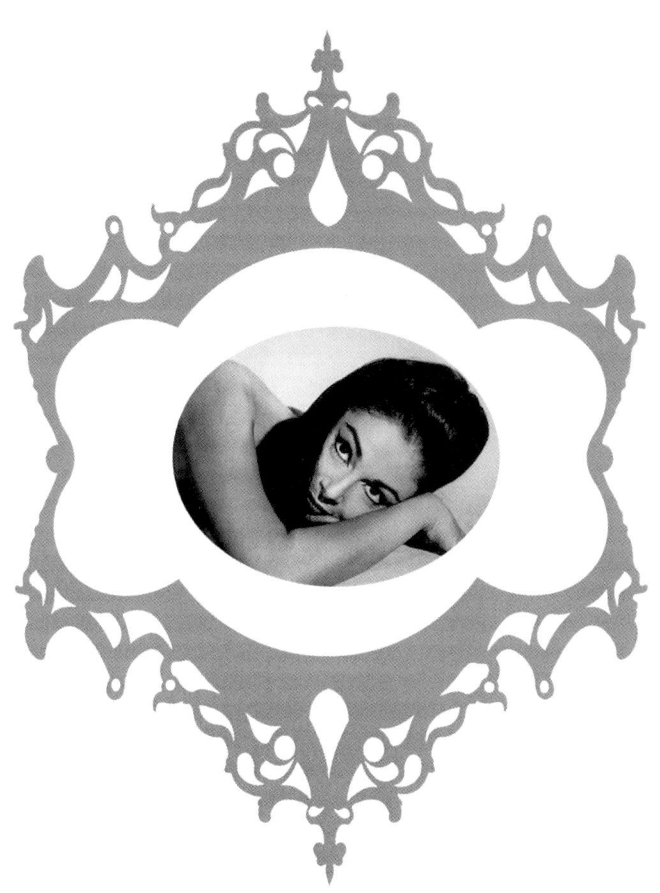

Both so young

Pierangeli is in love with James Dean
"He wanted me to love him unconditionally,
but Jimmy was not able to love someone
else in return . . . it was the troubled boy that
wanted to be loved very badly."

They meet each other during the shooting
of *The Silver Chalice* in 1954. Pierangeli is
22 and starting her career. James Dean
is 24 and a world-famous star so
near to his tragic end.
For a short time, not even one year, they
have a romantic relationship and, reportedly,
they are very much in love, even thinking
about marriage. For a very short time even
James promotes his love affair and Julie
Harries, Dean's co-star in *East of Eden* (1955),
reports that Jimmy tells her he is madly in
love with Pierangeli.

"I loved Jimmy as I have loved no one else
in my life, but I could not give him
the enormous amount that he needed.
Loving Jimmy was something that could
empty a person."

**But, Pierangeli's mother is contrary to
the relationship**
Dean is a teenager idol and he is not Catholic.
She breaks off the relationship, apparently.
Pierangeli accepts.
After one month Pierangeli marries the singer
actor Vic Damone. So strange . . . the following
month?! This marriage ends in a divorce four
years later together with a court battles
for the custody of their only son. Pierangeli
marries and divorces again with Armando
Trovaioli and she has another son.

Pierangeli's film career is full of ups and downs
and sorrow. Pierangeli's best and well-known
role is Norma Graziano in *Somebody Up There
Likes Me* (1956) opposite Paul Newman.
The film is a box-office hit and Pierangeli
dreams about her career's future. She plays in
some more films but she is always waiting for
a real change. After a handful of films between
1966 and 1970, Pierangeli realizes her dream
of superstardom doesn't exist.
Young, naïf, fragile, unlucky, and romantic,
she commits suicide at age 39.

Susan Peters

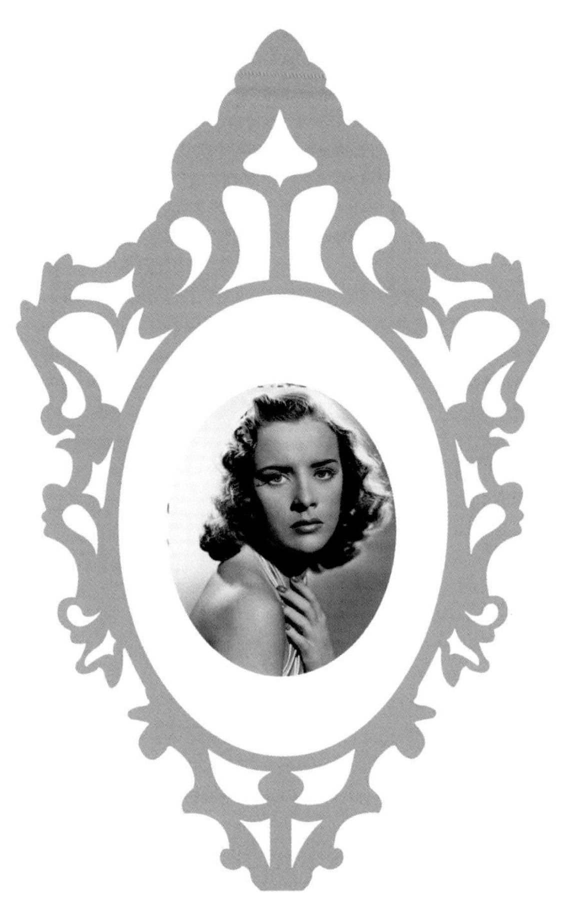

Too much

1942

MGM. The studio has a lovely, bright, full-face, and creative talent star. She plays her first important role in *The Big Shot* (1942), opposite Bogart.

Love. That same year Susan meets actor Richard Quine on *Tish* (1942) set. He plays the husband and they appear together in the film *Dr. Gillespie's New Assistant* (1942). The real-life marriage takes place in 1943.

Oscar Nomination. Susan wins an Academy Award nomination for best supporting actress for *Random Harvest* (1942) and the studio begins to cast her in several lesser productions that allow her to learn her craft, opposite such illustrious actors like James Stewart, Katharine Hepburn, Hedy Lamarr.

1945

The tragedy. Susan, her husband, and friends are together on vacation in early 1945 when a rifle accidentally goes off, lodging a bullet in her spine. The accident leaves her permanently paralyzed from the waist down. She needs a wheelchair to move.

MGM. The studio goes on paying her salary, but it's impossible to find suitable projects for her. Susan quits and tries radio.

Love. Susan and Richard adopt a son but two years later they divorce.

After 1945

A difficult actress to cast. Susan makes a film comeback with *The Sign of the Ram* (1948) where she plays a wheelchair-bound woman who tries to destroy the happiness around her, but the public does not react in a good way. On stage she plays again a wheelchair girl and she is a lawyer in the television series *Miss Susan* (1951) but the show runs for less than one season. She rejects the idea of playing the role of a famous ballerina who suffers a spinal injury.

1952

The hospital. She suffers from acute depression, she loses a lot of weight, and she is very weak. She continues to deteriorate, becoming physically and psychologically fragile. She develops anorexia nervosa.

The death. At age 31: "I'm getting awfully tired. I think it would be better if I did die." She passes away from kidney disease and pneumonia.

Tilly Losch

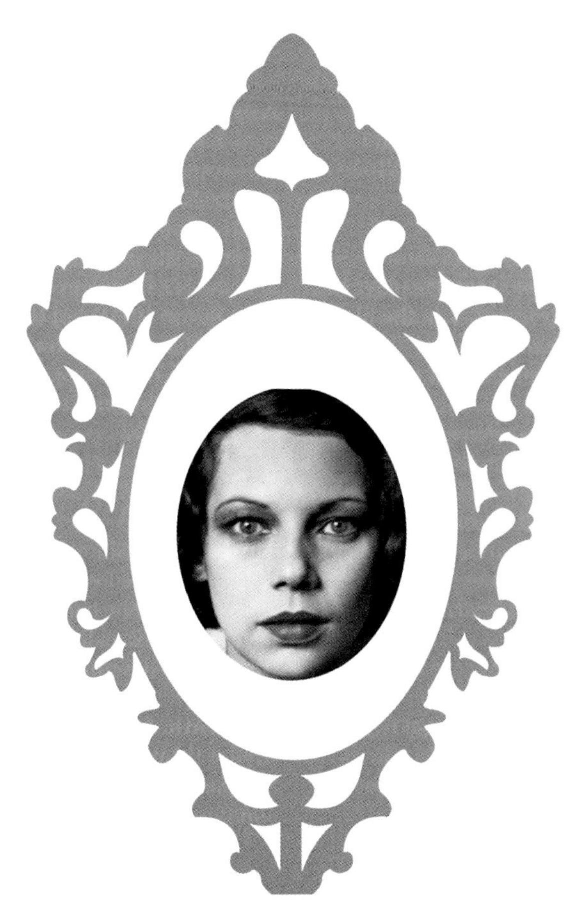

From dance to art crossing movies

Dance
She is born a dancer at the Vienna Imperial Opera ballet school, which she begins attending at age 6. In 1928 she lives in London and New York as both a dancer and choreographer. In *The Band Wagon* (1931) she dances with Fred and Adele Astaire.

Try to act
She believes she can act: some stage success leads her into Hollywood films including *Limelight* (1936), *The Garden of Allah* (1936), *The Good Earth* (1937).
Even if she is very well paid for these roles, she is unhappy in Hollywood: first of all she feels lonely and isolated with countless artists competing against each other for fame and, secondly, she is deeply dissatisfied with supporting film roles. She quits and returns to dance.

Depression and . . . painting for healing
At age 35 she is the victim of a severe clinical depression and she is recovered in a Swiss sanatorium. She quits dance, too. During this time she marries Henry Herbert, 6th Earl of Carnarvon, and the Countess of Carnavon, as she is called now, begins painting. First to help herself. She uses watercolors and oils to portray herself and friends and later she combines visual elements of dance into her paintings. Lord Carnarvon, afraid of Losch's delicate health and the growing danger of the war in Europe, sends her to America. The marriage ends in divorce.

Painting for a living - first solo show
At age 41 Tilly's debut show in New York is a hit; the collector and museum founder Albert C. Barnes buys some works.

World stardom
No star on the Walk of Fame but Tilly's painting is now purchased by various art organizations including the Tate Gallery in London, Philadelphia's Barnes Museum, the Sam Lewison Collection in New York, the Leonard C. Hanna Collection in Cleveland, the Maitland Collection in California, the C. Bliss Family, and by important collectors.

Vera-Ellen

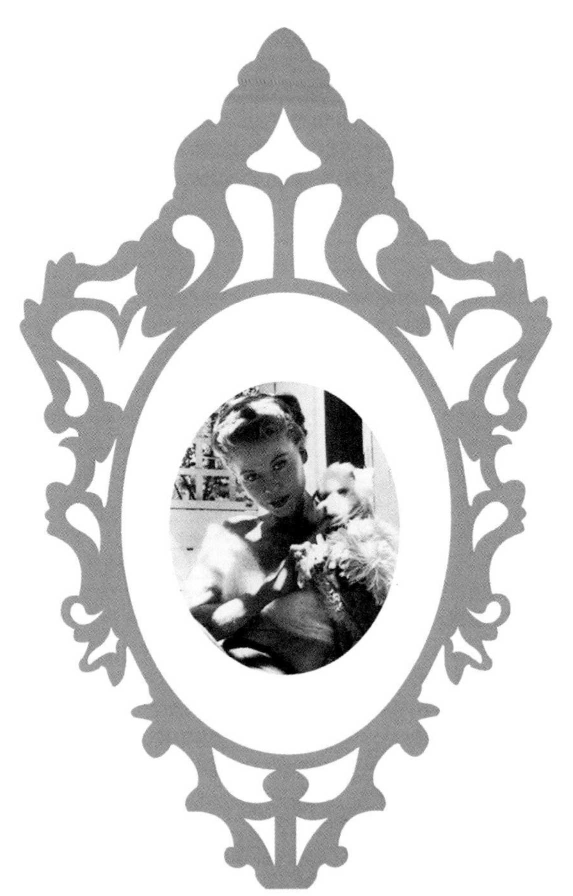

Oh . . . caviar?

White Christmas **with anorexia**
At age 33 her best role as Judy Haynes in
the movie *White Christmas* (1954) playing
opposite Bing Crosby, Danny Kaye,
and Rosemary Clooney but, despite the
success, MGM decides to make fewer musicals
and does not take her talent seriously enough
to give her many non-dancing parts.
During the 1950s, she is called the "smallest
waist in Hollywood."
She suffers from anorexia nervosa.
All of her costumes in *White Christmas*,
down to her robe and sleepwear, are designed
to cover her neck, which is aged beyond
her years due to her eating disorder.
At 36 her last film, *Let's Be Happy* (1957).
At 37 she retires from public life.
At 43 her only child, Victoria Ellen Rothschild,
dies of sudden infant death syndrome in 1963.

Anorexia nervosa is a psychiatric illness
that describes an eating disorder characterized
by extremely low body weight, body image
distortion, and an obsessive fear of gaining
weight. Individuals with anorexia nervosa
are known to control body weight commonly
through voluntary starvation.

Vera-Ellen is a strange figure in Hollywood
and, even now, people like to discuss her
and her "modern" illness and, sometimes,
to thank her.

Let's have a look at some web discussions:
"Vera-Ellen was indeed an anorexic before
the term was coined. It affected all of her life.
If you notice the high collars she wore, it was
to hide the damage to her neck caused
by the illness.
. . . Part of the mystery of her life is whether
she was anorexic before the term was "coined."
There is conjecture as to whether she
was anorexic, or just on a strict diet because
of MGM's "weight restrictions." Ask Judy
Garland!
. . . If you look at her legs in *White Christmas*
you can see how extremely thin they are
(unlike the healthy picture you have of her).
There are several pictures of her on a web page
that show her . . . well . . . maybe in her fifties
where she is so frail looking and yet so sweet.
. . . No matter the causes, she was a terrific
dancer who should have had a much longer
career.
. . . I've also somewhat suffered from anorexia
(not as badly as Vera did), and it comforts me
to know that I'm not alone. I look past her
anorexia and focus on her dancing.
How incredible. It's a shame there isn't more
footage of it to go around. She motivates me to
be the best dancer I can be . . . It's a shame that
she's not more well-known . . .
People say that she started having anorexia at
around the time she made *White Christmas*,
but I would argue she was already there by the
time she made *On the Town*, five years earlier.
She was horribly thin, and to think the camera
added ten pounds to her figure."
(www. uliabuckley.blogspot.com/mysterious-
vera-ellen.html)

Veronica Lake

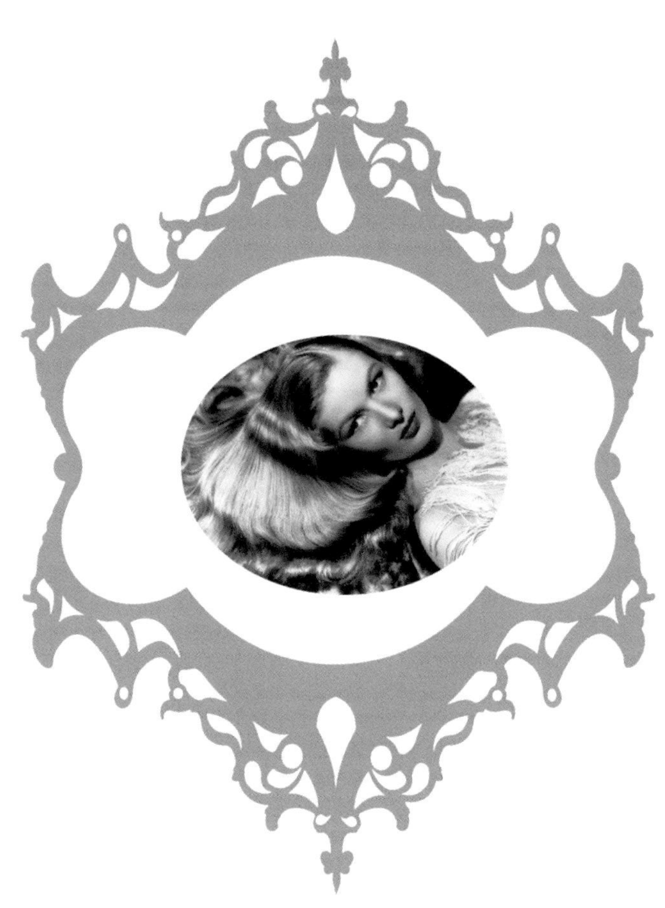

"I wasn't a sex symbol, I was a sex zombie."

Peek-a-boo bang icon
One eye, and almost half of the face, is hidden
behind a falling curl of hair. Every girl is crazy
about her hairstyle and even working women
in the defense industry copy her hairstyle,
which is dangerous when handling heavy
machinery that requires both eyes wide open.
The US government officially asks Lake to
change her hairstyle and publicize it. She does
so. Even later, in 1997, the Academy Award-
winning film *L.A. Confidential* pays homage
to Lake's image and manner with Kim
Basinger, and Jessica Rabbit from *Who
Framed Roger Rabbit* is modeled on Veronica
Lake and Rita Hayworth.

Peek-a-boo bang at home
You can obtain this look by using rag curlers
(sleep with the curlers if your hair loses curls
easily).
I usually use a ¾ inch curling iron, and having
a friend to help is good.
Part your hair the way you choose.
Start at the nape of the neck and wrap
the rest of your hair as you gradually work
yourself to the top.
Curl your whole head, after each curl,
a great tip is to pin the curls using your fingers
rolling the curls, pinning it to your head until
everything is done; this is to keep the shape
of the curls.
This way, you can prepare hours before
and walk around with rolled-up hair. You can
do your make-up in the meantime.
Make sure all the hair is going in the same
direction, making a repetitious pattern.
When you have finished, brush the hair with a
natural bristle hairbrush or wide-tooth comb.
Finish off with hairspray.
(the hair stylist advises)

Peek-a-boo bang reality
Lake's short and meteoritic career lasts during
the first-half of the 1940s, playing *femme
fatale* roles in film noir with Alan Ladd. At
first, the couple is teamed together merely
out of physical necessity: Ladd is just 5 feet 5
inches tall and Lake is just 4 feet 11½ inches.
Lake now is at the top, adored by the public.
Her films are an unquestionable hit.
However, *The Hour Before the Dawn* (1944)
is not well received. As Nazi sympathizer
Dora Bruckmann, Lake's role is dismal
at best. Critics dislike her accent because
it isn't true to life and her acting suffers
because of it. Paramount puts her in pathetic
and mostly forgotten films, except for *The Blue
Dahlia* (1946) in which she co-stars with Ladd.
At age 26 Paramount discharges her. At age 27,
after a single film, her career collapses.
She has a difficult personality to work
with and too many problems during her life
and too many marriages and divorces.
Her mother sues her for money, she loses
a child, she files for bankruptcy, she suffers
from untreated schizophrenia, she drinks
heavily. Her physical and mental health
decline steadily.
When Marlon Brando, her former lover,
reads in a newspaper that Veronica Lake
is working as a cocktail waitress in Manhattan,
he sends her a check for a thousand dollars.
She just keeps it to show her friends.
At age 51 Lake dies of hepatitis
and acute renal failure in Montreal.

seven
Discrimination

Alexis Smith

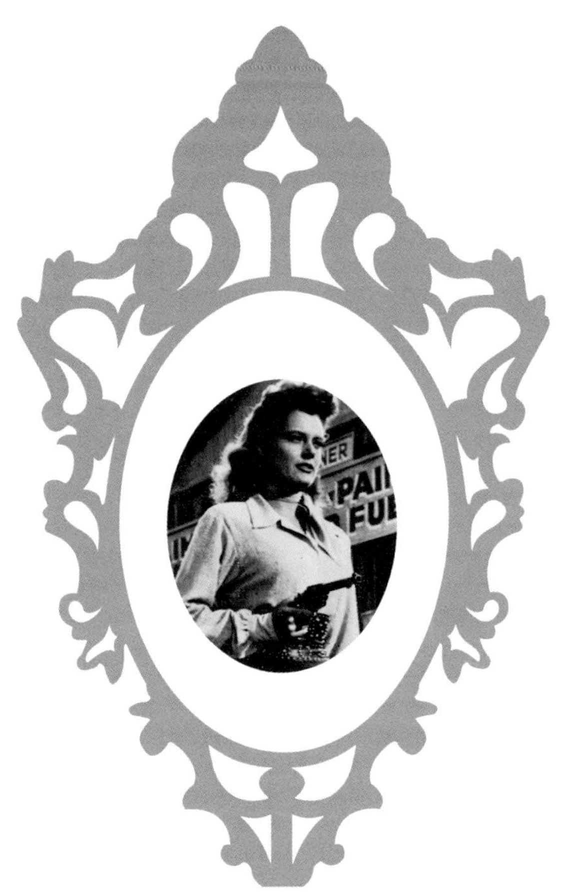

I wish I were a man

So Alexis cries to her lover Frank Clements/
Dick Bogarde one moment before giving
him a forceful slap, at age 23 (*The Sleeping
Tiger*, 1954). She is dressed like a man
wearing chic horse boots, with a firm posture
and long legs. Alexis is for sure an elegant,
tall, graceful, free and easy actress,
able to transform herself when acting.
Her charm remains even when she is sexy.

For seventeen years she co-stars with
important actors, including Errol Flynn (*San
Antoni*o, 1945), Humphrey Bogart (*The Two
Mrs. Carrolls*, 1947), and Cary Grant (*Night
and Day*, 1946). She signs with MGM.
She marries just once with actor Craig Steven,
living with him for forty-seven years until her
death at age 72.

Truth . . .
No children. No heirs.

She is a so-called big-hit actress, but when
her male partners are not as tall as she is . . .
over 5' 9"!

She stops at age 37 for no real reason.
She has no more calls. Just some stage
and television.

Rumors . . .
A lot of rumors about her homo
and bisexual nature:

Widespread gossip.

The writer Rita Mae Brown writes *Rubyfruit
Jungle* (1973) about the entire life
of a Floridian lesbian. This book is dedicated
to Alexis Smith.

After Alexis's death in 1993
the writer Boze Hadleigh declares her bisexual
inclination in his book entirely dedicated
to Hollywood lesbians.

"When they tell me one of my old movies is
on television, I don't look at it."

Cyd Charisse

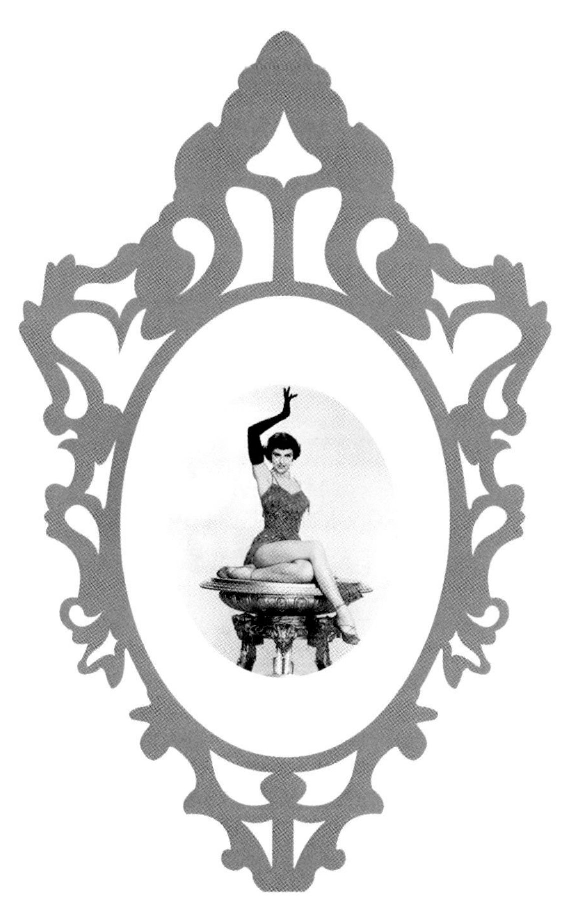

One or five million dollar legs . . .

"With apologies to my wife and the rest of the female population, can we all agree that actress Cyd Charisse simply had the best legs that ever walked the earth? If you don't believe me, just look at that amazing dance number in *Singin' in the Rain* (1952) when Cyd's legs, sheathed in green stockings, fill the entire length of the screen. Her gams were a work of art, strong, perfectly shaped, and proportioned, and more than capable of performing the best dancing ever seen on a movie screen And I mean EVER!" (Danny Miller, "Cyd Charisse's Legs" www.huffingtonpost.com)

Legs are insured for a million dollars, some say five million dollar at age 31 and they are among the most beautiful legs of all time along with those of with Betty Gable, Rita Hayworth, Marlene Dietrich, and Jane Russell.

Stylish and graceful.

Starts as Maria Istomina and Felia Sidorova when she is trained as a ballerina in the Russian tradition.When the Ballet Russe disbands Cdy moves to Hollywood with her new husband, ballet dancer Nico Charisse.

Gene Kelly: "When we were dancing, we didn't know what time it was."

Fred Astaire: "A beautiful dynamite" for her exceptional grace and good looks.

Gains fame playing the vamp in *Singin' in the Rain* with Kelly, and she goes on to play Kelly's leading lady in Vincente Minnelli's *Brigadoon* (1954). She plays and dances with Fred Astaire in *Silk Stockings* (1957). By 1957 musicals in general are out from the screen and Cyd, at age 35, never gets a decent part in a musical again. She makes appearances on television and performances in a nightclub revue. She is "the other woman" in *Something's Got to Give* (1962), the last and unfinished Marilyn Monroe film.

Dorothy Dandridge

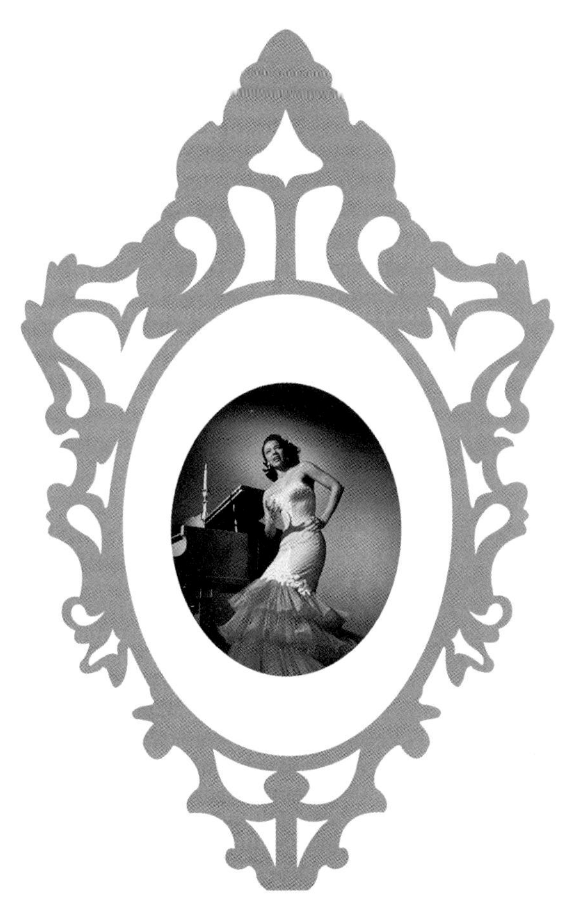

A racism victim

Dorothy Dandridge is one of the most well-known ladies of Hollywood
Extremely elegant, not expected from
a black lady.
Voluptuous beauty. Like Marilyn Monroe.
Dorothy Dandridge can eliminate
any memory of the nice girl next door.
She has everything, except a career.
She falls victim to bigotry, personal tragedy,
and one of Hollywood's great mistakes.

Dorothy performs for years as part
of The Dandridge Sisters, usually in black
Baptist churches throughout the country.
She makes her film debut in 1935. She is only
13 years old. Her film career spans almost
thirty years. And she is always a victim of
racism.

Since she can also sing which is clear
in the films *Atlantic City* (1944)
and *Pillow to Post* (1945), she is invited
to sing in the nation's finest hotel nightclubs
in New York, Miami, Chicago, and Las Vegas.
Due to racism, she cannot stay there.
It is said that one hotel empties the pool
to keep her from swimming.

Her role as the lead character in *Carmen Jones*
(1954) makes her a star. She receives
an Academy Award nomination.

Despite this nomination, her career declines
Hollywood is not ready for a black leading
lady. The only roles offered to her are variants
of the tragic mulatto theme.
She is the first Black on the cover
of *Life* magazine.
Dorothy is the first black woman to be held
in the arms of a white man in an American
movie in *Island in the Sun* (1957).
Her last movie is in 1961, *The Murder Men*.

She has problems with alcohol and is found
dead in her West Hollywood apartment
in 1965 at age 42, the victim of a barbiturate
overdose, an apparent suicide, with $2.14
in the bank.

Dorothy Lamour

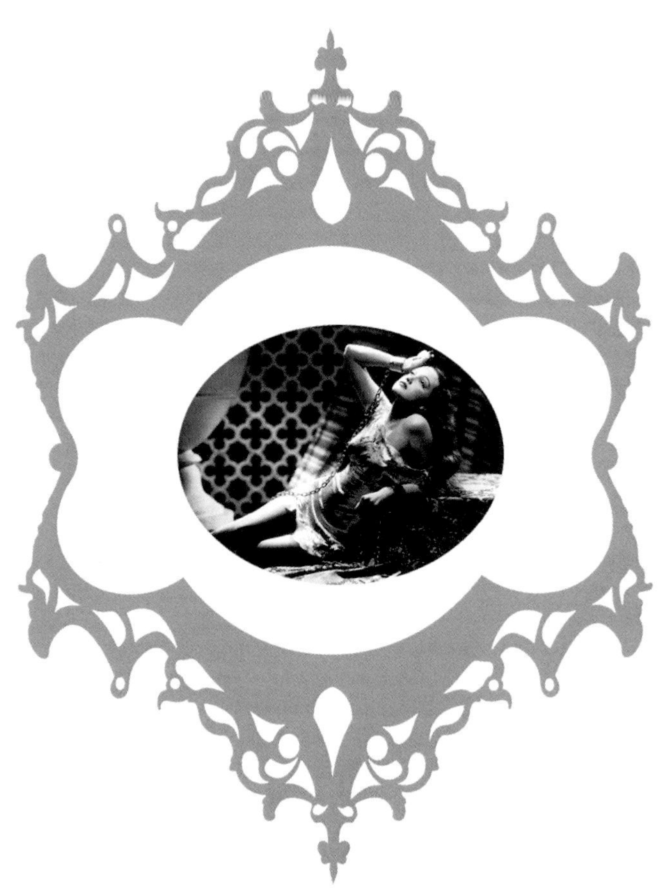

Much more than a sarong

A talented actress that never receives what she deserves
Dorothy Lamour contributes as much
to the Road movies as Hope and Crosby do.
But they are the ones that always get
the credit.

Lamour is also associated with over fifty films
she appears in.

Her voice is wonderful and she sings.

Her last Road film is *The Road to Hong Kong*
(1962). She is 48.

She has two stars on the Hollywood Walk of
Fame, a motion picture star and a radio star.

Although any person in Hollywood knows
about her extraordinary talent, the public
thinks of her as the sarong girl.

Not fair
She has no Hispanic descent, she has French
Louisiana roots, and both sides of her family
are American for several generations.
She does not speak Spanish.

"I made sixty motion pictures and only
wore the sarong in about six pictures, but it
did become a kind of trademark."

Eleanor Parker

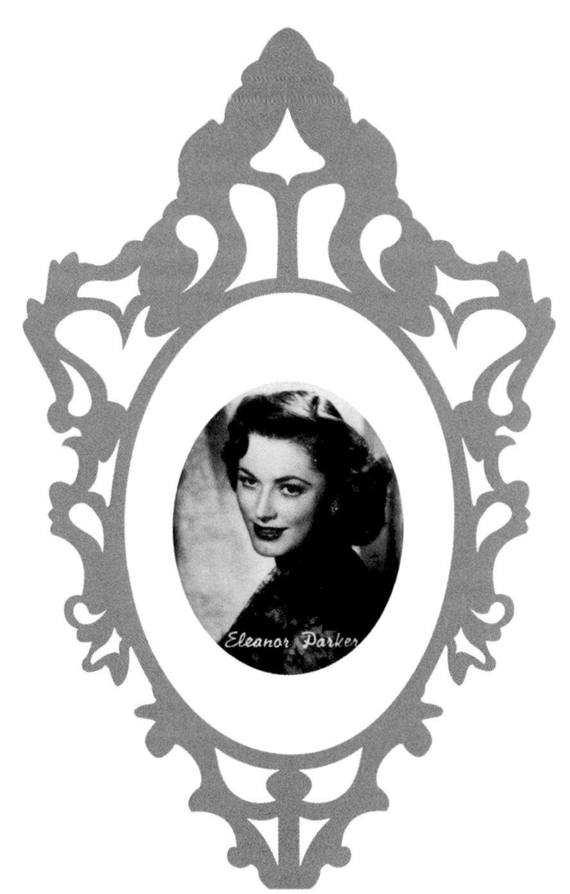

Not in sync

She is one of the great beauties and has
an incredible talent.

She is considered a true chameleon.

She wins several awards and nominations.

Fans have major crushes on her.
She is a sweetheart and responds to fans.

**Everyone believes she is destined
to stardom but she:**
Has an extremely shy nature . . . no good.

Avoids parties . . . no good.

Prefers to stay at home . . . no good.

Is not given high profile suitable roles
by Warner . . . no good.

Has modelled her look and mannerism not
in sync with time . . . no stardom.

Elena Verdugo

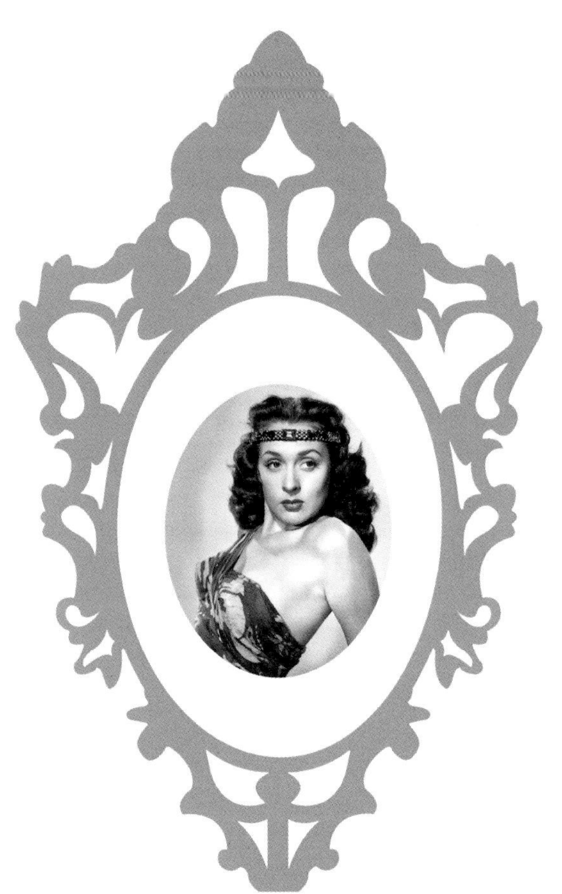

Weight vs. career

Universal Studios hires her frequently, but does not sign her to a studio contract because she refuses to lose weight. Hollywood wanted and still wants thin, tall, aristocratic, and white ladies.

Do not fool yourself. Elena gives autographs for less.

Be aware: USD 50 ebay average request for an autographed photo. USD 10 Verdugo's official web site request.

From an ebay user:
"I obtained this autograph after mailing this photo to Elena Verdugo in the early 90s. Photo is 8x10 and in good condition with a few light indentations, most of which are not visible unless photo is held up to direct light. Light wear in borders."

From Elena Verdugo herself:
Elena Verdugo
P.O. Box 2048
Chula Vista, CA 91912
Ms. Verdugo accepts fan mail and autograph requests at this address.
Autograph seekers should include a check for $10 payable to "Red Cross of Rosarito Beach, Baja, Mexico" for an 8x10 signed photo.

Franca Marzi

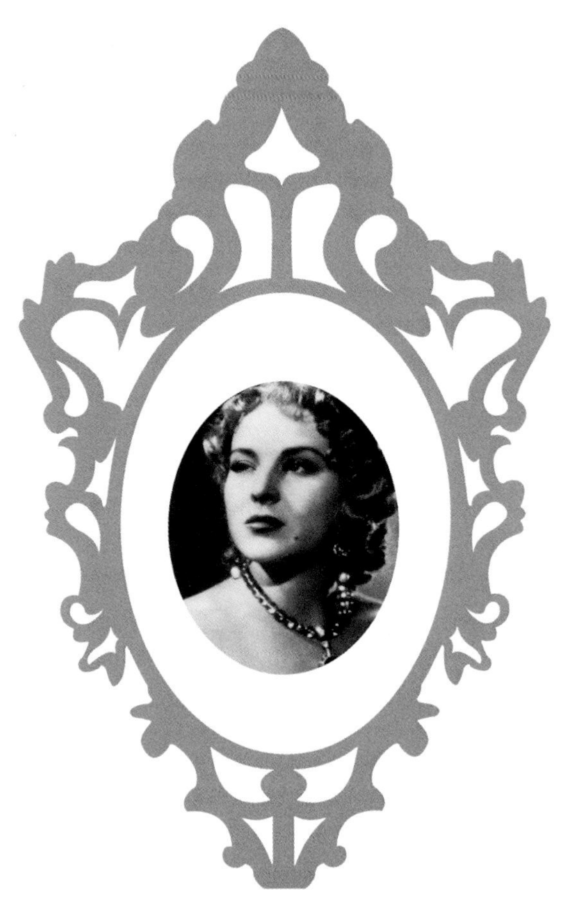

Voluptuous lady

Born in Rome, dies in Cinisello Balsamo.

Also known as Franca Marzi. Participates
in about 80 movies.

Femme fatale in melo movies.

Married until her death to Franco Festucci,
a boxer.

No awards except for a Silver Ribbon.

Known for her big tits and melo movies,
she ends up playing erotic roles.

Janet Leight

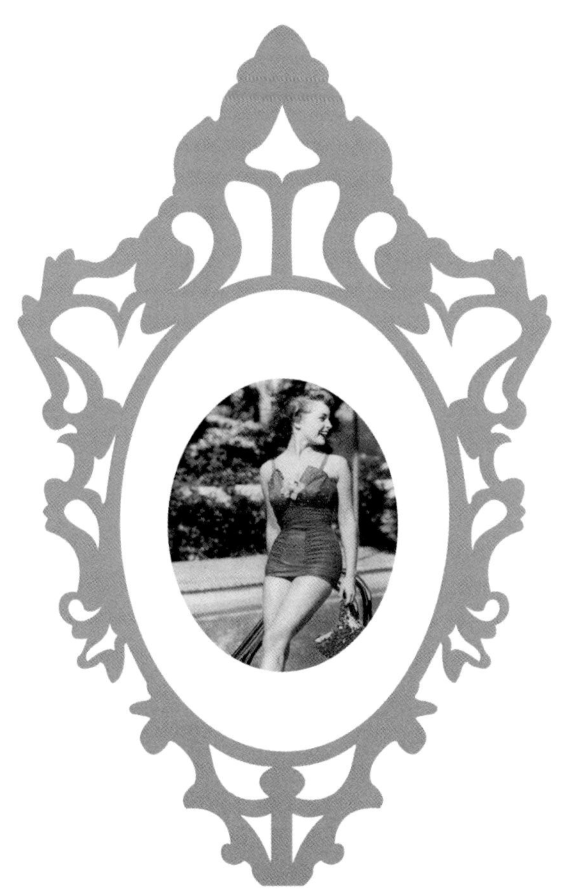

Forty-five minutes

Janet's best known role is the morally ambiguous Marion Crane in the Alfred Hitchcock film *Psycho* (1960), featuring its iconic shower murder scene in The Bates Motel (12 cabins, 12 vacancies, and 12 showers). Janet is 33.

Marion vs. Janet
Janet on Marion: "I saw that she was really a shabby, mousy little woman. She wasn't in any way glamorous or anything. So we chose clothes that she could have afforded. We didn't have a dressmaker do them; we just went out and bought clothes that she could have bought on her salay . . . She was lonely and poor."

For Marion's role Janet receives $25,000 and a Golden Globe Award for best supporting actress and she is nominated for the Academy Award for best supporting actress.

Janet is married to the very famous actor Tony Curtis and has two children. Janet is a very well-known actress. Norma Shearer sees a picture of her, and MGM, looking for a young naive country girl, signs her. She plays in a number of successful films with stars such as Errol Flynn, Gary Cooper, James Stewart, Orson Welles, and Judy Garland.

"*Psycho* gave me very wrinkled skin. I was in that shower for 7 days. 70 setups. At least Hitchcock made sure the water was warm."

Janet makes more than fifty movies, but she is still remembered for the forty-five minutes in that small-budget thriller *Psycho* directed by Alfred Hitchcock.

Janet's later appearances in films are rare. She does some television.

June Allyson

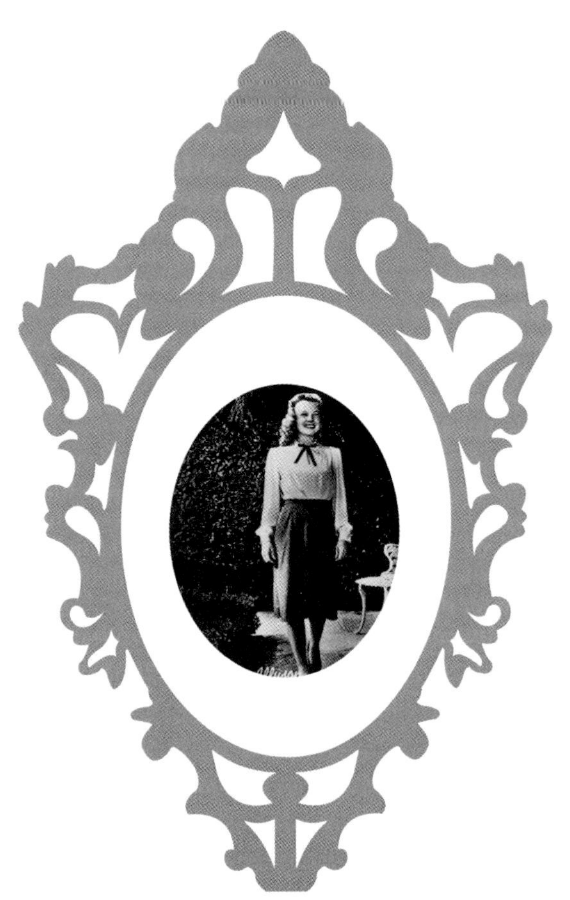

What kind of wife?

The perfect one

"I never did feel quite right about the roles I was called upon to portray—the gentle, kind, loving, perfect wife who will stand by her man through 'anything.' In real life I'm a poor dressmaker and a terrible cook; in fact, anything but the perfect wife."

June is the prototype MGM girl-next-door of American movies in the 1940s and early 1950s.

The cruel one

She wants to break out of the typecast: at age 38 she plays in *The Strike* (1955), a very extreme role: a vengeful wife, a cruel woman who drives her husband to a nervous breakdown but, to the rest of the world, however, Ann is a self-sacrificing saint, because that's the side of her personality that she prefers to show off. Allyson's acting is highly regarded, but audiences do not accept her in the role and the movie fails at the box office.

"The only parental authority I had was the studio. When I was a star, there was always somebody with me, to guard me. I was not allowed to be photographed with a cigarette, a drink, a cup of coffee, or even a glass of water because someone might think it was liquor. When I left the studio I was already married and had two children, but I felt as sad as a child leaving home for the first time." After that her film career suffers. She works in television with occasional appearances on her own anthology series. Occasional nightclub appearances and very few onscreen roles such as a lesbian murderess in *They Only Kill Their Masters* (1972) at age 55. She is survived by her husband and two children.

Lizabeth Scott

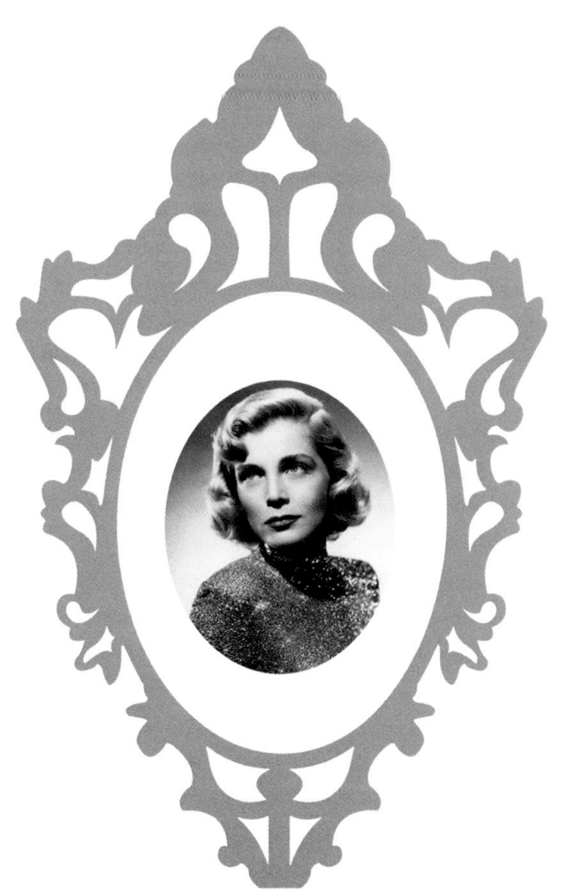

No husband. No child . . . so what?

Deep and strong. A nervy and sexy body.
Smoky sensuality and husky voice.

She plays the dark blonde and lost film
noir femme fatales. Film historian Eddie
Muller has noted that no other actress has
appeared in so many noir movies, with more
than three quarters of her 20 films. No way
for her to move away from this cliché.

For Paramount she is initially compared
to Lauren Bacall, because of a slight
resemblance and a similar voice. She plays
with Bacall's husband, Humphrey Bogart,
in the 1947 noir thriller *Dead Reckoning*.
Then she is compared to Veronica Lake,
but she doesn't obtain her stardom.
She co-stars with some of the bigs such as
Barbara Stanwyck, Van Heflin, Kirk Douglas,
Burt Lancaster, and Mary Astor.

***Confidential* lawsuit case**
In 1955 at age 33 Lizabeth, unmarried,
sues the magazine *Confidential* over
allegations concerning her private life,
stating that she spends her free time with
"Hollywood's weird society of baritone babes"
(an euphemism for lesbian). According
to *Confidential* there is a client list that
belongs to a call-girl agency, in which they
find Lizabeth's name. The suit is won thanks to
attorney Jerry Giesler and *Confidential*
pays $2,500,000 for ethical damage.

Maybe it is just a bizarre coincidence
but, starting in 1957 at age 35, Lizabeth's
film career comes to an end with her last
role in *Loving You* (1957). Later just few rare
television appearances and she spends most
of her private time attending classes
at the University of Southern California.

Lizabeth Scott never marries and has
no children.

Sandra Dee

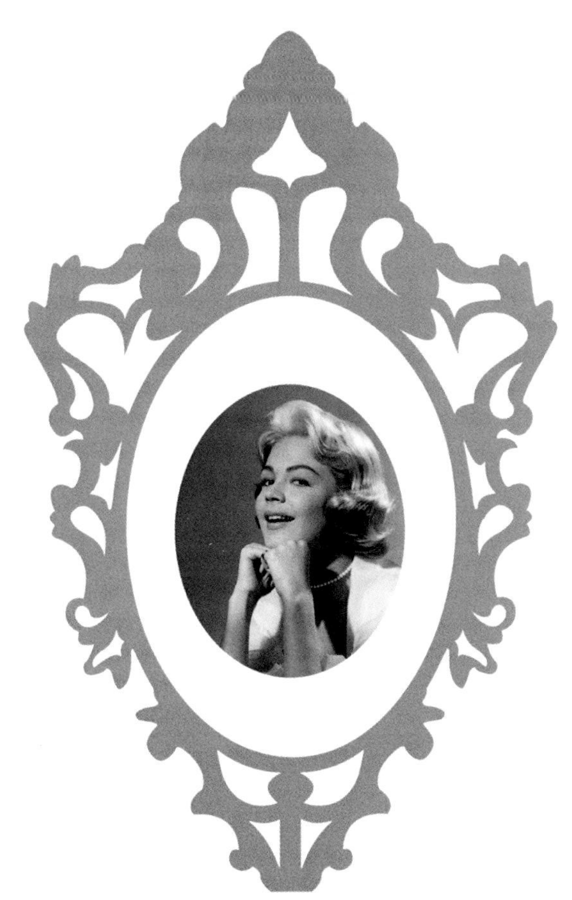

So difficult to grow up

Look at me I'm Sandra Dee
Lousy with virginity
Won't go to bed till I'm legally wed
I can't I'm Sandra Dee

Watch it! Hey, I'm Doris Day
I was not brought up that way
Won't come across even Rock Hudson lost
His heart to Doris Day

I don't drink I swear
I don't rat my hair
I get ill from one cigarette
Keep your filthy paws off my silky drawers
Would you pull that crap with Annette?

As for you Troy Donahue
I know what you wanna do
You've got your crust I'm no object of lust
I'm just plain Sandra Dee

Elvis, Elvis, let me be
Keep that pelvis far from me
Just keep your cool now your starting to drool

Hey, Fongul, I'm Sandra Dee

("Look at Me, I'm Sandra Dee," original
Broadway song from the musical *Grease*, 1972,
and from the film *Grease*, 1978)

She is not sultry or particularly sexy or
particularly beautiful but, during the late
1950s and early 1960s, she is a teen ideal.

She is always young, she has to look
even younger as her mother teaches her.
If you have to lie about your age, it doesn't
matter. You have to reach your goal. Sandra
is signed to do *Until They Sail* (1957)
at age 14 and, later, her two most popular
and international films, *Imitation of Life*
(1957) and *A Summer Place* (1959).

She marries teen idol Bobby Darin at age
18 and she divorces at age 25.

Her career is over at age 26. It is hard to get
a role in films when everybody knows you are
a divorcée and you are made to play just
a teenager. It's so unfair!

**"I was anorexic for many, many years, even
before people knew what it was. They didn't
even have a name for it back then."**

Sandra, for most of her life, fights anorexia
nervosa, depression, and alcoholism and
she is constantly under a doctor's supervision.
Painfully, she tries to become a woman.

Yvonne Sanson

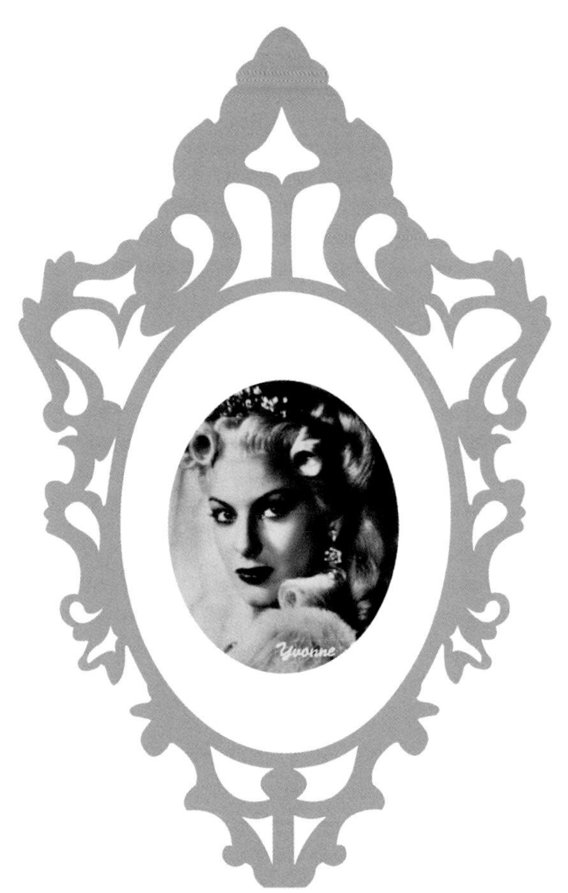

Melo lady

Greek origin.

Brownish.

Curved.

Migrates to Italy at age 17.

Femme Fatale in the *Il delitto di Giovanni Episcopo* (1947) by Alberto Lattuada.

Success comes when together with Amedeo Nazzari she interprets a series of melo movies for more than a decade.

But she never manages to free herself from this melo image.

She is only given roles as a sad and abandoned beautiful female.

Slowly vanishes from the screen as she ages and melo movies are not in demand.

Vera Miles

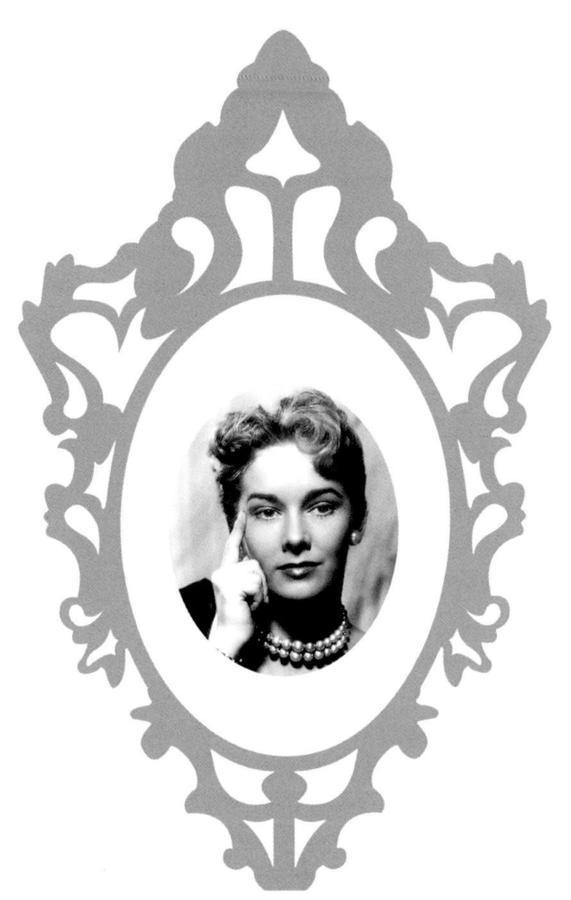

Too many pregnancies

Vera Miles loses the leading role in *Vertigo* (1958) because she is pregnant with Michael.

Alfred Hitchcock replaces Vera Miles with Kim Novak because of Miles's pregnancy.

François Truffaut many years later for the book *Hitchcock/Truffaut* asks him about Miles and he says: "She became pregnant just before the part that was going to turn her into a star. After that, I lost interest. I couldn't get the rhythm going with her again."

Hitchcock gives Miles a supporting role in *Psycho* (1960).

Miles says: "Over the span of years, he's had one type of woman in his films, Ingrid Bergman, Grace Kelly, and so on. Before that, it was Madeleine Carroll. I'm not their type and never have been. I tried to please him but I couldn't. They are all sexy women, but mine is an entirely different approach."

The pregnancies
Vera Miles is born in 1929.

With first husband Bob Miles (1948–1954), she has two daughters: Debra Miles (b. 1950) and Kelley Miles (b. 1952). She is in her mid-20s.

With second husband Gordon Scott (1954–1959), she has one son: Michael Scott (b. 1957). She is in her late 20s.

With third husband Keith Larsen (1960–1971), she has one son: Erik Larsen (b. 1961). She is in her early 30s.

Tallulah Bankhead

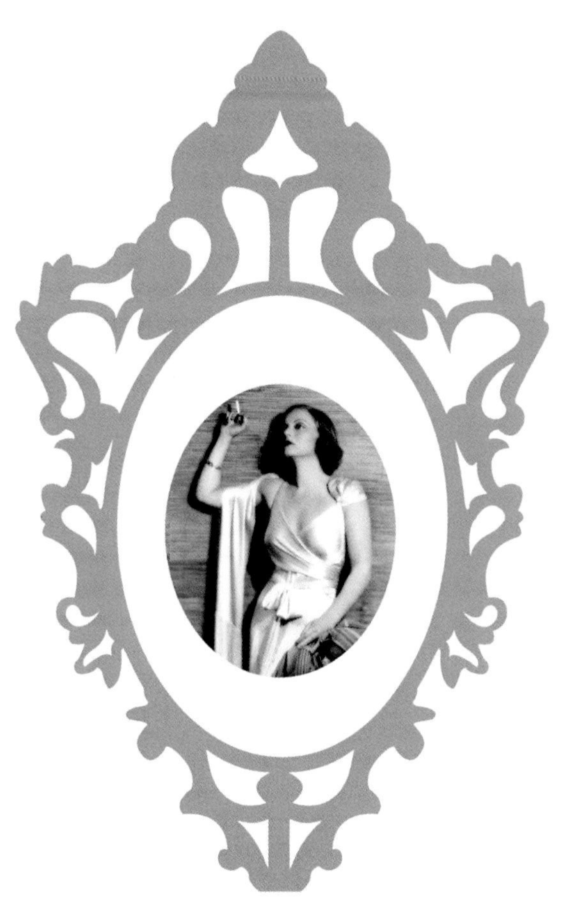

"If I had to live my life again, I'd make the same mistakes, only sooner."

"My father warned me about men and booze, but he never mentioned a word about women and cocaine."
Her father is a politician in the Democratic Party. Her mother dies during delivery. Her father sends his daughter to a Catholic convent in the unrealized hopes of educating her as a good woman.

"Nobody can be exactly like me. Even I have trouble doing it."
Tallulah starts on stage and she is great. She tries movies but with difficulty. She comes back from London and tries with Paramount. Her first two films are a flop and she goes back to theater. At age 29 she plays in *Tarnished Lady* (1931), but Tallulah's personality does not shine on film as Paramount hopes. And back to Broadway again. She does not appear on screen anymore for 11 years. But she does not care a lot. She says she moved to Hollywood just to sleep with Gary Cooper and . . . there is no place for her in Hollywood according to the Hays Code.

"I've tried several kinds of sex, all of which I hate. The conventional position makes me claustrophobic; the others give me a stiff neck and/or lockjaw."
Tallulah does her best to build up her legend. She is well known for her one-liners but mostly for her vulgarity. She adores to shock with her "unconventional" behavior, taking her clothes off and chatting in the nude while holding her bourbon and smoking 150 cigarettes a day. Parties for sure, especially if they are wild, bisex, and last for days.

"Hi I'm a lesbian, nice to meet you."
Rumors about her sex life are her favorite job for years. Rumors say she is romantically involved with a lot of female personalities, including Greta Garbo, Joan Crawford, Marlene Dietrich, Eva Le Gallienne, as well as writer Mercedes de Acosta and singer Billie Holiday with whom she has a long-term relationship. She is married to actor John Emery for four years. She has no children

"If you want to help the American theater, don't be an actress, be an audience."
At age 41 she returns just with a cameo but she has a big opportunity with Alfred Hitchcock's *Life Boat* (1944) that puts her back into the limelight, but just for a while. Later just a few television commercials and back to the stage. According to Marlon Brando, her co-star in the play *The Eagle Has Two Heads*, she could have been a great actress and a major movie star without her sex and alcohol addiction.

"Codeine . . . bourbon."
Tallulah's last coherent words before she dies at age 66.

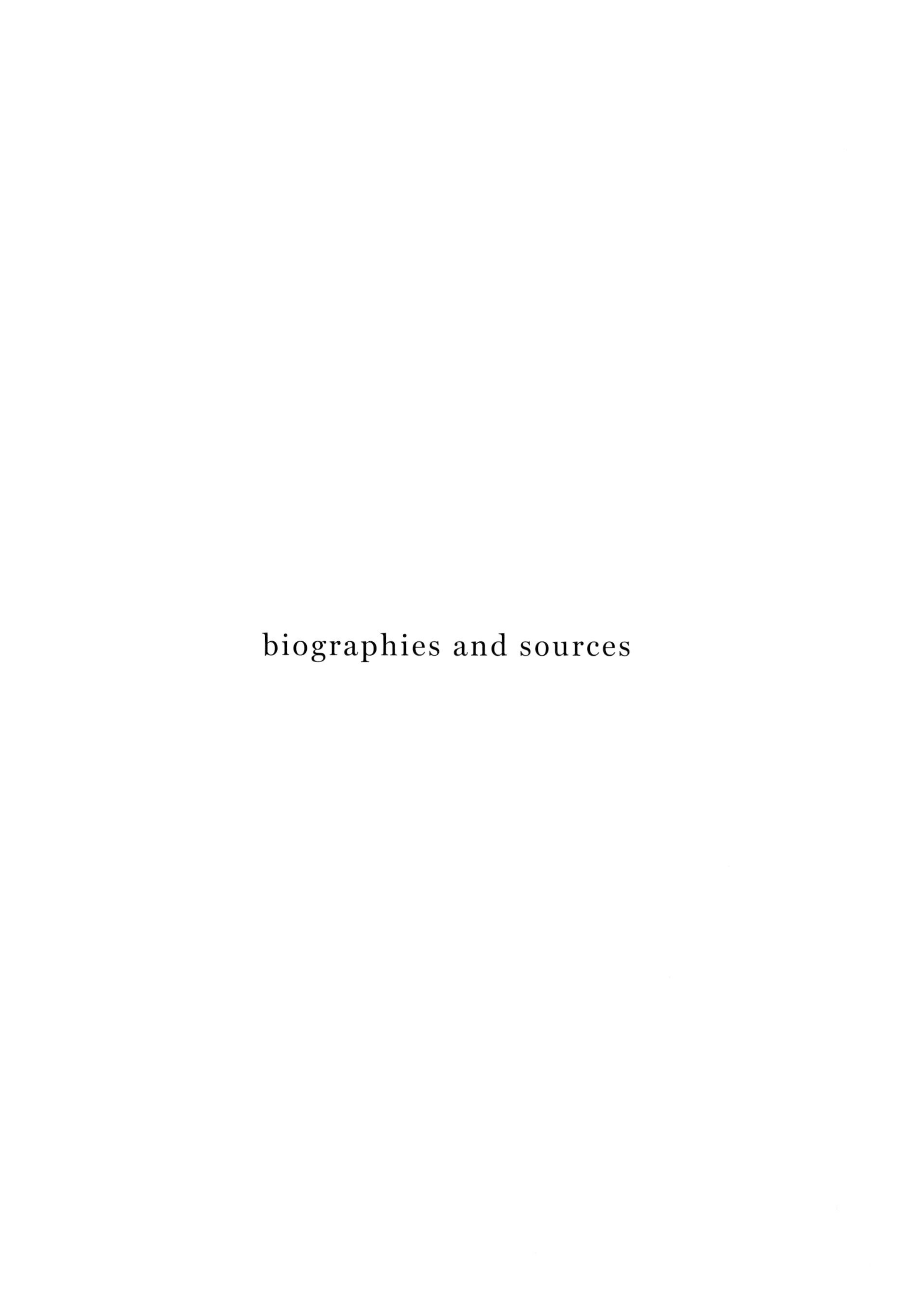

biographies and sources

A

JULIA(E) ADAMS
BORN: 10.17.1926,
Waterloo, Iowa
DIES: alive
NATIONALITY: American
MAIN MOVIES:
· *Creature from the Black Lagoon*
(1954)
RECOGNITIONS:
PERSONAL LIFE:
1 marriage
1 divorce
2 children
FRAMED: compromise with
television and low-profile roles

KAY ALDRIDGE
BORN: 07.09.1917,
Tallahassee, Florida
DIES: 01.12.1995,
Rockport, Maine
NATIONALITY: American
MAIN MOVIES:
· *Daredevils of the West* (1943)
· *Haunted Harbor* (1944)
· *The Man Who Walked Alone* (1945)
RECOGNITIONS:
PERSONAL LIFE:
3 marriages
1 divorce
twice widowed
4 children
FRAMED: only minor and decorative
roles as B-movie heroine

JUNE ALLYSON
BORN: 10.07.1917,
Bronx, New York
DIES: 06.08.2006,
Ojiai, California
NATIONALITY: American
MAIN MOVIES:
· *Two Girls and a Sailer* (1944)
· *Little Women* (1949)
· *The Stratton Story* (1949)
· *The Glenn Miller Story* (1955)
RECOGNITIONS:
· Golden Globe (1952) as best
picture actress musical comedy
for *Too Young to Kiss*
· photoplay awards (1954) most
popular female star
· box-office attraction (1954)
as prototype of girl-next-door
PERSONAL LIFE:
4 marriages
3 divorces
2 children
FRAMED: she pays the price
to change her image

HEATHER ANGEL
BORN: 02.09.1909,
Oxford, England
DIES: 12.13.1986,
Santa Barbara, California
NATIONALITY: English
MAIN MOVIES:
· *Orient Express* (1934)
· *Kitty Foyle: The Natural History
of a Woman* (1940)
· *Pride and Prejudice* (1940)
RECOGNITIONS: Walk of Fame
PERSONAL LIFE:
3 marriages
2 divorces
once widowed
FRAMED: no more calls since 1944

JEAN ARTHUR
BORN: 10.17.1900,
Plattsburgh, New York
DIES: 06.19.1991,
Carmel, California
NATIONALITY: American
MAIN MOVIES:
· *The More the Merrier* (1943)
· *A Lady Takes a Chance* (1943)
RECOGNITIONS:
· Oscar nomination (1943)
as best actress in a leading role
for *The More the Merrier*
· Walk of Fame
PERSONAL LIFE:
2 marriages
1 divorce
1 annulled
FRAMED: she suffers a kind
of stage fright

MARY ASTOR
BORN: 05.03.1906,
for *Too Young to Kiss*
Quincy, Illinois
DIES: 09.25.1987,
Woodland Hills, Los Angeles,
California
NATIONALITY: Czech
MAIN MOVIES:
· *Red Dust* (1932)
· *The Great Lie* (1941)
· *The Maltese Falcon* (1941)
RECOGNITIONS:
· Oscar (1942) as best actress
in a supporting role for *The Great Lie*
· Walk of Fame
PERSONAL LIFE:
4 marriages
3 divorces
once widowed
2 children
FRAMED: suffers from an scandal
(diary, adultery accusations,
daughter custody battle).
Uses alcohol and attempts suicide

CECILE AUBRY
BORN: 08.03.1928,
Paris, Ile-de-France, France
DIES: alive
NATIONALITY: French
MAIN MOVIES:
· *The Black Rose* (1950)
· *Blaubart* (1951)
· *Manon* (1949)
RECOGNITIONS:
PERSONAL LIFE:
1 marriage
1 child
FRAMED: quits after marrying
Si Brahim el Glaoui, pacha
Marrakech son

B

TALLULAH BANKHEAD
BORN: 01.31.1902,
Huntsville, Alabama
DIES: 12.12.1968,
New York City, New York
NATIONALITY: American
MAIN MOVIES:
· *The Cheat* (1931)
· *Devil and the Deep* (1932)
RECOGNITIONS: Walk of Fame

PERSONAL LIFE:
1 marriage
1 divorce
FRAMED: a rebel, too independent
and too untraditional

BARBARA BATES
BORN: 08.06.1925,
Denver, Colorado
DIES: 03.18.1969,
Denver, Colorado
NATIONALITY: American
MAIN MOVIES:
· *June Bride* (1948)
· *All about Eve* (1950)
· *Rhapsody* (1954)
RECOGNITIONS:
PERSONAL LIFE:
2 marriages
once widowed
FRAMED: with extreme mood shifts,
insecurity, ill health and chronic
depression, commits suicide after
one year from her husband's death

BELITA
BORN: 10.25.1923,
Nether Wallop, Hampshire
DIES: 12.18.2005,
South of France
NATIONALITY: English
MAIN MOVIES:
· *Silver Skates* (1943)
· *Suspense* (1946)
· *Silk Stokings* (1957)
RECOGNITIONS:
PERSONAL LIFE:
2 marriages
2 divorces
FRAMED: the flop of *Damn Yankees*
(1958). Definitively, no more calls

CONSTANCE CAMPBELL BENNETT
BORN: 10.22.1904,
New York City, New York
DIES: 07.24.1965,
Fort Dix, New Jersey
NATIONALITY: American
MAIN MOVIES:
· *Common Clay* (1930)
· *The Affairs of Cellini* (1934)
· *Ladies in Love* (1936)
· *Merrily We Live* (1938)

RECOGNITIONS: Walk of Fame
PERSONAL LIFE:
5 marriages
4 divorces
3 children
FRAMED: by the 1940s she works
less frequently in film but she is
in demand in radio and theatre

JOAN BENNETT
BORN: 02.27.1910,
Palisades, New Jersey
DIES: 12.07.1990,
Scarsdale, New York
NATIONALITY: American
MAIN MOVIES:
· *She Wanted a Millionaire* (1932)
· *Trade Winds* (1938)
· *The Woman on the Beach* (1947)
RECOGNITIONS: Walk of Fame
PERSONAL LIFE:
4 marriages
3 divorces
3 children
FRAMED: her third husband shoots and
injures her agent (maybe lover). Affair
is denied, but media is out of control

CLARA BOW
BORN: 07.29.1905,
Brooklyn, New York
DIES: 09.27.1965,
West Los Angeles, California
NATIONALITY: American
MAIN MOVIES:
· *It* (1927)
· *Wings* (1927)
· *Hoop-La* (1933)
RECOGNITIONS: Walk of Fame
PERSONAL LIFE:
1 marriage
2 children
FRAMED: with the advent of sound
her icon declines. Mental instability
and hospitalization

LOUISE BROOKS
BORN: 11.14.1906,
Cherryvale, Kansas
DIES: 08.08.1985,
Rochester, New York
NATIONALITY: American
MAIN MOVIES:

· *Pandora's Box* (1929)
· *Diary of a Lost Girl* (1929)
RECOGNITIONS: Walk of Fame
PERSONAL LIFE:
2 marriages
2 divorces
FRAMED: wants freedom above all.
Becomes a symbol of modernity

VIRGINIA BRUCE
BORN: 09.29.1910,
Minneapolis, Minnesota
DIES: 02.24.1982,
Woodland Hills, Los Angeles
NATIONALITY: American
MAIN MOVIES:
· *Jane Eyre* (1934)
· *The Bad Man of Brimstone* (1937)
· *The Invisible Woman* (1940)
RECOGNITIONS:
PERSONAL LIFE:
4 marriages
3 divorces
once widowed
2 children
FRAMED: no more call since 1949.
She stars in some Turkish films
unseen in America. Only occasional
television roles

C

CORINNE CALVET
BORN: 04.30.1925,
Paris, France
DIES: 06.23.2001,
Los Angeles, California
NATIONALITY: French
MAIN MOVIES:
· *Rope of Sand* (1949)
· *Sailor Beware* (1949)
RECOGNITIONS:
PERSONAL LIFE:
3 marriage
3 divorces
1 child
FRAMED: studies at the Sorbonne
before Hollywood. Becomes
a therapist at age 45

MARTINE CAROL
BORN: 05.16.1920,

Saint-Maudé, France
DIES: 02.06.1967,
Montecarlo, Monaco
NATIONALITY: French
MAIN MOVIES:
· *Caroline chérie* (1953)
· *Lucrezia Borgia* (1953)
· *Vanina Vanini* (1961)
RECOGNITIONS:
PERSONAL LIFE:
4 marriages
3 divorces
FRAMED: no more starring roles
after the arrival of Brigitte Bardot

ELISA CEGANI
BORN: 06.10.1911,
Turin, Italy
DIES: 02.23.1996,
Rome, Italy
NATIONALITY: Italian
MAIN MOVIES:
· *Aldebaran* (1935)
· *La contessa di Parma* (1937)
· *Altri tempi* (1952)
RECOGNITIONS:
PERSONAL LIFE:
1 marriage
FRAMED: dedicated to husband.
Moves to theatre and television

CYD CHARISSE
BORN: 03.08.1921,
Amarillo, Texas
DIES: 06.17.2008,
Los Angeles, California
NATIONALITY: American
MAIN MOVIES:
· *Ziegfeld Follies* (1946)
· *Singin' in the Rain* (1952)
· *Silk Stockings* (1957)
RECOGNITIONS: Walk of Fame
PERSONAL LIFE:
2 marriages
1 divorce
2 children
FRAMED: musicals fade from
the screen and so does her career

VIRGINIA CHERRILL
BORN: 04.12.1908,
Carthage, Illinois
DIES: 11.14.1996,

Santa Barbara, California
NATIONALITY: American
MAIN MOVIES:
· *City Lights* (1931)
· *Blonde Venus* (1932)
RECOGNITIONS: Walk of Fame
PERSONAL LIFE:
4 marriages
3 divorces
FRAMED: divorces Cary Grant.
Becomes the countess of Jersey

DOROTHY COMINGORE
BORN: 08.24.1913,
Los Angeles, California
DIES: 12.30.1971,
Stonington, Connecticut
NATIONALITY: American
MAIN MOVIES:
· *Citizen Kane* (1941)
· *The Hairy Ape* (1944)
· *Any Number Can Play* (1949)
RECOGNITIONS:
PERSONAL LIFE:
3 marriages
2 divorces
3 children
FRAMED: blacklisted, becomes
a psychopathic convinced of being
harassed by the government
for her political views

DOLORES COSTELLO
BORN: 09.17.1903,
Pittsburgh, Pennsylvania
DIES: 03.01.1979,
Fallbrook, California
NATIONALITY: American
MAIN MOVIES:
· *The Sea Beast* (1926)
· *Little Lord Fauntleroy* (1936)
· *The Magnificent Ambersons* (1942)
RECOGNITIONS: Walk of Fame
PERSONAL LIFE:
2 marriages
2 divorces
2 children
FRAMED: she is greatly damaged
due to harsh studio make-up.
She is forced into early retirement

JEANNE CRAIN
BORN: 05.25.1925,

Barston, California
DIES: 12.14.2003,
Santa Barbara, California
NATIONALITY: American
MAIN MOVIES:
· *Leave Her to Heaven* (1945)
· *Pinky* (1949)
· *A Letter to Three Wives* (1949)
RECOGNITIONS: Oscar nomination
(1950) as best actress in a leading
role for *Pinky*
PERSONAL LIFE:
1 marriage
7 children
FRAMED: no more calls and
retirement in the early 1960s

D

ARLENE DAHL
BORN: 08.11.1928,
Minneapolis, Minnesota
DIES: alive
NATIONALITY: American
MAIN MOVIES:
· *Journey to the Center
of the Earth* (1959)
RECOGNITIONS: Walk of Fame
PERSONAL LIFE:
6 marriages
5 divorces
3 children
FRAMED: suffers typecasting
syndrome. Becomes a beauty
columnist and writer,
and later founder of Arlene Dahl
Enterprises

DOROTHY DANDRIDGE
BORN: 11.09.1922,
Cleveland, Ohio
DIES: 09.08.1965,
West Hollywood, California
NATIONALITY: American
MAIN MOVIES:
· *Atlantic City* (1944)
· *Carmen Jones* (1954)
· *Porgy and Bess* (1959)
RECOGNITIONS:
· Oscar (1955) as best actress
in a leading role for *Carmen Jones*
· Bafta film awards nomination

(1956) as best foreign actress
for *Carmen Jones*
· Golden Globe nomination (1960)
as best motion picture
actress for *Porgy and Bess*
· Laurel awards nomination (1960)
as top female musical
performance for *Porgy and Bess*
· Walk of Fame
· first African-American
to be nominated as Oscar
best actress
PERSONAL LIFE:
2 marriages
2 divorces
1 child
FRAMED: victim of racism her entire
career, suicides by overdose after
suffering from manic depression
and alcoholism

LINDA DARNELL
BORN: 10.16.1923,
Dallas, Texas
DIES: 06.10.1965,
Glenview, Illinois
NATIONALITY: American
MAIN MOVIES:
· *My Darling Clementine* (1946)
· *Forever Amber* (1947)
RECOGNITIONS: Walk of Fame
PERSONAL LIFE:
3 marriages
3 divorces
1 child
FRAMED: suffers from alcoholism
during her entire career.
She dies of burns

YVONNE DE CARLO
BORN: 09.01.1922,
Vancouver, Canada
DIES: 01.08.2007,
Woodland Hills, California
NATIONALITY: Canadian
MAIN MOVIES:
· *The Ten Commandments* (1956)
· *Bando of Angels* (1957)
RECOGNITIONS: Walk of Fame
PERSONAL LIFE:
1 marriage
1 divorce
2 children

FRAMED: invitations only for minor
appearances

FRANCES DEE
BORN: 11.26.1909,
Los Angeles
DIES: 03.06.2004,
Norwalk, Connecticut
NATIONALITY: American
MAIN MOVIES:
· *Blood Money* (1933)
· *Walked with a Zombie* (1943)
RECOGNITIONS: Walk of Fame
PERSONAL LIFE:
1 marriage
3 children
FRAMED: devotes herself
to her husband as of 1953

SANDRA DEE
BORN: 04.23.1942,
Bayonne, New Jersey
DIES: 02.20.2005,
Thousand Oaks, California
NATIONALITY: American
MAIN MOVIES:
· *Imitation of Life* (1959)
· *A Summer Place* (1959)
RECOGNITIONS: Golden Globe
(1958) as most promising female
newcomer
PERSONAL LIFE:
1 marriage
1 divorce
1 child
FRAMED: there is little room
for a teenage movie star to play
a daughter when everyone knows
she is a divorcée

CARLA DEL POGGIO
BORN: 12.02.1925,
Naples, Italy
DIES: alive
NATIONALITY: Italian
MAIN MOVIES:
· *Maddalena, zero in condotta* (1940)
· *Luci del varietà* (1950)
RECOGNITIONS:
PERSONAL LIFE:
1 marriage
once widowed (of Italian director
Alberto Lattuada)

2 children
FRAMED: devotes herself to family

PEGGY DOW
BORN: 03.18.1928,
Columbia, Mississippi
DIES: alive
NATIONALITY: American
MAIN MOVIES:
· *Harvey* (1950)
· *Bright Victory* (1951)
RECOGNITIONS:
PERSONAL LIFE:
1 marriage
5 children
FRAMED: retires after only three
years, never looks back and raises
five sons. Avid charity worker

BETSY DRAKE
BORN: 09.11.1923,
Paris, France
DIES: alive
NATIONALITY: French-American
MAIN MOVIES:
· *Every Girl Should Be Married* (1948)
RECOGNITIONS:
PERSONAL LIFE:
1 marriage
1 divorce
FRAMED: addicts to LSD.
Divorces from Cary Grant (1962)

IRENE DUNNE
BORN: 12.20.1898,
Louisville, Kentucky
DIES: 09.04.1990,
Los Angeles, California
NATIONALITY: American
MAIN MOVIES:
· *Love Affair* (1939)
· *My Favorite Wife* (1940)
· *Anna and the King of* Siam (1945)
· *I Remember Mama* (1948)
RECOGNITIONS:
· 5 Oscar nominations (1931, 1937,
1938, 1940, 1949) as best actress
in a leading role for *Cimarron,
Theodora Goes Wild, The Awful
Truth, Love Affair, I Remember
Mama*
· Walk of Fame
PERSONAL LIFE:

1 marriage
1 adopted daughter
FRAMED: dedicated to philanthropic
and public work. Becomes
an alternate delegate
to the UN General Assembly

F

FRANCES FARMER
BORN: 09.19.1913,
Seattle, Washington
DIES: 08.01.1970,
Indianapolis, Indiana
NATIONALITY: American
MAIN MOVIES:
· *Come and Get It* (1936)
· *Son of Fury* (1942)
RECOGNITIONS:
PERSONAL LIFE:
3 marriages
2 divorces
FRAMED: a rebel, passes eleven
years in a mental hospital because
of a mistake. Her mother
is accomplice of the doctors

SUSAN FLEMING
BORN: 02.19.1908,
New York City, New York
DIES: 12.22.2002,
Rancho Mirage, California
NATIONALITY: American
MAIN MOVIES:
· *Million Dollar Legs* (1932)
· *Gold Diggers* (1936)
RECOGNITIONS:
PERSONAL LIFE:
1 marriage
4 adoptions
FRAMED: ends Hollywood career
when she marries Harpo Marx
(1936) with whom she adopts four
children. Artist and activist

ANNE FRANCIS
BORN: 09.16.1930,
Ossining, New York
DIES: alive
NATIONALITY: American
MAIN MOVIES:
· *Forbidden Planet* (1956)

RECOGNITIONS:
· Emmy nomination (1966)
as best actress in a leading role
for *Honey West* (TV series)
· Golden Globe (1966) best TV
female for *Honey West*
· Walk of Fame
PERSONAL LIFE:
2 marriages
2 divorces
2 children
FRAMED: compromise
with glamour television roles

KAY FRANCIS
BORN: 01.13.1905,
Oklahoma City, Oklahoma
DIES: 08.26.1968,
New York City, New York
NATIONALITY: American
MAIN MOVIES:
· *Trouble in Paradise* (1932)
· *Living on Velvet* (1935)
· *Confession* (1937)
RECOGNITIONS: Walk of Fame
PERSONAL LIFE:
5 marriages
5 divorces
FRAMED: the highest-paid American
film actress of the 1930s. Declining
health and an accident stop her career

G

GLORIA GRAHAME
BORN: 11.28.1923,
Los Angeles, California
DIES: 10.05.1981,
New York City, New York
NATIONALITY: American
MAIN MOVIES:
· *Crossfire* (1947)
· *The Bad and the Beautiful* (1952)
RECOGNITIONS:
· Oscar (1953) as best actress
in a supporting role for *The Bad
and the Beautiful*
· Oscar nomination (1948)
as beast actress in a supporting
role for *Crossfire*
· Walk of Fame
PERSONAL LIFE:

4 marriages
4 divorces
4 children
FRAMED: suffers typecasting
syndrome as shady after noir acting
marital and child-custody issues
damage her image. Moves to stage
and television

KATHRYN GRAYSON
BORN: 02.09.1922,
North Carolina
DIES: 02.17.2010,
Los Angeles, California
NATIONALITY: American
MAIN MOVIES:
· *Show Boat* (1951)
· *Kiss Me Kate* (1953)
RECOGNITIONS: Walk of Fame
PERSONAL LIFE:
2 marriages
2 divorces
1 child
FRAMED: no more calls since 1957.
Only nightclub jobs

H

HAYA HARAREET
BORN: 09.20.1931,
Haifa, Palestine
DIES: alive
NATIONALITY: Palestinian
MAIN MOVIES:
· *Hill 24 Doesn't Answer* (1955)
· *Ben-Hur* (1959)
RECOGNITIONS: Cannes Film
Festival award (1956) for *Hill 24
Doesn't Answer*
PERSONAL LIFE:
1 marriage
once widowed
FRAMED: after *Ben-Hur*, no more
news about her. Even fans cannot
find her current photos and address

DOLORES HART
BORN: 10.20.1939,
Chicago, Illinois
DIES: alive
NATIONALITY: American
MAIN MOVIES:

· *Loving You* (1957)
RECOGNITIONS: Golden Laurel
(1961) 3rd top new personality
female
PERSONAL LIFE: not available
FRAMED: enters Benedictine Regina
Laudis monastery and is called
Reverend Mother Dolores Hart

JUNE HAVER
BORN: 06.10.1926,
Rock Island, Illinois
DIES: 06.04.2005,
Brentwood, California
NATIONALITY: American
MAIN MOVIES:
· *Look for the Silver Lining* (1949)
· *Love Nest* (1951)
· *The Girl Next Door* (1953)
RECOGNITIONS:
PERSONAL LIFE:
2 marriages
1 divorce
once widowed
adopted twin girls
FRAMED: becomes a nun (1954),
enters a convent, but leaves
after six months

SUSAN HAYWARD
BORN: 06.30.1917,
Brooklyn, New York
DIES: 03.14.1975,
Hollywood, California
NATIONALITY: American
MAIN MOVIES:
· *Tap Roots* (1948)
· *David and Bathsheba* (1951)
· *I Want to Live!* (1958)
RECOGNITIONS:
· Oscar (1959) as best actress
in a leading role for *I Want to Live!*
· Oscar nominations (1948, 1950,
1953, 1956) as best actress
in a leading role for *Smash-Up:
The Story of a Woman*, *My Foolish
Heart*, *With a Song in My Heart*,
I'll Cry Tomorrow
· Walk of Fame
PERSONAL LIFE:
2 marriages
1 divorce
2 children

FRAMED: dies from brain cancer,
probably as a result of exposure
to nuclear fallout during the filming
of *The Conqueror* (1956)

JOYCE HOLDEN
BORN: 09.01.1930,
Kansas City, Missouri
DIES: alive
NATIONALITY: American
MAIN MOVIES:
· *The Werewolf* (1956)
· *Terror from the Year 5000* (1958)
RECOGNITIONS:
PERSONAL LIFE:
2 marriages
1 divorce
FRAMED: leading lady of B-horror
and crime drama. No more calls
since 1960

MIRIAM HOPKINS
BORN: 10.19.1902,
Savannah, Georgia
DIES: 10.09.1972,
New York City, New York
NATIONALITY: American
MAIN MOVIES:
· *Dr. Jekyll and Mr. Hyde* (1932)
· *Trouble in Paradise* (1932)
· *Becky Sharp* (1935)
RECOGNITIONS:
· Oscar nomination (1936)
as best actress in a leading role
for *Becky Sharp*
· Walk of Fame
PERSONAL LIFE:
4 marriages
4 divorces
1 child
FRAMED: in 1939 slowdown
in film work, only stage
appearances

RUTH HUSSEY
BORN: 10.30.1911,
Providence, Rhode Island
DIES: 04.19.2005,
Newbury Park, California
NATIONALITY: American
MAIN MOVIES:
· *The Philadelphia Story* (1940)
· *Fight Command* (1940)

RECOGNITIONS:
· Oscar nomination (1941)
as best actress in a supporting role
for *Philadelphia Story*
· Walk of Fame
PERSONAL LIFE:
1 marriage
3 children
FRAMED: no more calls since 1945.
Dedicated to Broadway

J

JENNIFER JONES
BORN: 03.02.1919,
Tulsa, Oklahoma
DIES: 12.17.2009,
Malibu, California
NATIONALITY: American
MAIN MOVIES:
· *The Song of Bernadette* (1943)
· *Duel in the Sun* (1946)
· *Lover Is a Many-Splendored
Thing* (1955)
RECOGNITIONS:
· Oscar (1944) as best actress
in a leading role for *The Song
of Bernadette*
· Oscar nominations (1946,
1947, 1956) as best actress
in a leading role for *Love Letters,
Duel in the Sun, Lover Is a
Many-Splendored Thing*
· Oscar nomination (1945)
as best actress in a supporting role
for *Since You Went Away*
· Golden Globe (1944)
as best motion picture actress
for *The Song of Bernadette*
· Golden Globe nomination (1975)
as best supporting actress
for *The Towering Inferno*
· Walk of Fame
PERSONAL LIFE:
3 marriages
1 divorce
once widowed
3 children
FRAMED: with Selznick's death
(her second husband), loses
guidance. Attempts suicide.
Daughter commits suicide

K

SUSAN KOHNER
BORN: 11.11.1936,
Los Angeles, California
DIES: alive
NATIONALITY: American
MAIN MOVIES:
· *Imitation of Life* (1959)
· *Freud* (1962)
RECOGNITIONS:
· Oscar nomination (1960) as best
actress in a supporting role for
Imitation of Life
· Golden Globe (1959) as most
promising female newcomer
· Golden Globe (1960) as best
actress in a supporting role
for *Imitation of Life*
PERSONAL LIFE:
1 marriage
2 children
FRAMED: retires at age 26
to raise a family

L

VERONICA LAKE
BORN: 11.14.1919,
Brooklyn, New York
DIES: 06.07.1973,
Burlington, Vermont
NATIONALITY: American
MAIN MOVIES:
· *Sullivan Story* (1941)
· *So Proudly We Hail!* (1943)
· *The Blue Dahlia* (1946)
RECOGNITIONS: Walk of Fame
PERSONAL LIFE:
4 marriages
3 divorces
4 children
FRAMED: her career stumbles
in 1944. She dies from alcoholism

HEDY LAMARR
BORN: 11.09.1914,
Vienna, Austria-Hungary
(now Austria)
DIES: 01.19.2000,
Orlando, Florida
NATIONALITY: American

MAIN MOVIES:
· *Ecstasy* (1933)
· *White Cargo* (1942)
· *Experiment Perilous* (1944)
RECOGNITIONS:
· Walk of Fame
· Volpi Cup nomination (1934)
for *Ecstasy*
PERSONAL LIFE:
6 marriages
6 divorces
3 children
FRAMED: co-invents (with composer
George Antheil) "frequency
hopping"

DOROTHY LAMOUR
BORN: 12.10.1914,
New Orleans, Louisiana
DIES: 09.22.1996,
Los Angeles, California
NATIONALITY: American
MAIN MOVIES:
· *The Jungle Princess* (1936)
· *Uragano* (1937)
· *Dixie* (1943)
RECOGNITIONS: Walk of Fame
PERSONAL LIFE:
2 marriages
1 divorce
once widowed
2 children
FRAMED: suffers typecasting
syndrome. Although Dorothy
actually only wore a sarong
in six of her fifty-nine pictures,
it defined her career

CAROLE LANDIS
BORN: 01.01.1919,
Fairchild, Wisconsin
DIES: 07.05.1948,
Pacific Palisades, California
NATIONALITY: American
MAIN MOVIES:
· *I Wake Up Screaming* (1941)
· *Having Wonderful Crime* (1945)
RECOGNITIONS: Walk of Fame
PERSONAL LIFE:
5 marriages
3 divorces
1 annulled
FRAMED: poor health, failed

marriages, financial problems.
Suicide at age 29

PRISCILLA LANE
BORN: 06.12.1915,
Indianola, Iowa
DIES: 04.04.1995,
Andover, Massachusetts
NATIONALITY: American
MAIN MOVIES:
· *Saboteur* (1942)
· *Arsenic and Old Lace* (1944)
RECOGNITIONS:
PERSONAL LIFE:
2 marriages
1 annulled
4 children
FRAMED: retires twice
to domestic life

JANET LEIGH
BORN: 07.06.1927,
Merced, California
DIES: 10.03.2004,
Beverly Hills, California
NATIONALITY: American
MAIN MOVIES:
· *Act of Violence* (1948)
· *Psycho* (1960)
· *The Manchurian Candidate*
(1962)
RECOGNITIONS:
· Oscar nomination (1961)
as best actress in a supporting role
for *Psycho*
· Golden Globe (1961) as best
supporting actress for *Psycho*
· Walk of Fame
PERSONAL LIFE:
4 marriages
2 divorces
1 annulled
2 children
FRAMED: suffers typecasting
syndrome for *Psycho*

NAN LESLIE
BORN: 06.04.1926,
Los Angeles, California
DIES: 07.30.2000,
San Juan Capistrano, California
NATIONALITY: American
MAIN MOVIES:

· *The Woman on the Beach* (1947)
· *The Devil Thumbs a Ride* (1947)
PERSONAL LIFE:
2 marriages
twice widowed
FRAMED: only B movies
and TV Westerns

VIVECA LINDFORS
BORN: 12.29.1920,
Uppsala, Sweden
DIES: 10.25.1995,
Uppsala, Sweden
NATIONALITY: Swedish
MAIN MOVIES:
· *Night unto Night* (1949)
RECOGNITIONS: Berlin
International Film Festival (1962),
Silver Berlin Bear as best actress for
No Exit
PERSONAL LIFE:
4 marriages
4 divorces
3 children
FRAMED: moves to theatre
and television

MARGARET LOCKWOOD
BORN: 09.15.1916,
Karachi, British India
(now Pakistan)
DIES: 07.15.1990,
Kensington, London
NATIONALITY: British
MAIN MOVIES:
· *The Lady Vanishes* (1938)
· *The Man in Grey* (1943)
· *The Wicked Lady* (1945)
RECOGNITIONS:
PERSONAL LIFE:
1 marriage
1 child
FRAMED: films take a nose-dive
in quality

TILLY LOSCH
BORN: 11.15.1903,
Vienna, Austria
DIES: 12.24.1975,
New York City, New York
NATIONALITY: American
MAIN MOVIES:
· *The Good Earth* (1937)

· *Duel in the Sun* (1946)
RECOGNITIONS:
PERSONAL LIFE:
2 marriages
2 divorces
1 child
FRAMED: victim of depression.
Spends several years in
sanatorium. She starts painting
with acclaim

DIANA LYNN
BORN: 10.07.1926,
Los Angeles, California
DIES: 12.18.1971,
Los Angeles, California
NATIONALITY: American
MAIN MOVIES:
· *The Major, and the Minor*
(1942)
· *Every Girl Should Be Married*
(1948)
RECOGNITIONS: Walk of Fame
PERSONAL LIFE:
2 marriages
1 divorce
4 children
FRAMED: few roles as from age 30,
but a lot of television.
She dies at 45, just before
a comeback in film

M

JAYNE MANSFIELD
BORN: 04.19.1933,
Bryn Mawr, Pennsylvania
DIES: 06.29.1967,
Slidell, Louisiana
NATIONALITY: American
MAIN MOVIES:
· *The Girl Can't Help It* (1956)
· *Kiss Them for Me* (1957)
RECOGNITIONS: Walk of Fame
PERSONAL LIFE:
3 marriages
3 divorces
5 children
FRAMED: her film career begins
to decline and nightclub acts
and store appearances begin to
rise

FRANCA MARZI
BORN: 08.18.1926
Rome, Italy
DIES: 03.06.1989
Cinisello Balsamo, Italy
NATIONALITY: Italian
MAIN MOVIES:
· *Amanti in fuga* (1947)
· *Le notti di Cabiria* (1957)
RECOGNITIONS:
PERSONAL LIFE:
not available
FRAMED: once a star with melo,
she ends up playing erotic roles

VIRGINIA MAYO
BORN: 11.30.1920,
St. Louis, Missouri
DIES: 01.17.2005,
Thousand Oaks, California
NATIONALITY: American
MAIN MOVIES:
· *The Secret Life of Walter Mitty*
(1947)
· *White Heat* (1949)
RECOGNITIONS: Walk of Fame
PERSONAL LIFE:
1 marriage
1 child
FRAMED: only B movies
and Westerns by age 40

MARIE MCDONALD
BORN: 10.28.1923,
Burgin, Kentucky
DIES: 10.21.1965,
Calabasas, California
NATIONALITY: American
MAIN MOVIES:
· *It's a Pleasure* (1945)
· *Living in a Big Way* (1947)
· *Tell It to the Judge* (1949)
RECOGNITIONS:
PERSONAL LIFE:
7 marriages
4 divorces
3 children
FRAMED: addiction to alcohol
and prescription drugs.
Suicide at age 42

VERA MILES
BORN: 08.23.1929,

Boise City, Oklahoma
DIES: alive
NATIONALITY: American
MAIN MOVIES:
· *The Searchers* (1956)
· *Psycho* (1960)
RECOGNITIONS: Walk of Fame
PERSONAL LIFE:
3 marriages
3 divorces
4 children
FRAMED: becomes pregnant,
Hitchcock loses interest

MARIA MONTEZ
BORN: 06.06.1912,
Barahona, Dominican Republic
DIES: 09.07.1951,
Paris, France
NATIONALITY: Dominican
MAIN MOVIES:
· *The Invisible Woman* (1940)
· *Arabian Nights* (1942)
· *Ali Baba and the 40 Thieves*
(1944)
RECOGNITIONS:
PERSONAL LIFE:
2 marriages
1 divorce
1 child
FRAMED: she dies at 39 after
suffering a heart attack in her bath

N

ANNA QUIRENTIA NILSSON
BORN: 03.30.1888,
Ystad, Skåne Län, Sweden
DIES: 02.11.1974,
Hemet, California
NATIONALITY: Swedish
MAIN MOVIES:
at least 197 movies
RECOGNITIONS: Walk of Fame
PERSONAL LIFE:
2 marriages
2 divorces
FRAMED: violent eclipse
with the advent of sound

MABEL NORMAND
BORN: 11.10.1895,

New Brighton, Staten Island,
New York
DIES: 02.22.1930,
Monrovia, California
NATIONALITY: American
MAIN MOVIES: at least 227 movies,
director and producer to many
Charles Chaplin films
RECOGNITIONS: Walk of Fame
PERSONAL LIFE:
1 marriage
FRAMED: uses alcohol and
cocaine. Suspected of murdering
Paramount director William
Desmond Taylor, dies of
tuberculosis at age 34

O

MAUREEN O'HARA
BORN: 08.17.1920,
Renelagh, Dublin, Ireland
DIES: alive
NATIONALITY: Irish
MAIN MOVIES:
· *The Hunchback
of Notre Dame* (1939)
· *Rio Bravo* (1950)
· *The Quiet Man* (1952)
RECOGNITIONS:
· Laurel awards nomination (1964)
top female star
· Walk of Fame
PERSONAL LIFE:
3 marriages
1 divorce
1 annulled
1 child
FRAMED: quits at the beginning
of the 1960s. Some years after
an airplane crash kills her husband

NANCY OLSON
BORN: 07.14.1928,
Milwaukee, Wisconsin
DIES: alive
NATIONALITY: American
MAIN MOVIES:
· *Sunset Boulevard* (1950)
· *Big Jim McLain* (1952)
RECOGNITIONS: Oscar nomination
(1951) as best actress in a

supporting role for *Sunset
Boulevard*
PERSONAL LIFE:
2 marriages
1 divorced
3 children
FRAMED: first is not serious about
her acting career. Then becomes too
old to play the girl-next-door type
she was known for

P

ELEANOR PARKER
BORN: 06.22.1922,
Cedarville, Ohio
DIES: alive
NATIONALITY: American
MAIN MOVIES:
· *Human Bondage* (1946)
· *Caged* (1950)
RECOGNITIONS:
· 3 Oscar nominations (1951,
1952, 1956) as best actress in a
leading role for *Caged, Detective
Story, Interrupted Melody*
· Venice Film Festival (1951)
· Volpi Cup for *Caged*
PERSONAL LIFE:
4 marriages
3 divorces
4 children
FRAMED: is not in sync with look
change of the 1960s

MARISA PAVAN
BORN: 06.19.1932,
Cagliari, Italy
DIES: alive
NATIONALITY: Italian
MAIN MOVIES:
· *The Rose Tattoo* (1955)
RECOGNITIONS:
· Oscar nomination (1956) as best
actress in a supporting role for
The Rose Tattoo (1956)
· Golden Globe (1955)
as best supporting actress for
The Rose Tattoo
PERSONAL LIFE:
1 marriage
once widowed

2 children
FRAMED: quits to sing with
husband

SUSAN PETERS
BORN: 07.03.1921,
Spokane, Washington
DIES: 10.23.1952,
Visalia, California
NATIONALITY: American
MAIN MOVIES:
· *Random Harvest* (1942)
· *Song of Russia* (1944)
· *Keep Your Powder Dry* (1945)
RECOGNITIONS:
· Oscar nomination (1943)
as best actress in a supporting role
for *Random Harvest*
· Walk of Fame
PERSONAL LIFE:
1 marriage
1 divorce
1 child
FRAMED: at age 24 permanent
paralyses. MGM pays for her bills
but is forced to settle her contract.
Suicide at age 31

ANNA MARIA PIERANGELI
BORN: 06.19.1932,
Cagliari, Italy
DIES: 09.10.1971,
Beverly Hills, Los Angeles,
California
NATIONALITY: Italian
MAIN MOVIES:
· *The Silver Chalice* (1954)
· *Somebody Up There Likes
Me* (1956)
RECOGNITIONS: Golden Globe
(1952) as most promising
newcomer for *Teresa*
PERSONAL LIFE:
2 marriages
2 divorces
2 children
FRAMED: ups and downs in her
career till the end. Suicide at age 39

JANE POWELL
BORN: 05.01.1929,
Portland, Oregon
DIES: alive
NATIONALITY: American

MAIN MOVIES:
· *Seven Brides for Seven Brothers*
(1954)
RECOGNITIONS:
PERSONAL LIFE:
5 marriages
4 divorces
3 children
FRAMED: her innocent girl-next-door
image starts declining due to age

R

LUISE RAINER
BORN: 01.12.1910,
Düsseldorf, Germany
DIES: alive
NATIONALITY: German
MAIN MOVIES:
· *The Great Ziegfeld* (1936)
· *The Good Earth* (1937)
RECOGNITIONS:
· Oscar (1937, 1938) as best actress
in a leading role for *The Great
Ziegfeld, The Good Earth*
· Walk of Fame
PERSONAL LIFE:
2 marriages
1 divorce
once widowed
1 child
FRAMED: demands serious roles
and higher salary

PAULA RAYMOND
BORN: 11.23.1924,
San Francisco, California
DIES: 12.31.2003,
West Hollywood, California
NATIONALITY: American
MAIN MOVIES:
· *City That Never Sleeps* (1953)
· *The Beast from the 20,000
Fathoms* (1953)
RECOGNITIONS:
PERSONAL LIFE:
1 marriage
1 divorce
1 child
FRAMED: dramatic car accident.
One year of plastic surgery and,
later, a series of falls and accidents

RUTH ROMAN
BORN: 12.22.1922,
Lynn, Massachusetts
DIES: 09.09.1999,
Laguna Beach, California
NATIONALITY: American
MAIN MOVIES:
· *Strangers on a Train* (1951)
RECOGNITIONS: Golden Globe
nomination (1950) as most
promising female newcomer
for *Champion*
PERSONAL LIFE:
3 marriages
2 divorces
1 child
FRAMED: no more calls.
Only television roles after the end
of the 1950s

ROSALIND RUSSELL
BORN: 06.04.1907,
Waterburg, Connecticut
DIES: 11.28.1976,
Los Angeles, California
NATIONALITY: American
MAIN MOVIES:
· *The Women* (1939)
· *Sister Kenny* (1946)
· *Mourning Becomes Electra* (1947)
· *Auntie Mame* (1958)
RECOGNITIONS:
· 4 Oscar nominations (1943, 1947,
1948, 1959) as best actress in
a leading role for *My Sister Eileen,
Sister Kenny, Mourning Becomes
Electra, Auntie Mame*
· 5 Golden Globes (1947, 1948,
1959, 1962, 1963) as best motion
picture actress for *Sister Kenny,
Mourning Becomes Electra, Auntie
Mame, A Majority of One, Gypsy*
· Walk of Fame
PERSONAL LIFE:
1 marriage
1 child
FRAMED: moves to theatre
and television

PEGGY RYAN
BORN: 08.28.1924,
Long Beach, California
DIES: 10.30.2004,

Las Vegas, Nevada
NATIONALITY: American
MAIN MOVIES:
· *What's Cookin'?* (1942)
· *Private Buckaroo* (1942)
RECOGNITIONS:
PERSONAL LIFE:
3 marriages
2 divorces
1 child
FRAMED: decides to retire
after her third marriage

S

YVONNE SANSON
BORN: 01.01.1926,
Salonika, Greece
DIES: 07.23.2003,
Bologna, Italy
NATIONALITY: Greek
MAIN MOVIES:
· *L'imperatore di Capri* (1949)
· *Nobody Children* (1951)
· *Tormento* (1953)
RECOGNITIONS:
PERSONAL LIFE:
1 marriage
1 child
FRAMED: disappears with the death
of melo movies

GIA SCALA
BORN: 03.03.1934,
Liverpool, England
DIES: 04.30.1972,
Hollywood, California
NATIONALITY: English
MAIN MOVIES:
· *The Angry Hills* (1959)
· *The Guns of Navarone* (1961)
RECOGNITIONS:
PERSONAL LIFE:
1 marriage
1 divorce
FRAMED: deep-rooted insecurities
and alcoholism. Suicide at age 38

LIZABETH SCOTT
BORN: 09.29.1922,
Scranton, Pennsylvania
DIES: alive

NATIONALITY: American
MAIN MOVIES:
· *The Strange Love of Martha
Ivers* (1946)
· *I Walk Alone* (1948)
· *Loving You* (1957)
RECOGNITIONS: Walk of Fame
PERSONAL LIFE: never married
FRAMED: rumors about her lesbian
sexuality damage her career

JEAN SEBERG
BORN: 11.13.1938,
Marshalltown, Iowa
DIES: 08.30.1979,
Paris, France
NATIONALITY: French
MAIN MOVIES:
· *Breathless* (1960)
· *Lilith* (1964)
· *Airport* (1970)
RECOGNITIONS: Golden Globe
nomination (1965) as best motion
picture actress for *Lilith*
PERSONAL LIFE:
4 marriages
3 divorces
1 child
FRAMED: no more calls since age 30.
She commits suicide at age 41

NORMA SHEARER
BORN: 08.10.1902,
Montréal, Québec, Canada
DIES: 06.12.1983,
Woodland Hills, Los Angeles,
California
NATIONALITY: Canadian
MAIN MOVIES:
· *The Divorcee* (1930)
· *The Barretts of Wimpole Street*
(1934)
· *Romeo and Juliet* (1936)
RECOGNITIONS:
· Oscar (1930) as best actress
in a leading role for *The Divorcee*
· 5 Oscar nominations (1930, 1931,
1935, 1937, 1939) as best actress
in a leading role for *Their Own
Desire, A Free Soul, The Barretts of
Wimpole Street, Romeo and Juliet,
Marie Antoinette*
· Volpi Cup (1938) for best actress

in *Marie Antoinette*
· Walk of Fame
PERSONAL LIFE:
2 marriages
once widowed
2 children
FRAMED: retires at age 40
and marries a sky instructor twenty
years younger than herself. They
stay together until her death

ANN SHERIDAN
BORN: 02.21.1915,
Denton, Texas
DIES: 01.21.1967,
Los Angeles, California
NATIONALITY: American
MAIN MOVIES:
· *Torrid Zone* (1940)
· *They Drive by Night* (1940)
· *I Was a Male War Bride* (1949)
RECOGNITIONS: Walk of Fame
PERSONAL LIFE:
3 marriages
2 divorces
FRAMED: she ages prematurely
because she is a chain smoker. Only
occasional television appearances

ANNE SHIRLEY
BORN: 04.17.1918,
New York City, New York
DIES: 07.04.1993,
Los Angeles, California
NATIONALITY: American
MAIN MOVIES:
· *So Big!* (1932)
· *Stella Dallas* (1937)
· *Murder, My Sweet* (1944)
RECOGNITIONS:
· Oscar nomination (1938)
as best actress in a supporting role
for *Stella Dallas*
· Walk of Fame
PERSONAL LIFE:
3 marriages
2 divorces
2 children
FRAMED: infant prodige, becomes
an actress just to pleaseher mother

SIMONE SIMON
BORN: 04.23.1910,

Marseille, France
DIES: 02.22.2005,
Paris, France
NATIONALITY: French
MAIN MOVIES:
· *Seventh Heaven* (1927)
· *Ladies in Love* (1936)
· *The Human Beast* (1938)
RECOGNITIONS:
PERSONAL LIFE:
never married
FRAMED: no more calls after 1949.
She is very well known for her
gold key

ALEXIS SMITH
BORN: 06.08.1921,
Penticton, British Columbia,
Canada
DIES: 06.09.1993,
Los Angeles, California
NATIONALITY: Canadian
MAIN MOVIES:
· *Rhapsody in Blue* (1945)
· *Human Bondage* (1946)
· *The Sleeping Tiger* (1954)
RECOGNITIONS:
PERSONAL LIFE:
1 marriage
FRAMED: rumors about her
lesbian sexuality damage her
career

CONSTANCE SMITH
BORN: 01.22.1928,
Limerick, Ireland
DIES: 06.30.2003,
Islington, London
NATIONALITY: Irish
MAIN MOVIES:
· *Man in the Attic* (1953)
RECOGNITIONS:
PERSONAL LIFE:
not available
FRAMED: no more calls
and missing information

INGER STEVENS
BORN: 10.18.1934,
Stockholm, Sweden
DIES: 04.30.1970,
Hollywood, California
NATIONALITY: Swedish

MAIN MOVIES:
RECOGNITIONS: Golden Globe
(1964) as Best TV Star - Female
for *The Farmer's Daughter*
PERSONAL LIFE:
2 marriages
1 divorce
FRAMED: her television career
is better than movie career.
She commits suicide at age 36

T

SHEILA TERRY
BORN: 03.05.1910,
Warroad, Minnesota
DIES: 01.19.1957,
New York City, New York
NATIONALITY: American
MAIN MOVIES:
· *'Neath the Arizona Skies* (1934)
· *A Girl's Best Years* (1936)
RECOGNITIONS:
PERSONAL LIFE:
not available
FRAMED: second lead of the 1930s
for Warner Bros. Appears opposite
John Wayne in a few of his early
Westerns

PHYLLIS THAXTER
BORN: 11.20.1921,
Portland, Maine
DIES: alive
NATIONALITY: American
MAIN MOVIES:
· *Act of Violence* (1948)
RECOGNITIONS: Walk of Fame
PERSONAL LIFE:
2 marriages
1 divorce
2 children
FRAMED: a poliomyelitis attack
at age 31. Later she works mostly
in television

GENE TIERNEY
BORN: 11.19.1920,
Brooklyn, New York
DIES: 11.06.1991,
Huston, Texas
NATIONALITY: American

MAIN MOVIES:
· *Laura* (1944)
· *Leave Her to Heaven* (1945)
RECOGNITIONS:
· Oscar nomination (1945) as best
actress in a leading role for *Laura*
· Walk of Fame
PERSONAL LIFE:
2 marriages
1 divorce
2 children
FRAMED: her first daughter is born
mentally retarded. Suffers from
bi-polar disorder and suicidal
depression

THELMA TODD
BORN: 06.29.1905,
Laurence, Massachusettes
DIES: 12.16.1935,
Pacific Palisades, California
NATIONALITY: American
MAIN MOVIES:
· *Nevada* (1927)
· *Misses Stooge* (1935)
RECOGNITIONS: Walk of Fame
PERSONAL LIFE:
1 marriage
1 divorce
FRAMED: mystery surrounds
her death: suicide or murder?

V

LUPE VÉLEZ
BORN: 07.18.1908,
San Luis Potosi, Mexico
DIES: 12.13.1944,
Beverly Hills, Los Angeles
NATIONALITY: Mexican
MAIN MOVIES:
· *Stardust* (1937)
· *Mexican Spitfire's Blessed Event*
(1943)
RECOGNITIONS: Walk of Fame
PERSONAL LIFE:
Gary Cooper's lover
1 marriage
1 divorce
1 child
FRAMED: commits suicide
while pregnant

VERA-ELLEN
BORN: 02.16.1921,
Norwood, Ohio
DIES: 08.30.1981,
Los Angeles, California
NATIONALITY: American
MAIN MOVIES:
· *Happy Go Lovely* (1951)
· *White Christmas* (1954)
RECOGNITIONS: Walk of Fame
PERSONAL LIFE:
2 marriages
2 divorces
1 child
FRAMED: anorexic throughout
much of the 1950s

ELENA VERDUGO
BORN: 04.25.1925,
Paso Robles, California
DIES: alive
NATIONALITY: American
MAIN MOVIES:
· *Down Argentine Way* (1940)
· *Little Giant* (1946)
· *Cyrano* (1950)
plays in many scripts in whatever
ethnic role is necessary
RECOGNITIONS: Walk of Fame
PERSONAL LIFE:
2 marriages
1 divorce
1 child
FRAMED: refuses to lose weight

W

TERESA WRIGHT
BORN: 10.27.1918,
New York City, New York
DIES: 03.06.2005,
New Haven, Connecticut
NATIONALITY: American
MAIN MOVIES:
· *The Pride of Yankas* (1942)
· *Shadow of a Doubt* (1942)
RECOGNITIONS:
· Oscar (1943) as best actress
in supporting role for *Mrs. Miniver*
· Oscar nomination (1943) as best
actress in a leading role for
The Pride of Yankas

· Emmy nomination (1958)
as best single performance for
Playhouse 90
· Walk of Fame
PERSONAL LIFE:
2 marriages
2 divorces
2 children
FRAMED: compromise with
television

PATRICE WYMORE
BORN: 12.17.1926,
Miltonvale, Kansas
DIES: alive
NATIONALITY: American
MAIN MOVIES:
· *Tea for Two* (1950
· *Rocky Mountain* (1950)
· *The Big Trees* (1952)
RECOGNITIONS:
PERSONAL LIFE:
1 marriage
once widowed
1 child
FRAMED: separates from Errol
Flynn. Attempts a comeback after
his death. Retires in Jamaica

Y

LORETTA YOUNG
BORN: 01.06.1913,
Salt Lake City, Utah
DIES: 08.12.2000,
Los Angeles, California
NATIONALITY: American
MAIN MOVIES:
· *Man's Castle* (1933)
· *Born to Be Bad* (1934)
· *The Stranger* (1946)
RECOGNITIONS:
· Oscar (1948) as best actress
in a leading role for *The Farmer's
Daughter*
· Oscar nomination (1950) as best
actress in a leading role for *Come to
the Stable*
PERSONAL LIFE:
1 marriage
1 child,
FRAMED: gives her child (with

married Clark Gable) to an
orphanage to avoid a scandal,
then adopts her

SOURCES

Acker, Ally. *Reel Women: Pioneers of the Cinema 1896 to the Present*. New York: Continuum, 1991.

Alleman, Richard. *Hollywood: The Movie Lover's Guide*. New York: Broadway Books, 2005.

Anger, Kenneth. *Hollywood Babilonia I*. Milan: Adelphi Editore, 1979.

Armes, Roy. *A Critical History of the British Cinema*. New York: Oxford University Press, 1978.

Auiler, Dan. *Vertigo: The Making of a Hitchcock Classic*. New York: St. Martins Press, 1998.

Barlett, Donald L., and James B. Steele. *Empire: The Life, Legend, and Madness of Howard Hughes*. New York: Norton, 1979.

Barnouw, Erik. *The Golden Web, A History of Broadcasting in the United States 1933-1953*. New York: Oxford University Press, 1968.

Bergman, Ingrid, and Alan Burgess. *My Story*. New York: Delacorte Press, 1980.

Bernstein, Walter. *Inside Out: A Memoir of the Blacklist*. New York: Alfred A. Knopf, 1996.

Best, Marc. *Those Endearing Young Charms: Child Performers of the Screen*. New York: A. S. Barnes & Co., 1971.

Biskind, Peter. *Seeing Is Believing: How Hollywood Movies Taught Us to Stop Worrying and Love the Fifties*. New York: Pantheon, 1983.

Bogdanovich, Peter. *Who the Devil Made It: Conversations with Legendary Film Directors*. New York: Alfred A. Knopf, 1997.

Bowers, Ronald. *The Selznick Players*. Cranbury, NJ: A. S. Barnes, 1976.

Bret, David. *Tallulah Bankhead: A Scandalous Life*. London: Robson Books, 1998.
Camerino, Vincenzo. *Il divismo a Hollywood. Primordi e dintorni*. Manduria (TA): Barbieri Editore, 2000.

Carotenuto, Aldo. *L'anima delle donne. Per una lettura psicologica al femminile*. Milan: Bompiani, 2001.

Chaplin, Charles. *My utobiography*. New York: Simon & Schuster, 1964.

Corey, Melinda, and George Ochoa. *The American Film Institute Desk Reference*. New York: Dorling Kindersley, 2002.

Cottom, J.V. *Amours et scandales a Hollywood*. Brussels: Editions J.M. Collet, 1985.

Cross, Robin. *The Big Book of "B" Movies or How Low Was My Budget*. New York: St. Martins Press, 1981.

Crowther, Bosley. *Hollywood Rajah: The Life and Times of Louis B. Mayer*. New York: Henry Holt, 1960.

Debot, Georges. *Martine Carol ou la vie de Martine chérie*. Paris: France-Empire, 1979.

DeMille, Cecil B. *The Autobiography of Cecil B. DeMille*. Edited by Donald Hayne. Englewood Cliffs, NJ: Prentice-Hall, 1959.

Ford, Charles. *Hollywood Story*. Paris: La Jeune Parque, 1968.

Freedland, Michael. *The Warner Brothers*. New York: St. Martin's Press, 1983.

Gans, Eric Lawrence. *Carole Landis: A Most Beautiful Girl*. Jackson, MS: University of Mississippi Press, 2008.

Guidi, Silvia. "A colloquio con madre Dolores Hart, negli anni Cinquanta star del cinema e oggi suora di clausura." *L'Osservatore Romano* (July 17-18, 2008).

Hay, Peter. *Accadde a Hollywood: Notizie, curiosità e aneddoti dal mondo del cinema*. Edited by Filippo Castelli. Recco (GE): Le Mani-Microart's Edizioni, 2008.

Katz, Ephraim. *The Film Encyclopedia*. New York: HarperCollins, 1998.

Leaming, Barbara. *Orson Welles: A Biography*. New York: Viking Press, 1985.
Lobenthal, Joel. *Tallulah!: The Life and Times of a Leading Lady*. New York: HarperCollins, 2008 .

Lockwood, Margaret. *Lucky Star:*

The Autobiography of Margaret Lockwood.
London: Odhams Press, 1955.

O'Brien, Scott. *Virginia Bruce: Under My Skin.*
Duncan, OK: BearManor Media, 2008.

O'Brien, Scott. *Kay Francis: I Can't Wait to Be
Forgotten.* Duncan, OK: BearManor Media, 2008.

O'Hara, Maureen, and John Nicoletti. *Tis Herself.*
New York: Simon & Schuster, 2004.

Osborne, Robert. *Leading Couples.*
San Francisco: Chronicle Books, 2008.

Peske, Nancy, and West Beverly. *Cinematerapia 2:
Un film dopo l'altro verso la felicità.*
Milan: Feltrinelli Editore, 2005.

Powell, Jane. *The Girl Next Door
. . . and How She Grew.*
New York: William Morrow & Co., 1988.

Ribeiro, Tete. *Divas Abandonadas.*
São Paulo: Jaboticaba, 2007.

Sartori, Carlo. *La fabbrica delle stelle.*
Milan: Mondadori Editore,1983.

Schessler, Ken. *This Is Hollywood.*
Los Angeles: Ken Schessler Productions, 1984.

Schickel, Richard, and Perry George.
You Must Remember This: The Warner Bros. Story.
Philadelphia, PA: Running Press, 2008.

Schneider, Steven Jay. *501 Movie Stars:
A Comprehensive Guide to the Greatest Screen Actors.*
London: Quintessenze Editions Limited, 2008.

Siegenthaler, Danny and Susan Siegenthaler.
"Aging Gracefully, Skin Care in Your 20's, 30's, 40's,
and Beyond." www.ezinearticles.com

Sikov, Ed. *Dark Victory: The Life of Bette Davis.*
New York: Henry Holt, 2007.

Sorlin, Pierre. *Sociologia del cinema.*
Milan: Garzanti Editore, 1979.
Steed, Tobias, and Ben Reed. *Hollywood Cocktails.*
London: Octopus Publishing Group Limited, 1999.

LINKS

www.afi.com
www.allmovieportal.com
www.amazon.com
www.ancestry.com
www.bombshells.com
www.brainyquote.com
www.britannica.com
www.chicagotribune.com
www.cinekolossal.com/star/
www.classicmovies.org
www.cmgww.com
www.cooplover.com
www.culturagay.it
www.dailynews.com
www.editorsguild.com
www.famousandgay.com
www.fandango.com
www.fanpix.net
www.findagrave.com
www.frieze.com
www.glamourgirlsofthesilverscreen.com
www.guardian.co.uk
www.heraldsun.com.au
www.heraldtribune.com
www.hollywood.com
www.hollywoodreporter.com
www.hdfoundation.org
www.imdb.com
www.independent.co.uk
www.latimes.com
www.life.com
www.lycos.com
www.theasc.com/magazine
www.theasc.com
www.mixonline.com
www.movies.nytimes.com
www.moviesoundnewsletter.com
www.mpse.org
www.msnbc.msn.com
www.museum.tv
www.online.wsj.com
www.oscars.org.
www.ProfilesInHistory.com
www.reelclassics.com
www.rollingstone.com
www.silentladies.com
www.starpulse.com
www.thegoldenyears.org
www.tate.org.uk
www.time.com
www.variety.com
www.vogue.com
www.warhol.org
www.warholfoundation.org
www.washingtonpost.com

www.whitney.org
www.wikipedia.org
www.whosdatedwho.com
www.youtube.com

www.moharamagazine.com
www.maureen-ohara.com
www.maureenohara.org
www.loretta-young.com
www.elvis.com.au (rev_mother_dolores)
www.abbeyofreginalaudis.com
www.loti.com/fifties_movies (Jane Leigh)
www.ingerstevens.org/bio.html
www.wickedlady.com (Margaret Lockwood)
www.filmstarpostcards.blogspot.com
www.briansdriveintheater.com/joyceholden.html
martinklasch.blogspot.com (Quirentia)
www.epinions.com (Ben-Hur, Haya Harareet)
www.flickr.com/photos/castlekay/2434423451
www.filesofjerryblake.netfirms.com (Kay Aldridge)
www.saintjean.co.uk
www.ezinearticles.com (Symptoms-of-Stage-Fright)
www.kayfrancis.net
www.emol.org/celebrities/costello
www.operator_99.blogspot.com (Dolores Costello)
www.rubyemporium.com (hair&makeup)
www.trovacinema.repubblica.it/attori (Virginia Mayo)
www.virginiamayo.com
www.cinekolossal.com/star2/m/mayo
oldhollywood.tumblr.com (Constance Bennett)
www.pokerplayernewspaper.com/viewarticle.php
www.altfg.com/blog (Miriam Hopkins)
www.blog.allanellenberger.com/tag/michael-hopkins
www.lindadarnell.com
www.classicmoviefavorites.com/darnell
www.glamourgirlsofthesilverscreen.com (Linda Darnell)
juliabuckley.blogspot.com (Vera Ellen)
www.mariemcdonald.org
www.cheleinwonderland.blogspot.com (Veronica Lake)
www.guillermito2.net/archives/2005_02_05.html
www.amazon.co.uk (Kay-Francis)
www.kayfrancis.net
www.gadflyonline.com (Clara Bow)
www.trivia-library.com/wherearetheynow-
simonesimon.htm
www.altfg.com/blog/actors/simone-simon/
www.glbtq.com/sfeatures/lesbianshollywood.html
www.huffingtonpost.com (Cyd Charisses)
www.legs.free.fr
www.entertainment.timesonline.co.uk
www.juneallyson.com
www.bobbydarin.net/liveagain.html
www.caringonline.com/eatdis/celebrities_s.html
www.newprophecy.net/firetragedy.htm

To find out more about Charta,
and to learn about our most recent publications, visit

www.chartaartbooks.it

Printed in June 2010
by arti grafiche BIANCA&VOLTA, Truccazzano,
for Edizioni Charta